A Point to Ponder

Biblical Verses Applied With Stimulating Stories and Thought-provoking Ideas

G. Michael Cocoris

A Point to Ponder

Biblical Verses Applied With Stimulating Stories and Thought-provoking Ideas

G. Michael Cocoris

© 2012, 2024 G. Michael Cocoris
All rights reserved. This publication may not be reproduced (in whole or in part, edited, or revised) in any way, form, or means including, but not limited to, electronic, mechanical, photocopying, recording or any kind of storage and retrieval system for sale, except for brief quotations in printed reviews, without the written permission of G. Michael Cocoris, 2016 Euclid #20, Santa Monica, CA 90405, michaelcocoris@gmail.com, or his appointed representatives. Permission is hereby granted, however, for the reproduction of the whole or parts of the whole without changing the content in any way for free distribution, provided all copies contain this copyright notice in its entirety. Permission is also granted to charge for the cost of copying.

Unless otherwise indicated, all Scripture quotations are taken from the New King James Version ®, Copyright © 1979, 1980, 1982 by Thomas Nelson, Inc. Used by permission. All rights reserved.

TABLE OF CONTENTS

INTRODUCTION	1
AN ACT OF LOVE	3
WALK IN WISDOM	5
WHY NOT RUN?	7
WHEN WEARY IN WELL-DOING	9
HOW DO YOU PRAY WITHOUT CEASING?	11
IS PROPHECY PROFITABLE?	13
THERE IS NO WAY OUT OF THIS ONE!	15
WHY ARE THERE ALWAYS SO MANY PROBLEMS?	17
IMPROVING YOUR MARRIAGE	19
SINGING IN THE RAIN	21
LAY HOLD ON ETERNAL LIFE	23
THE SMELL OF HEAVEN	25
A ONE-WORD MESSAGE	27
THE PROBLEM OF FELLOWSHIP WITH GOD	29
SHOULD YOU INVITE A CULTIST INTO YOUR HOME?	31
THE USE OF YOUR HOUSE	33
HOW TO GROW	35
WHAT IS SPIRITUAL GROWTH?	37
KEEP YOURSELF IN THE LOVE OF GOD	39
A SILENT WITNESS	41
JUDGE RIGHTEOUSLY	43
HOW TO CATCH FISH	45

GOD'S INCREDIBLE PROMISE	47
BELIEVING PRAYER	49
YOU CAN BE CONTENT	51
ASK HIM IN FOR WHAT?	53
LAMP OR LAMP POST?	55
THE WISE OR OTHERWISE	57
ARE BELIEVERS TO REJOICE *ALL* THE TIME?	59
THE AUDIENCE MAKES THE DIFFERENCE	61
ARE BELIEVERS TO GIVE THANKS IN *EVERY* SITUATION?	63
HOW TO GET YOUR PRAYERS ANSWERED	65
HOW TO GET STARTED	67
HOW TO BE HAPPY	69
MINISTERING TO THE MINISTER	71
A DEED IS WORTH A THOUSAND WORDS	73
TRY THE RESURRECTION	75
DO YOU YEARN TO BE LIKE CHRIST?	77
THE APPROPRIATE RESPONSE	79
GREETINGS!	81
IS BAPTISM NECESSARY FOR SALVATION?	83
SHOULD YOU SEEK THE BAPTISM OF THE HOLY SPIRIT?	85
TONGUES THEN AND NOW	87
THE PERFECT STORM	89
WHY SO MUCH JUDGMENT?	91
GLASSES COME IN PAIRS	93
WHY SO MUCH ABOUT THE CHURCH?	95

REFLECTIONS ON AN ELECTION	97
FOR ME TO LIVE IS MAINTENANCE	99
FROM COMMON SENSE TO NONSENSE	101
LEFT BEHIND	103
OWNERS OR GUARDIANS?	105
FROM HONEYMOON HARMONY TO DIVORCE	107
FOR GOODNESS SAKE	109
A PERFECT PRAYER	111
NO IS NOT A NEGATIVE	113
WHAT MY SHOES HAVE TAUGHT ME	115
FOR MERCY SAKE	117
THE 9/11 ATTACK ON AMERICA	119
THE MOTIVATION OF A SUICIDE TERRORIST	121
HOW TO HANDLE THE ANTHRAX SCARE	123
REAL THANKSGIVING	125
I HAVE BEEN ROBBED!	127
CHURCH MATH	129
MARRIAGE MATH	131
HOW SAD	133
THE ANATOMY OF AN AFFAIR	135
"I HAVE A PROBLEM"	137
SPORTS HISTORY	139
UNDER GOD	141
AN "HONEST" THIEF	143
WHY DOES LIFE HAVE TO BE SO DIFFICULT?	145
WHAT JESUS' WORDS HAVE TAUGHT ME	147
WHO MINISTERS TO THE MINISTER?	149

THE WHINER	151
RECKONED RIGHTEOUS BY WORKS	153
NEW YEAR'S RESOLUTIONS BIBLICAL?	155
ONE OF THE GREATEST NEEDS IN AMERICA	157
YOUR MEMORIAL TABLE	159
THE PROBLEM WITH GAMBLING	161
LEARNING TO LISTEN	163
GEORGE W. BUSH VERSUS SADDAM HUSSEIN	165
THE PROBLEM WITH GAMBLING	167
MEMORIAL DAY	169
MY ENCOUNTER WITH AN ORTHODOX JEW	171
SCOTT FREE	173
WHAT MY AUTO ACCIDENT TAUGHT ME	175
THE DECLINE IN FAMILY LIVING	177
GIVE ME A PROBLEM	179
DECODING THE DA VINCI CODE	181
THANKSGIVING IS NOT A HOLIDAY	183
WHAT A CHRISTMAS PRESENT!	185
WHAT DO YOU MEAN BY THAT?	187
WHAT ARE PARENTS TO DO?	189
"THE PASSION OF THE CHRIST"	191
MARTHA STEWART'S GREATEST LESSON	193
SAME-SEX MARRIAGE	195
TRIBUTE TO A SERVANT	197
ELEMENTS OF A HAPPY MARRIAGE	199
INDEPENDENCE	201
KERRY'S LOGIC CONCERNING ABORTION	203

THE OLYMPIC SPIRIT	205
PLAYING CARDS	207
THE CARDINAL VIRTUES	209
NOW THAT THE ELECTION IS OVER	211
A TRIBUTE TO MY MOTHER	213
REAL SPIRITUAL GROWTH	215
NO TIME TO THINK	217
THE TEN COMMANDMENTS CONTROVERSY	219
DO WE NEED A POPE?	221
EVERYBODY LOVES RAYMOND	223
EXAMPLES WORTHY OF NOTE	225
HOW DIFFERENT MEN LEARNED TO GET ALONG	227
SOME SAY, "JESUS NEVER LIVED"	229
KATRINA AND NOW RITA!	231
WOULD YOU SAY "NO" TO $4 MILLION?	233
"IN GOD WE TRUST"	235
THE REDEMPTION OF TOOKIE WILLIAMS	237
IS RELIGION A PROBLEM?	239
THE RIGHTS OF THE BORN	241
DID YOU HEAR WHAT SHE SAID ABOUT MUSLIMS?	243
JUDAS: BETRAYER OR BEST FRIEND?	245
WEEKEND OR WEEK BEGINNING?	247
A TRIBUTE TO MY (SPIRITUAL) FATHER	249
YOUR RELATIONSHIP TO THE WORD	251
AMERICA'S FOUR GODS	253
HOW TO DEAL WITH YOUR ENEMIES	255

THE CASE FOR SYSTEMATIC EXPOSITION	257
DON'T MISS THE MESSAGE	259
I CAN AFFORD IT!	261
THE GOSPEL ACCORDING TO PATRICIA	263
THE FUNCTIONAL CHURCH	265
WHO WANTS TO DEAL WITH A TAXMAN?	267
VITAL VIRTUES	269
HAVE YOU GROWN UP YET?	271
THE VOLUME OF SILENCE	273
BIBLICAL ILLITERACY	275
A MODEST POLITICAL PROPOSAL	277
HOW TO HANDLE CREDIT CARDS	279
ROMNEY'S RELIGION	281
CONTINUE!	283
A TRIBUTE TO JACK	285
WHY GOOD FRIDAY?	287
HAPPY BIRTHDAY	289
THE MOST IMPORTANT ROOM IN THE HOUSE	291
THE 80-20 RULE	293
BE SENSIBLE	295
TO BE LIKE CHRIST	297
SWEET REASONABLENESS	299
THE OTHER BENEFIT OF CHRISTMAS	301
WHAT DETERMINES WHO OBTAINS ETERNAL LIFE?	303
THE HEALING TOUCH	305
THE FUNCTION OF DYSFUNCTION	307
WHEN YOUR WORLD FALLS APART	309

24-7-365	311
TO COMPLAIN OR NOT COMPLAIN	313
"SUGGESTIONS!"	315
MAKING A MARK	317
GOD'S TIMING	319
JESUS WEPT	321
ANDREW	323
THE COST OF SERVICE	325
AWARENESS OF SIN	327
INDEX	329

A Point to Ponder

INTRODUCTION

Twice, I have written one-page articles. The first time was when I had a radio broadcast in the 1980s. When I thanked people for supporting the broadcast, I included a one-page "devotional" called "Doorkeeper's Diary." The doorkeepers kept the "door" of the broadcast open with their financial support.

Years later, beginning in 2000, I did another series of one-page articles entitled "A Piece of My Mind." A footnote at the end of each article explained that "A Piece of My Mind" is a periodic publication by G. Michael Cocoris. It is the musing of Mike, consisting of whatever comes out of his reflections on life in general and spiritual things in particular. It is published as the urge hits him." Those articles were sent to people on my mailing list.

Both series are given here under the title "A Point to Ponder." The first 43 articles (pp. 2-44) are from the "Doorkeeper's Diary." Following that are the articles from "A Piece of My Mind."

Changes have been made. A few original articles, such as eulogies to a deceased person, have been omitted. A couple of titles have been altered. For example, "Kerry's Logic" is now "Kerry's Logic Concerning Abortion." Some of the articles have been slightly revised; in some, a verse and sometimes two verses have been added.

Here, the articles are arranged chronologically in the order in which they were written. The articles that mention a specific date

A Point to Ponder

were usually written shortly after that date. A name in parenthesis identifies the author of the quotation or the idea in that sentence.

Although at least a single verse is mentioned in each article, these articles are not intended to just interpret a verse or several verses. Instead, these articles are more concerned with a application. They contain stimulating stories and thought-provoking ideas that explore applications of biblical truth. The aim is to offer a biblical point that needs to be pondered.

May these brief articles not only stimulate thought. May they provoke thought that produces a change in attitude and actions. The object is not just to know; it is to grow.

G. Michael Cocoris
Santa Monica, CA

A Point to Ponder

AN ACT OF LOVE

One book of the New Testament was written to give believers a practical illustration of love. That book is Philemon. Philemon was a wealthy Christian who had a slave named Onesimus. Onesimus ran away to Rome, where he met Paul. Paul introduced Onesimus to Christ and then instructed him to return to his human master to request forgiveness and restoration. Paul penned the little postcard of *Philemon* for Onesimus to deliver to his owner. It contains a great illustration of love. In it, Paul requests that Philemon "receive him (Onesimus) as you would me, but if he has wronged you, or owes you anything, put that on my account. I, Paul, am writing with my own hand. I will repay" (Phm. 17-19).

Evidently, before running away, Onesimus stole money from Philemon (he had to have money to travel and live). In a grand gesture of love, Paul told Philemon to put Onesimus' debt in his (Paul's) account and that he would repay it. Love does that; it pays.

A large Christian publisher salesman once told me, "I carry samples in the trunk of my car and I would like to give you whatever you wish." I was thrilled because I love books. I chose one or two and thanked him. He then said, "Let me send you a catalog and you can choose from it whatever you wish and I will see to it that you get them." I was hesitant, but I said OK. He then asked if I could send him a tax-deductible receipt. I explained that I could not give him a tax deduction for a personal gift. He accepted that and insisted that he still wanted to send me books.

A Point to Ponder

When the catalog arrived, I limited myself to a small order. He sent me the books and then a strong letter asking for a receipt. I was floored. I didn't know what to do. I wrote him apologetically and explained that I could not legally send him a tax-deductible receipt. I felt terrible.

Sometime later, in a philosophical discussion with a seminary professor, I brought up the situation and asked him what he would have done. He told me the loving thing to do would have been to pay. He suggested that I contribute in that man's name and send him the receipt. I missed that opportunity, but I learned a great lesson. Love pays.

When someone has wronged you, love them. Like Christ, you pay their debt. When someone is in trouble over their head, you pay to pull them out of hot water. Like Paul, you pay for their wrong. These are acts of love.

A Point to Ponder

WALK IN WISDOM

Imagine a man risking his honor, job, and life in prison by selling a few government secrets to a foreign country for a few shekels. Stupid, you say. Imagine a teenager endangering his life, limb, and friends in the family car by driving ninety miles an hour down a busy boulevard. Not smart, you think. Imagine a bag lady living in a fleabag apartment and wandering the streets, rummaging through garbage cans for food when she has thousands of dollars stuffed in a mattress. Foolish, you believe. Imagine a star athlete on a major team throwing his cash and career after a cocaine habit. Ridiculous, you exclaim.

Before you look down your nose at these people, look at your life. Have you ever done anything foolish or stupid? Who hasn't? Some not only do stupid things occasionally, but they also live foolish lives.

It is no wonder that Paul exhorts believers to "see then that you walk circumspectly, not as fools, but as wise" (Eph. 5:15).

The Greek word translated "wise" means skill. A wise walk is a careful, skillful walk. A foolish fellow is careless concerning his walk. He does not watch where he is going. He doesn't think about what he is doing. Consequently, he trips and falls and gets hurt. Don't be stupid; be smart. Don't be foolish; be wise. Walk circumspectly, a Greek word that means "exactness, carefully."

A Point to Ponder

Let me illustrate. Two men lived adjacent to each other. One had a beautiful orchard with luscious fruit. The other had a cat with a lot of natural curiosity. Because vandals constantly picked fruit from the man's orchard, he built a wall around his house with sharp objects, such as nails and pieces of glass, embedded in the top.

Curiosity almost killed the cat. To see what was on the other side of the well, he leaped on top of it, landed on a piece of glass, and cut his paw.

The next time he tried walking on the wall, he was wiser. He found an appropriate place to land and walked gingerly along the entire length of the barrier, carefully and deliberately picking each succeeding step. He was walking wisely; he was walking circumspectly.

Since the world is full of nails and broken glass, believers must be careful how they walk. Don't be foolish. Watch where you're going and walk circumspectly. Walk in wisdom.

A Point to Ponder

WHY NOT RUN?

When problems pile up, troubles mount, and difficulties increase, the tendency is to run. A teenager has problems with his parents and thinks of running away from home. A man has trouble at work and contemplates changing jobs. Difficulties develop in a marriage and the wife dreams of a divorce. Why not run away?

Before you bow out, James says you need to know something. "My brethren, count it all joy when you fall into various trials, knowing that the testing of your faith produces patience. But let patience have its perfect work that you may be perfect and complete, lacking nothing" (Jas. 1:2-4).

The thought of these verses is this: You can count a trial a joy if you know a trial endured produces maturity. In other words, God allows trouble to come into our lives to develop us. Adversity does to our character what fire does to iron—refines it into steel. Problems need not impair us; they can improve us. When you begin to understand that you'll not run away, you can even count a trial as joy. James does not suggest the trial itself is a joy. He simply insists that we can count it a joy if we understand that God allowed it to conform us to the image of Christ. Eventually, You may thank God for His goodness in allowing you to have the trial (1 Thess. 5:18)!

Many years ago, a boy was born with a deformed foot. Two surgeons tried to straighten the foot but failed. The father, an engineer, studied the foot for months and then made a strange-looking box

A Point to Ponder

with rods that screwed into the side. On the end of each rod was a felt tip. Then, he had the surgeon operate again, cutting the muscle and tendons in different places. The foot was then placed in the box and the rods were screwed until the felt tips pressed to bring pressure to bear on the other part of the foot, again almost breaking the bone.

For months the boy's foot was kept in the box. The suffering was indescribable. The child wept. When the father came home, the boy begged him to take off the box and let him be a cripple. The father, mingling his tears with those of his son's, turned the screws tighter. The child was in agony. During those weeks and months, he felt the father was harsh.

Finally, the boy stood erect. Years later, the son, now a gray-haired man, stood over his father's grave. With tears trickling down his cheek, he thanked God that he had a father who cared enough to continue the suffering until the deformity was straightened.

God cares enough about you that He has prepared a box just to straighten out your deformity. Don't run away. Hang in there. When the foot is straightened, you'll be glad you did.

A Point to Ponder

WHEN WEARY IN WELL-DOING

Doing good works is work. Work is tiring. Helping people and even serving the Lord can be exhausting. Visiting the sick, counseling, teaching a Sunday school class, ushering, working in the nursery, etc., makes one grow weary after a while. Faithful servants get tired and become discouraged. The temptation is to relax, slack off, and possibly give up and quit.

What do you do when you grow weary in well-doing? Paul advises, "Let us not grow weary in doing good for in due season we will reap if we do not lose heart" (Gal. 6:9).

The word translated "weary" comes from the Greek word for "coward." The phrase "lose heart" is the translation of a single Greek word that means "to loosen, to release, to unloose as a bow string, to relax." It also means to be faint and was used for mental weariness. These words describe the tired servant who craves to relax, perhaps to retreat from the weariness of the work.

Paul admonishes, however, that when it comes to doing good, we should not relax our effort like we would release a string on a bow. Don't be cowardly; he says, be courageous. He reminds us that if we keep on keeping on, we will reap in due season. To say the same thing another way, if you are to reap, you must have continual effort and constant toil.

When you grow weary in well-doing, remember the law of the harvest. It's not the reaper who decides the kind and size of the harvest; it's the sower. If you focus on the work of sowing, your

A Point to Ponder

weariness will persuade you to slack off or quit, but if you remember the harvest ahead, you will endure the weariness of the moment.

Charles Haddon Spurgeon tells of a poor woman desperately needing coal to heat her house. To help her, a friend ordered a supply and had it delivered. Soon after, the lady's little daughter came out of the house with a small shovel, picked up a scoop full of coal, and took it inside. Spurgeon, who happened by there, saw her do this several times and asked, "Do you expect to get all the coal in with that little shovel?" Confidently, she answered, "Yes, sir, if I work long enough."

She might have given up if she had mused on the massive pile of coal or thought about the weariness in her little arms. Instead, she persisted and endured, knowing that if she stuck with the task eventually, it would get done.

A Point to Ponder

HOW DO YOU PRAY WITHOUT CEASING?

Paul says believers are to "Pray without ceasing (1 Thess. 5:17). That verse has always troubled me. What does it mean? Sounds like a believer is to pray constantly without interruption like a running faucet, but that's impossible!

"Without ceasing" does not mean without interruption. Instead, the idea is "constantly reoccurring," like a periodic dripping faucet. The Greek term translated "without ceasing" was used of a hacking cough. A person with a cough does not cough non-stop all day, but she does cough every few minutes.

The phrase "without ceasing" occurs only four times in the New Testament. Three of these are in 1 Thessalonians. In 1 Thessalonians 1:2, 3, Paul says he mentioned them in his prayers, remembering without ceasing their work and patience. In 1 Thessalonians 2:13, he told the Thessalonians he thanked God without ceasing for how they received the gospel. Then, in 1 Thessalonians 5:17, he tells them to pray without ceasing. He preached what he practiced.

Furthermore, notice that 1 Thessalonians is punctuated with prayer and praise. Paul began by recording his thanksgiving for them (1 Thess. 1:2-10). Then, after he discussed his first visit with them (1 Thess. 2:1-12), he tells them again that he thanked God for them (1 Thess. 2:13-16). The next subject with which Paul deals in this book is the sending of Timothy (1 Thess. 2:17-3:9), and after

A Point to Ponder

that discussion, he prays for them (1 Thess. 3:10-13). In other words, the subjects of prayer and thanksgiving came from Paul's pen periodically as drops from a dripping faucet.

The issue is not how long you pray; it's how long you wait to pray. If you prayed for a person every time you thought of him or her, you would be praying without ceasing.

Stonewall Jackson said, "I have so fixed my habit of mine that I never raise a glass of water to my lips without asking God's blessing; never seal a letter without putting a word of prayer under the seal; never take a letter from the post without a brief sending of my thoughts heavenward; never change my class in the lecture room without a minute's petition for the cadets who go out and for those who come in."

James Gilmore, the pioneer missionary to Mongolia, had a habit of *never* using a blotter. When he reached the bottom of any page, he prayed while waiting for the ink to dry.

Why not make prayer a habit—a constant, often-repeated habit?

A Point to Ponder

IS PROPHECY PROFITABLE?

Is prophecy really profitable? Consider the problems it causes. Prophecy has caused divisions. Christians do not agree on the details of the Second Coming and their differences cause divisions. Prophecy causes divergence. Some believers get so caught up in the details of prophecy that they get diverted from the major task. Prophecy also causes disturbance. Upon learning of the Lord's imminent return, some immature believers have gone so far as to quit their jobs and move to the country. Is the study of prophecy really profitable?

God's answer is yes. When the Bible was written, as much as twenty-five percent was prophetic. Some predictions have been fulfilled. Many have not. While there are many reasons for knowing things to come, Paul mentions one specific reason when he says, 'Now brethren, concerning the coming of our Lord Jesus Christ and our gathering together to Him, we ask you not to be soon shaken in mind or troubled, neither by spirit, nor by word, nor by letter as from us, as though the day of Christ had come" (2 Thess. 2:1-2).

The believers at Thessalonica thought the Tribulation had begun and were deeply disturbed. Either "by spirit" (the exercise of a spiritual gift), "by word," meaning a conversation, or "by letter," they had been given false information concerning prophecy.

Paul exhorts them not to "be soon shaken in mind or troubled."

A Point to Ponder

Paul reveals prophetic events to prevent them from being troubled. He tells them that before the Tribulation can begin, three things must happen: 1) There must be a falling away first, 2) the man of sin must be revealed, and 3) the restrainer must be removed (2 Thess. 2:6-12). In other words, if believers have the correct information about the future, they will not be shaken or troubled (2 Thess. 2:2) or deceived (2 Thess. 2:3). Some think prophecy is unprofitable because it disturbs people. The truth of the matter is that the opposite is true. Prophecy may produce disturbance if false information is believed, but correct teaching concerning prophecy is designed to prevent disturbance and promote stability.

Years ago, before the interstate freeway system was complete, I lived in Tennessee. Once, while traveling in the mountainous terrain between Manchester and Murfreesboro, Tennessee, I found myself sandwiched between a slow-moving trailer ahead of me and a tailgater behind me. I could not pass because of the curves and hills. There was no freeway. I began to get frustrated. I became impatient and aggravated, but I had been over that road many times before and knew it well. I was aware that in a few miles, and thus in a few minutes, I would come up to a red light outside Murfreesboro. I remembered that after that light, there were two lanes on my side of the road and I could pass the trailer in front of me. That made me relax and wait. My knowledge of the future made me patient.

Knowledge of the future affects the present. Study prophecy and be stable. Ignore it and be shaken by false information.

A Point to Ponder

THERE IS NO WAY OUT OF THIS ONE!

Imagine being a pilot in a military jet fighter (for some, that will be difficult, but try anyway). You're on a solo reconnaissance flight high over an enemy country. All is going well—until you notice a red light on the instrument panel blinking on and off. The message of that flashing light hits you like a fist in the face. It means that a radar-guided missile is locked in on your plane. Panic seizes you. There is no escape. If you turn to the right, the missile will hound you. If you turn to the left, it will hunt you until it finds you. If you climb, you will lose power and the missile will gain speed. If you nose down, the missile again moves faster and swifter than you. There is no way out of this one!

You may have never flown a jet, but you no doubt have felt like you were in a situation without escape. A radar-guided temptation was locked in on you and you knew that you couldn't get away. A habit hounds you. No matter which way you turn, it follows in hot pursuit. After a few battles with equal losses, you feel there is no way out of this one. There is no escape.

The facts disagree with you. Consider some of them as reported by Paul, who said, "No temptation has overtaken you except as is common to man, but God is faithful who will not allow you to be tempted above that you're able but will with the temptation also make the way of escape that you may be able to bear it" (1 Cor. 10:13).

A Point to Ponder

These words form Paul's comfort to the tempted. The consolation is two-fold: manward and Godward. First, believers can only experience what is common to man. When we think there's no way out, it is because we think, "I'm different" or "This is different." If anyone else had the same set of circumstances, they could feel trapped, too. Paul assures us that no one encounters an exceptional, extraordinary, or superhuman temptation. Others have faced *this* problem and won. Details may differ, but the underlying difficulty is the same. Therefore, the temptation can be resisted.

Second, God is faithful. He will not allow a believer to be hemmed in so that the only way out is sin. He has promised to preserve His people and He is faithful.

Furthermore, God will provide a way of escape. You may have to think about finding it. You will have to exercise your will (see "flee" in the next verse), but the way out is there. You are not the victim of your circumstance. It is like an army trapped in the mountains, escaping from a seemingly impossible situation through a pass.

The Air Force figures out how a jet could escape a radar-guided missile. Someone discovered that bats operate on radar and attack moths. So, how does a pursued moth escape a radar-guided bat? Answer: He flips over on his back and dives down. Lo and behold, when a jet does that, it escapes the missile. More recently, the Air Force has found other ways of escape. They release metal particles and the missile attacks one of them.

You may feel there is no way out of this one, but there is. There are probably several ways out. Remember, God is faithful. He has provided a way of escape. Search until you find it.

A Point to Ponder

WHY ARE THERE ALWAYS SO MANY PROBLEMS?

Does it seem to you that you are always facing a problem of such magnitude that you sometimes think you're on the brink of disaster? The truth is all believers feel that way. Some conclude that it is because God is punishing them. Even those who have a close walk with the Lord have this experience. Christian leaders are not exempt. Why does God do this to us?

Paul, himself, had the experience. He said, "we are hard pressed on every side, We are perplexed...persecuted...struck down" (2 Cor. 4:8-9). He felt pressure, perplexity, persecution, and pushed down.

Yet, he also said, "Yet not crushed ... not in despair ... not forsaken ... not destroyed" (2 Corinthians 4:8-9). He felt pressure, perplexity, persecution, and pushed down, but he was not distressed, in despair, deserted, or destroyed. Though he constantly felt that he was on the brink of destruction, he was never over the edge.

Why did God allow even the Apostle Paul to live on the edge constantly? Paul himself explains, "For we have this treasure in earthen vessels that the excellency of the power may be of God and not of us (2 Corinthians 4:7), always carrying about in the body the dying of the Lord Jesus that the life of Jesus also may be manifested in our body (2 Cor. 4:10).

Believers are earthen vessels with the life of Jesus Christ inside. God allows the vessel to be treated in such a way that the contents

A Point to Ponder

inside can be seen.

Andrew Murray, a Dutch Reformed leader of South Africa, noticed a beautiful silver mug containing milk on a table. Beside it was an ordinary brown earthenware jar filled with cream. He commented that God puts his richest treasures in lowly vessels. I would add that He sometimes takes that earthenware jar filled with cream, shakes it up and even turns it upside down so that everyone can see what is inside. That just may be, my friend, why you feel shaken up and turned upside down at times.

A Point to Ponder

IMPROVING YOUR MARRIAGE

Some marriages are "on the rocks" and need rescuing; all can be improved. There are many ways that this can be done. May I suggest one of the most basic?

In Colossians 3, Paul addresses the husband/wife relationship, telling husbands to love their wives and wives to submit to their husbands (Col. 3:18-19), but before he spoke directly to believers as married partners, he had a great deal to say to them about being godly. What he said about being spiritually mature is assumed when he addresses them as mates. For example, earlier in the passage, he said, "Bearing with one another and forgiving one another, if anyone has a complaint against another, even as Christ forgave you, so you also must do" (Col. 3:13). A growing, godly believer manifests a forgiving spirit as well as individual acts of forgiveness. One way then to improve your marriage is to practice forgiveness.

Forgive him when the dinner gets cold because he gets home late. Forgive her when she blows the budget on a new outfit. Forgive him when he forgets to fix the faucet. Forgive her when she fails to iron your shirt.

"But," you object, "he/she doesn't deserve it." "He could have called and he didn't." "I had reminded her I needed that shirt today." Granted, your spouse may not deserve it. Forgive anyway! That's what Christian forgiveness is all about—Christ forgave us when we didn't deserve it!

A Point to Ponder

An employee caught embezzling was summoned to the office of the firm's senior partner. Entering the office, the guilty man expected a blistering dismissal and the possibility of criminal prosecution. The elderly boss asked if he was guilty of the crime. The employee was embarrassed and humiliated, confessed his guilt, and admitted he had no defense. "I won't press charges," said the employer, "If I let you stay, can I trust you?" The surprised and repentant clerk assured the boss that he had learned his lesson and that given another chance would prove his trustworthiness, to which the employer said, "You are the second man who has fallen and been pardoned in this business—I was the first."

Let's practice forgiving others at home the way Christ forgave us, that is, though we didn't deserve it, He forgave us anyway. Let's make His pattern our practice. Forgiveness will improve your marriage.

A Point to Ponder

SINGING IN THE RAIN

Most people complain when their circumstances are in any way against them and celebrate only when something good happens to them. Then there are those rare individuals who seem to be able to sing in the rain as well as in the sunshine. What is their secret? What goes on in their head and their heart that makes it possible for them to be glad when their circumstances are sad? For the Christian, the solution is simple. Paul admonishes: "Rejoice in the Lord always, again I say rejoice!' (Phil. 4:4)

The Scripture repeatedly admonishes the believer to rejoice. In this case, Paul commands the believer to rejoice twice in one verse. But how can the believer do that when things in his life are falling apart? Notice that Paul does not say rejoice "in your circumstances" or "good fortune." He says rejoice *in the Lord*. No matter what happens to believers, they can rejoice in the spirit of the Lord. They can be grateful that they know the Lord. They can be thankful that their sins are forgiven. They can be joyful in the prospect that heaven is their future home.

Notice also that Paul says rejoice in the Lord *always*. Believers can always rejoice in the Lord, no matter their circumstances. They can rejoice in the morning, in the afternoon, and in the evening. They can rejoice on Monday as well as Sunday. They can rejoice in January as well as in June. They can rejoice in the Lord in the inner sanctuary of their soul regardless of what is happening in their lives.

A Point to Ponder

There is a difference between happiness and joy. Our word happiness comes from the word happenings. The modern concept of happiness is that when your happenings are in our favor, we are happy, and when your happenings are against us, we are not. The biblical concept of joy is radically different. Believers can rejoice in the Lord; since the Lord never changes, they can always rejoice in the Lord.

Among birds, robins are one of the few birds that sing as cheerfully in the rain as it does in the bright sunshine. When other birds are silent, the songs of the robin can be heard. Don't be an old crow. Be a robin singing in the rain because you are rejoicing in the Lord, not your circumstances.

A Point to Ponder

LAY HOLD ON ETERNAL LIFE

Even if you have trusted Jesus Christ for eternal life, you do not yet have it! Before you can accuse me of heresy, remember what no less than the apostle Paul said, "Lay hold on eternal life, to which you were also called" (I Tim. 6:12)

Now let me explain. In the New Testament, eternal life is both a present possession and a future possibility. If you have trusted Jesus Christ, and Him alone, to get you to heaven, you possess eternal life right now. The Scripture proclaims, "He who believes in the Son has (present tense) everlasting life" (Jn. 3:36). Furthermore, if you have trusted Jesus Christ, you have eternal life and nothing can change that. You will "never perish." Jesus said, "I give them eternal life, and they shall never perish" (Jn. 10:28). Yet, the New Testament also speaks of eternal life as something we do not have at the moment but will obtain in the future. For example, Paul says, "in hope of eternal life" (Titus 1:2). He also teaches, "He who sows to the spirit will of the spirit reap everlasting life" (Gal. 6:8). In other words, in the New Testament eternal life is the gift to be received (Rom. 6:23) and it is the reward to be earned (Mt. 19:28-30). Eternal life is like physical life. You first receive it as a gift, but what you make of your life in the future depends on how hard you work in the present.

Hence, Paul can say, "Lay hold on eternal life." The question is, "How do you do that?" Later in the passage, Paul explains, "Let them do good, that they may be rich in good works, ready to give, willing to share, storing up for themselves a good foundation for the time to come that they may lay hold on eternal life" (I Timothy 6:18-19). In other words, the believer lays hold on eternal life by doing good works and giving money! (see also Mt. 6:19-21 and Gal. 6:6-8.)

D. L. Moody told of a rich man who lay dying. After overhearing that from a friend of her father's, a little girl asked for her dying father, "Are you going away?" When her father confirmed her fears, she asked, "Have you got a nice house and a lot of friends over where you are going?" After a long silence and tears, he said, "Oh, what a fool I've been. I have built a great business here but will be a pauper there." That rich man possessed eternal life, but he had not laid hold on eternal life.

A Point to Ponder

THE SMELL OF HEAVEN

You sense your need for spiritual food, or you wouldn't be reading such an article as this. I appreciate you reading what I have written, and I pray it may be profitable. But I must ask: "Have you read the Scriptures lately?" Every believer must consume, concentrate on, and continue in the Word of God. Why is it so necessary for believers to have hands-on experience with the Scriptures? Paul explains what the Scripture does for us: "But as for you continue in the things which you have learned and been assured of knowing that from whom you have learned them and from childhood, you have known the Holy Scriptures which are able to make you wise for salvation through faith which is in Christ Jesus. All scripture is given by inspiration of God and is profitable for doctrine, for reproof, for correction, for instruction in righteousness that the man of God may be complete thoroughly equipped for every good work." (2 Tim. 3:14-17)

The Scriptures are not only inspired, that is, God-breathed, they are profitable. The Scriptures are profitable for salvation (2 Tim. 3:15). Both the Old Testament (Genesis 15:6) and the New Testament (Gal. 2:16) teach that salvation is by faith alone in Christ. The Scriptures are profitable for the spiritual life (2 Tim. 3:16). All Scripture rebukes us and reminds us that we are to walk in righteousness. Both the Old Testament (Leviticus 19:18) and the New Testament (Jn. 13:14) teach that love is the ultimate

A Point to Ponder

in the spiritual life. The Scriptures are profitable for service (2 Tim. 3:17). With material like Psalm and Proverbs on one hand and Romans and Revelations on the other, the people of God are "equipped" for good work. Thus, the Scriptures are profitable for salvation, sanctification, and service. While what people say about the Scriptures may be helpful, there is no substitute for first-hand exposure to the Scriptures themselves.

John Bunyon, the author of *Pilgrim's Progress*, once said, "Although you may have no commentaries at hand, continue to read the Word and pray, for a little from God is better than a great deal received from man. Too many are content to listen to what comes from men's mouths without searching and kneeling before God to know the real truth. That which we receive directly from the Lord through the study of the Word is from the 'minting house' itself. Even old truths are new if they come to us with the smell of heaven upon them."

A Point to Ponder

A ONE-WORD MESSAGE

May I have a word with you? Normally, that question means, "May I have a short conversation with you," but, in this case, the whole conversation can be condensed to one brief word. The word I wish to share with you is a virtue that virtually all believers need to develop more of in their lives. Paul repeatedly uses this one-word message in Titus. For example: "Likewise exhort the young men to be sober-minded."(Titus 2:6)

Paul has a one-word message for young men: that they be sober-minded. A careful consideration of the whole book of Titus indicates that he did not intend to limit this one-word message to just men. Titus 1:8 lists sober-mindedness as a virtue an elder must possess. Older men are commanded to be sober-minded (see 2:2, where sober-minded is translated "temperate"). The verb form of the word sober-minded is used to describe what older women are to tell younger women to be (see 2:4, where sober-minded is translated "admonish"). Clearly, in Paul's mind, every believer should be sober-minded (Titus 2:12, where sober-minded is translated "soberly").

In *Poor Richard's Almanac*, Benjamin Franklin said, "At twenty years of age, the will reigns; at thirty the wit; at forty the judgment, but God says all men at every age level should be sober-minded."

The Greek word translated "sober-minded" is rich in meaning. (Here's where the "word with you" becomes a brief conversation.) The Greek word means soundness of mind, good sense, and sanity,

A Point to Ponder

but it also contains the nuance of self-control, restraint, and self-discipline. Being sane, sensible, sober-minded, and self-controlled seems to say it all. The essence of the concept consists of two basic elements: sensibility and self-control.

The most godly men I've known have been the most down-to-earth, practical, and sensible men I've known. The men I have respected the most in my life have been cut from that cloth. As a young man, I met a man in his thirties whom I admired greatly. Watching what he did, I thought, "That makes sense. He's a level-headed, thoughtful, common sense kind of guy." His other outstanding characteristic is his discipline, which manifested in everything he did, from jogging to his church work. As a young man, I looked at him and said, "Lord, I need to be like that." I've not arrived yet, but it's one of the major virtues I've always wanted to own. May this word we have shared together become the desire of your heart and the goal of your life.

A Point to Ponder

THE PROBLEM OF FELLOWSHIP WITH GOD

When people trust Jesus Christ as their Savior, they establish a relationship with God. God becomes their Father; they become a child of God. The relationship between father and child grows increasingly intimate as the two communicate and share everything with each other. The Father communicates to believers through His Word and His children share their needs and concerns to Him through prayer. The problem is that His children sin and fellowship, not the relationship, is broken.

What is the solution to this broken fellowship? There are two approaches believers can take toward their sin. John spells them out in his first epistle.

If we say we have no sin, we deceive ourselves, and the truth is not in us. If we confess our sins, He is faithful and just to forgive us our sins and to cleanse us from all unrighteousness (1 Jn. 1:8-9).

Believers can deny their sin. If they do, they deceive themselves (1 Jn. 1:8), lie to others (1 Jn. 1:6) and contradict God (1 Jn. 1:10). If, however, they allow the light of God's nature to expose their sin (1 Jn. 1:7) and confess their sin (1:9), the blood of Jesus Christ will cleanse them "from all sin" (1 Jn. 1:7). The Greek word translated "confess" means "to say the same thing, to agree, to acknowledge." If we acknowledge the sins we're aware of, God will forgive and cleanse *all* unrighteousness. First John 1:9 does not say that if we confess "all" our sins, He will forgive them all. It says if we confess, implying the ones we're aware of because the light has exposed them, He will forgive *all*. There is no need for believers to agonize over sin they are unaware of. As long as they walk in the light, confessing the sins they are aware of, God will forgive them and cleanse them of *all* unrighteousness.

The solution, then, to sin in the life of a believer begins by acknowledging that sin to the Lord. But God only forgives sins, not excuses, so say the same thing God says: Admit sin is sin.

Someone has put it like this:

Man calls sin an accident; God calls it an abomination.
Man calls it a blunder; God calls it blindness.
Man calls it chance; God calls it choice.
Man calls it error; God calls it enormity.
Man calls it heredity; God calls it a habit.
Man calls it liberty; God calls it lawlessness.
Man calls it a mistake; God calls it madness.
Man calls it a relapse; God calls it rebellion.
Man calls it a trifle; God calls it a tragedy.
Man calls it weakness; God calls it wickedness.

A Point to Ponder

SHOULD YOU INVITE A CULTIST INTO YOUR HOME?

The doorbell rings and you go to the door. When you open it, you discover two cultists standing on your doorstep. As you look at them, you feel mixed emotions and even tensions inside of you. In the first place, you're a little annoyed because they've come at an inconvenient time, but the real problem is, what do you do now? The spiritual side of you would like to invite them into your living room, tell them about Christ, and have them trust Him on the spot. The problem is that someone has told you the Bible says you should not let a cultist into your home. 2 John says explicitly, "If anyone comes to you and does not bring this doctrine, do not receive him into your house or greet him; for he who greets him shares in his evil deeds (2 Jn. 10-11).

Does that verse mean that you, as a believer, should not invite a cultist to sit down in your living room so that you can tell him about Christ? Precisely, what does this passage mean?

The issue of what is the meaning of the word "house." Many interpret the word house in this verse to mean a private residence and conclude that John is saying, do not give one peddling false doctrine about Christ hospitality. Such an interpretation is possible. There are reasons, however, for taking "house" as a reference to the church. In the first place, this letter is addressed to a church, not an individual (see verse 1, where "elect lady" refers to a church). "You" in verse 10 is in the plural, suggesting a visit to a group. Furthermore, since there was no church building in the first century, believers assembled for church in a house (Rom. 16:5: 1 Cor. 16:19; Col. 4:15; Phm. 2). If the word "house" refers to the church, then 2 John says do not officially welcome a false teacher as a speaker in your church. For that matter, do not encourage false teachers in any way.

I would not recommend that all believers invite cultists into their homes. Witnessing to a cultist can be tricky. Before you attempt to win any cultist to Christ, you need to know what you're doing. Nevertheless, I do not believe that this verse is teaching that believers should not invite cultists into their homes.

I have witnessed to cultists on my doorstep, and I've also invited them into my living room and presented the gospel to them inside my house. I listened to their presentation first and, as courteously, kindly, and graciously as I can, I give them my testimony (when talking to a cultist, avoid an argumentative attitude at all costs). I usually begin by asking if they know *for sure* that their sins are forgiven and they are going to heaven. When they hedge, I ask why I should trade the assurance I have in Christ for their doubt. That can be most effective.

So, if you know how to handle cultists, don't hesitate to invite them into your living room to give them the gospel.

A Point to Ponder

THE USE OF YOUR HOUSE

For what do you use your house? Obviously, you use it to meet the needs of you and your family. There's a kitchen where you prepare meals, a bathroom for you to shower, and a bedroom where you sleep. You and the family probably spend most of your time at home in the den. All of that is necessary and proper, but can it be wrong? How can using your home to eat, sleep, bathe, and live in be wrong?

The Bible contains the tale of two men who lived in two houses. One used his home properly and the other did not.

"Beloved, you do faithfully whatever you do for the brethren and for strangers who have borne witness of your love before the church. If you send them forward on their journey in a manner worthy of God, you will do well, because they went forth for His name's sake, taking nothing from the Gentiles. We therefore ought to receive such, that we may become fellow workers for the truth" (3 Jn. 5-8).

In 3 John, the apostle John commended a man named Gaius for using his house for hospitality. In practicing hospitality, Gaius was faithful to the truth of God. His faithfulness to the truth produced acts of love in the form of hospitality. Those who experienced Gaius' kindness were so impressed they related it to the whole congregation. John acknowledges Gaius' gracious hospitality in the past and encourages him to continue it in the future. John urged him to continue such hospitality because Gaius was not entertaining mere

A Point to Ponder

traveling tourists; instead, he was assisting traveling teachers for Jesus Christ. By aiding them, John assures Gaius, he was becoming a fellow worker of the truth.

In stark contrast to Gaius, Diotrephes, who loved to have the preeminence, did not practice hospitality. Diotrephes loved himself and used his house only for himself. He did not like, or would not allow, others to use his home for the Lord. He rejected traveling teachers. It is wrong to only use your house for you and your family.

Gaius loved the brethren and used his house for the Lord even though he was sick! He received traveling teachers. Are you hospitable like Gaius or hostile like Diotrephes?

A. T. Robertson, a famous Greek scholar, once wrote an article that was published in a Christian periodical. In the article, he rebuked those who followed the footsteps of Diotrephes. In response to the article, he received at least 25 letters from church officials demanding that their subscription to the magazine be canceled. Their complaints were all the same, "You have personally attacked me in your paper." A. T. Robertson didn't know any of them personally, but apparently, he hit a nerve. Unfortunately, too many believers use their house selfishly instead of for the Lord.

A Point to Ponder

HOW TO GROW

Over the years, many young Christians and young people born again as children have asked me, "How can I grow spiritually?" Perhaps the young, physically and spiritually, have asked that question the most because growth is on their mind. Candidly, all believers should ask: Would you like to grow? How does one do that?

In his first epistle, Peter gives us the formula for spiritual growth. "Therefore, laying aside all malice, all guile, hypocrisy, envy, and all evil speaking, as newborn babes, desire the sincere milk of the Word that you may grow thereby if indeed you have tasted that the Lord is gracious." (1 Pet. 2:1-3).

In 1 Peter 1:22-25, Peter taught that believers are born again by the eternal Word of God and that they have been cleansed from their sins so that they can love one another. Now he concludes (cf. "Therefore") that we should grow so that we can love. But how do we grow? Peter tells us two things to do.

First, sin must be removed so the purified soul can love sincerely and steadfastly. Peter mentions five sins, like taking off a coat, need to be put off. A well-dressed believer does not wear malice, deceit, hypocrisy, envy, or slander. These are out of style for the child of God. Take off these old rags of the old life. They will hinder your spiritual development.

Second, Peter says that believers are to desire the "pure milk of the Word." The Scripture is milk; it supplies nourishment.

A Point to Ponder

This spiritual milk is also "pure," a word that means genuine, unadulterated. Feeding on unadulterated milk produces a clean heart that is without deception (1 Pet. 2:1), so there can be sincere love (1 Pet. 1:22). The purpose of consuming milk is that "you may grow thereby." As physical babes cannot grow without milk, so spiritual newborns cannot grow without spiritual milk. The incentive is that "you have tasted that the Lord is gracious." The taste of grace should excite the appetite for more.

To grow, one must put off sin and desire the milk of the Word. In these verses, Peter *commands* us to desire the Word. If you don't desire the Word, it is probably because of sin. As D.L. Moody said, "Either this book will keep you from sin, or sin will keep you from this book."

Would you like to grow? Then take off sin and drink milk. A medical doctor once wrote, "The best way to begin gaining weight is on a simple diet of milk. I once was on a diet of nothing but milk for nine months and gained weight. For nine months, I did not eat one particle of food other than milk and I DOUBLED MY WEIGHT. IT WAS THE FIRST NINE MONTHS AFTER I WAS BORN." Dr. M. R. DeHaan, the famous medical doctor who became a Bible teacher, was right. The way to grow is to drink the milk of the Word.

A Point to Ponder

WHAT IS SPIRITUAL GROWTH?

When plants or animals grow, they get larger. When children grow, they get taller. But what is spiritual growth? In his first epistle, Peter, who could be called "the apostle of spiritual growth," commands all believers to desire the sincere milk of the Word so that they may grow by it (1 Pet. 2:1-3). In his second epistle, he commands believers to grow and tells us exactly what spiritual growth is. He says, "But grow in grace and knowledge of our Lord and Savior, Jesus Christ. To Him be the glory both now and forever. Amen." (2 Pet. 3:18).

The Greek word translated "grow" means "to increase, to become greater." Believers are to increase in grace and knowledge. The phrase "of our Lord and Savior, Jesus Christ" can modify 1) grace and knowledge or 2) just knowledge. Both are possible. The first option is preferable. Jesus Christ gives grace and believers are to grow in becoming more gracious. He is also the object of our knowledge. Believers need to increase their knowledge *about* Christ and their knowledge *of* Christ, that is, their acquaintance with Him.

Spiritual growth, then, is increasing in the grace of Christ. To grow spiritually is to increase in my realization of His sufficiency to meet my insufficiency. As I do that, I become more and more gracious. A dishonest and immoral man was radically changed when he trusted Jesus Christ. But a short time later, severe physical infirmities made him cantankerous. He heard the sermon, which convicted him of his sin and, as a result, began to depend more and more on the Lord. As he did, he became more and more gracious.

Spiritual growth is knowledge about and personal acquaintances with Jesus Christ. Through His Word, we learn about Him, and as we obey that Word, depending on Him, we get acquainted more and more with Him (see Jn. 14:21, 23).

All believers need to grow. In this passage, Peter acknowledges that his readers knew what he had written to them (2 Pet. 1:13-15, 3:1, 17), yet he commanded them to grow (1 Pet. 3:18). If you are not growing in grace, it is a disgrace. The tragedy is that some believers, even some leaders, have not grown much.

The Associated Press reported, "The promising youth of the 1960s are today's newly arrived executives, but corporate bosses are discovering that their heirs apparently can't read." The article quoted an educator who said, "I met a thirty-year-old executive at a reading clinic who was reading at the second-grade level."

The nature of growth is simple. It is growth in the grace and knowledge of Jesus Christ. The tragedy is too many believers haven't grown in either knowledge or grace.

A Point to Ponder

KEEP YOURSELF IN THE LOVE OF GOD

God loves you and His love is unconditional. No matter what you do, He will still love you, but there is a sense in which you, as a believer in Jesus Christ, can keep yourself in a place of His love. That doesn't mean that you could ever get to the place where God would not love you because, as Paul says, nothing can separate us from the love of God (Romans 8:35-39). Yet Jude says, "But you, beloved, building yourselves up in the most holy faith, praying in the Holy Spirit, keep yourselves in the love of God, looking for the mercy of the Lord Jesus Christ unto eternal life" (Jude 20-21).

This long, complex sentence's main verb and main point is "keep yourselves in the love of God." Clustered around that verb are three participles: building, praying, and looking. The participles explain how the action of the verb is to be accomplished. In other words, the believer is to keep himself in the love of God by building himself up, praying and looking for the Lord.

"Building" depicts spiritual growth under the figure of erecting a house or temple. The "holy faith" is the faith spoken of in the New Testament, an objective body of truth (see Jude 3; Acts 2:42). This requires knowing and obeying the Scripture. Polycarp wrote to the Phillippians, "If you study the epistles of the blessed apostle Paul, you can be built up in the faith given you." Praying in the Holy Spirit is connected with praying according to the Word of God, which the Spirit authored (Eph. 6:18). Finally, believers are to keep looking for the coming of Christ until He arrives. Eternal life is both a present possession and a future prospect. Here it is, the future prospect. By keeping the age to come in view, the believer will not be blinded by the present age.

If believers obey the Word, continue in prayer in the Holy Spirit, and are constantly looking for Christ, they will keep themselves in the love of God and keep themselves from the contamination of false teachers about whom Jude warned us. (Notice that each member of the Trinity is involved in this process of spiritual growth.) You may not be able to keep yourself physically healthy, but you can keep yourself spiritually healthy. You may not be able to keep yourself in your parent's love or your mate's love, but you can keep yourself in God's love.

When Billy Sunday, the famous evangelist, was first saved, a fellow believer said to him, "William, there are three simple rules I wish you'd practice. If you do, no one will ever write "backslider" after your name. Take fifteen minutes each day to let God talk to you: allow fifteen minutes to talk to Him; and then spend fifteen minutes telling others about the Savior." Sunday did that for years. He faithfully spent time with the Lord every morning. Years later, when he became a nationally known evangelist, he attributed much of the blessing of his ministry to the fact that his first impressions of the day came directly from heaven itself. If you want the warmth and intimacy of fellowship with Christ, keep yourself in the love of God by keeping yourself in His Word and be in prayer, looking for His return.

A Point to Ponder

A SILENT WITNESS

I know a man who claims he is a silent witness. According to him, he witnesses with his life, not with his lips. I have even heard preachers suggest something similar. One I know points to Acts 1:8, which says: "But you shall receive power when the Holy Spirit has come upon you and you shall be witnesses to Me in Jerusalem and in all Judea and Samaria, and unto the uttermost parts of the earth" (Acts 1:8). He claims Acts 1:8 teaches you are to "*be* witnesses unto me." According to him, witnessing is not something you *do* as much as it is something you *are*. Is it possible to be a silent witness?

My answer is NO! The Greek word "witness" is a forensic term, a courtroom term. A witness is someone who *tells* the court what he knows. He is not the judge, the jury, or the prosecuting attorney. He is a witness; he must relate what he has seen and heard. Likewise, a witness for Christ is not to try people or judge them or condemn them; he is to tell them what he knows. So, the word's very meaning indicates you cannot be a *silent* witness. Furthermore, just going to Jerusalem, Judea, Samaria, and the rest of the world without saying something will not communicate anything about Jesus. To be a witness of Jesus, His name, who he is, and what He did must be spoken,

A silent witness could never convey a message, convince a jury, or convert anyone. He would frustrate the judge and fail the court. He would be in contempt of court! It just wouldn't work.

A Point to Ponder

Please don't misunderstand. The issue is not, "Can you witness with your life?" Obviously, we can and we must. The question is, "Can one witness with his life only, never opening his mouth?" The answer to that is NO! No matter how good or godly your life is, if you never said anything about Jesus Christ, no one would ever know your godly life was because of Him!

Let me illustrate. Suppose someone afflicted with polio is in a hospital ward with other patients. All the patients in that ward are bedridden and unable to walk. Then, one day, our "someone" finds a cure. Now he can walk! Immediately, he wants to tell all the other patients. So, he bounces out of bed and does cartwheels down the ward every day, but he never says a word. The sick might know he had found the cure, but they would never know how to be cured.

You can be silent, or you can be a witness, but you cannot be a silent witness.

A Point to Ponder

JUDGE RIGHTEOUSLY

Believers, who would never think of committing murder, adultery, or armed robbery, sin regularly by judging unrighteously. They judge situations and people merely on appearance; motives and actions are criticized before all the facts are known.

In chapter 7 of the Gospel of John, the Jews made that mistake. A year earlier, Christ had healed a man on the sabbath. When He comes to observe the Feast of Tabernacles, He discovers that people are angry with Him for that act. He draws their attention to the fact that, according to Mosaic Law, a baby was to be circumcised when he was eight days old, even if that day fell on the Sabbath. Jesus then asks why, if such a ritualistic act as circumcision could be performed on the sabbath, He should be judged for performing an act of mercy.

It appeared that His act was a breach of the Sabbath. In reality, it was not. So Jesus says to them: "Do not judge according to appearance, but judge with righteous judgment" (Jn. 7:24). In other words, don't judge a situation by the way it looks to you, but by the way it looks to God.

A pair of crutches was being sold at an auction. A crippled boy was the first to bid on them, but a well-dressed older man offered more. The people in the crowd showed their disapproval. One lady cried, "Shame on you! Let the boy have them." Nevertheless, whatever price the youngster cried out, the man would top it.

A Point to Ponder

Finally, the little boy held up all he had—a five-dollar bill. The man offered more and bought the crutches. The young lad turned away in tears. Then, the gentleman presented the crutches to the boy saying, "When I saw that you were crippled, my heart went out to you, so I decided to buy the crutches for you." The crowd, realizing they had completely misjudged the situation, applauded.

Beware of superficial judgment. Don't judge a situation by how it looks, but by how it really is—by the way it looks to God. Judge righteously!

A Point to Ponder

HOW TO CATCH FISH

Why do some win more people to Christ than others? Although there are several answers to that question, one essential truth is taught in Luke 5:1-11.

Jesus said, "Launch out into the deep and let down your nets for a catch" (Luke 5:4). These words must have stunned the disciples. The fish came to the surface at night in the Sea of Galilee. During the day, they went to the bottom in very deep waters. If they hadn't caught anything all night, they would not likely catch anything during the day. Therefore, Peter answered, "Master, we have toiled all night and caught nothing; nevertheless, at Your word, I will let down the net" (Lk. 5:5).

Peter decided to obey anyway. The result was a net-breaking, boat-sinking catch. Christ then said to Simon, "Do not be afraid. From now on, you will catch men" (Lk. 5:10).

One of the things Christ stressed was that when He said do it, do it! But there is another truth here, as the remainder of the passage illustrates. The more they fished, the more they caught.

Several years ago, the men of my church took an annual deep-sea fishing trip. We boarded the boat in Long Beach at about 11:00 p.m. Friday night. While we slept, the boat traveled toward San Clemente. At 6:00 a.m., the boat stopped; we all piled out of the bunks and dropped our lines into the water. After fishing all morning, we headed back.

A Point to Ponder

As we compared notes, I discovered that everyone else caught several fish, but I caught only one! The reason was simple. At the same time, the others were catching fish between 8:00 and 10:a.m. I was catching 40 more winks. Besides that, it was sprinkling when I got out of bed the second time. Not wanting to fish in the rain, I went to bed again.

It took a lot to get me going, but it didn't take much to stop me. I suspect I would have caught more fish had it been reversed.

A Point to Ponder

GOD'S INCREDIBLE PROMISE

Most of us are so preoccupied with making more money to pay for a bigger house and a newer car that we don't have time to serve the Lord. The more materialistic our society has become, the more difficult it is for pastors to get believers to work in the church nursery, with teenagers, or with the aged. But, you say, "If I am not concerned about these things, who will be?"

Jesus answered that in Matthew 6. He told us not to worry about our lives, including what we eat and drink. He then made this incredible promise: "But seek first the kingdom of God and His righteousness and all these things will be added to you." (Mt. 6:33).

The phrase "these things" in the context of Matthew 6 includes food, clothing, and tomorrow (Mt. 6:25, 31, 32, 34). Jesus invites us to consider the birds of the air and the lilies of the field. God provides for those and will provide for those who first seek His kingdom and righteousness. God's incredible promise is if we do His work and will, He will provide for us.

Queen Elizabeth chose a busy merchant to fulfill an important ambassadorial mission. When informed of this honor, he asked to be excused, explaining that it would cost him great monetary loss and severely interrupt the supervision of his industrial activities. The queen responded, "You look after my business abroad and I will look after yours at home." The merchant accepted the appointment and was gone for several years. When he returned, he found that

A Point to Ponder

the queen, true to her word, had more than adequately taken care of his affairs.

Is God able to provide for us? Is He able to provide for us better than we can provide for ourselves? To discover the reality of the answer in your life, begin to live by Matthew 6:33.

A Point to Ponder

BELIEVING PRAYER

We don't get answers to prayer because we don't pray! James reminds us, "You do not have because you do not ask" (Jas. 4:2). But some will argue that they do ask and don't get an answer. To them, I would say we must pray according to His will. John insists, "If we ask anything according to His will He hears us and if we know He hears us whatever we ask we know that we have the petitions that we have asked Him" (1 Jn. 5:14-15). If you tell me that you are praying according to His will, which you learned from His Word, then I would say the issue is that you must believe. That's what Jesus said. "Therefore, I say to you whatever things you ask when you believe that you received them and you will have them" (Mk. 11:24).

We don't receive answers to prayer because 1) we don't pray, 2) we don't pray according to His will, and 3) when we pray according to His will, we don't believe He will answer. We must pray in His will, believing He will answer. As someone has said, a faith that prays for rain takes an umbrella to work.

When Hudson Taylor went to China, he made a voyage on a sailing ship. As the channel between the Southern Malay peninsula and the Island of Sumatra neared, he heard an urgent knock on his stateroom door. When he opened the door, he discovered the captain of the ship. "Mr. Taylor," he said, "We have no wind. We are drifting toward an island where the people are heathen and I fear

A Point to Ponder

they are cannibals." "What can I do?" asked Taylor. "I understand you believe in God and I want you to pray for wind." "All right, Captain, I will, but you must set the sails." "Why, that's ridiculous! There's not even the slightest breeze. Besides, the sailors will think I'm crazy." But finally, because of Taylor's insistence, the captain agreed to set the sails. When he returned forty-five minutes later, he found Hudson Taylor on his knees, praying to God for wind. "You can stop now," said the Captain, "We've got more wind than we know what to do with."

When you pray, make sure you prepare to receive the answer.

A Point to Ponder

YOU CAN BE CONTENT

Covetousness is the key to contentment. If you covet what you do not have, you will be discontented and dissatisfied. On the other hand, if you covet what you already have, you will be content with it, provided you can never lose it. But that's the problem, isn't it? Everything we have, we can lose, so how, then, is it possible for a person to be content? The answer is in Hebrews. "Let your conduct be without covetousness; be content with such things as you have. For He Himself has said, 'I will never leave you nor forsake you'" (Heb. 13:5)

Believers in Jesus Christ can be content with what they have because what they have is Jesus Christ and they can never lose Him. The most emphatic statement in the New Testament is "I will never leave you nor forsake you." In English, a double negative negates an assertion. In Greek, a double negative is emphatic. The statement in Hebrews 13:5, "I will never leave you nor forsake you," contains two double negatives. This is the only place in the New Testament where that emphatic construction occurs twice in the same statement!

If you covet what you do not have or more of what you do have, you will be perpetually discontent no matter how much you have. If you covet what you have and cannot lose, you will be content. Since, as a believer, you have Christ and cannot lose Him, desire Him first and foremost, and you will be content. You have within you *who* it takes for you to be content.

A Point to Ponder

An ancient Persian legend tells of a wealthy man named Al Haffed, who owned a large farm. A visitor told him of a fabulous amount of diamonds that could be found in other parts of the world. The vision of all that wealth made Al feel poor by comparison, so he sold his farm and set out to find greater riches. His search proved to be fruitless. Finally, penniless and in despair, he committed suicide by jumping into the sea. In the meantime, the man who purchased his farm noticed the glitter of an unusual stone in a shallow stream on the property. He reached into the water and to his amazement, he pulled out a huge diamond. Later, when working in his garden, he uncovered more valuable stones. Al had what he desired within his farm, but he looked every place but the right place.

A Point to Ponder

ASK HIM IN FOR WHAT?

One of the most well-known verses in the Bible is Revelation 3:20. It is also one of the most misapplied verses in the Scripture. The verse says, "Behold, I stand at the door and knock. If anyone hears My voice and opens the door, I will come in to him and dine with him and he with Me." (Rev. 3:20)

The popular treatment of this verse suggests that Jesus is standing outside the door of a sinner's heart. If the sinner invites Him in, Jesus will come in to *save* him. Is Revelation 3:20 a salvation verse?

The answer is no. The context of the verse is Jesus speaking to a church (3:14). Contrary to popular opinion, this church was filled with Christians, for He tells them that He will chasten them (3:19). The Greek word translated "chasten" means "child train." Furthermore, the Lord did not say He would come "into" him, but "in to" him. The Greek word translated "to" means to be before someone, but it stops short of entry. If entry was the idea, another Greek preposition would have been used. In other words, Revelation 3:20 says that Jesus is knocking at the door of a church. If any individual invites Him in, Jesus will come in the building and stand before the person (see "Don't ask Jesus to come into your heart" in my book *Evangelism, A Biblical Approach*, for a more detailed discussion of this verse).

The question is, what is Jesus coming in to do? To save? No. The text clearly says if He comes in to the person, He will dine

A Point to Ponder

with that person. Revelation 3:20 is an invitation to fellowship, not salvation. Jesus Christ wants to fellowship with you today. Talk to Him like you would an intimate friend over dinner.

Many years ago, King George V and Queen Mary were vacationing by the seaside. One day, they took a long walk along the ocean front. While on the walk, the queen sprained her ankle. They made it to the nearest cottage and knocked. A voice from within the house said, "Who's there?" "King George and Queen Mary," was the reply. "You don't expect me to believe that do you?" exclaimed the occupant. "See for yourself," said the King. Opening the door, the man and his wife immediately invited the royal couple into their home, giving them hospitality and help. For years, the lady of the house retold the story and always concluded by saying, "You know, we almost refused to let them in the house."

Don't make that mistake. Invite the Lord in for fellowship today.

A Point to Ponder

LAMP OR LAMP POST?

Do you use your Bible as a lamp or a lamp post? The Bible claims that it is a lamp. Unfortunately, many use it as a lamp post. Let me explain. The Psalmist said: "Your Word is a lamp to my feet and a light to my path" (Ps. 119:105).

The Word of God is a lamp; it gives light so we can see where to walk. The truth of the Word of God illuminates our minds so we can see God's direction. We decide to walk the path He has designated in His Book.

Some people use the Bible like a drunk uses a lamp post, not as a light to show them the way but as a post to support their instability. When they read it, they really do not understand its message. Its truth does not give them light and direction; instead, they read it to get emotional support. Reading the Bible makes them "feel" better.

A woman once told me, "I have been reading the Bible more lately than anything in my entire life, yet I do not have peace." She looked deeply troubled, so I asked, "Is there something that is really bothering you?" She replied, "Yes." "Do you want to talk about it?" I queried. "No," she said, "but I guess I need to talk to someone, so here goes." What followed was the story of a conflict she had with another believer.

My advice to her was simple. Stop reading the Bible to get peace. If you do what the Bible says, you will get the peace the Bible promises. I also suggested she go to that person and make things right.

That lady did not have peace because she was using the Bible as a lamp post for emotional support. She was hurt and she wanted God to comfort her. She was not using the Bible as a lamp for light. She was not following its instructions.

By the way, she took my advice, followed the light from the lamp and found harmony, peace, and joy.

May I ask if you use the Bible as a lamp or a lamp post?

A Point to Ponder

THE WISE OR OTHERWISE

Teenagers often ask, "What's wrong with ...?" Sometimes the answer is simple: God says, "Thou shalt not ...!" But for some issues, it's not that simple. God has not explicitly spoken about everything. Furthermore, the thing may not be wrong in itself. What do you do then?

Frankly, a great deal depends on the problem being discussed, but as a general rule, I've often suggested a principle in Proverbs. "Get wisdom! Get understanding! Do not forget, nor turn away from the words of my mouth" (Prov. 4:5).

The principle is "get wisdom." There is something beyond "what is right and wrong;" it is "what is wise and foolish." The issue is right and wrong in Exodus 20, where the 10 Commandments are recorded. In Proverbs, the issue is not only righteousness and unrighteousness but wisdom and stupidity. God wants us to do what is right, but that doesn't cover everything. Beyond that, He wants us to walk in wisdom. Use sanctified common sense. Beyond asking what is right, ask what is wise.

Let me illustrate. A man lived at the top of a tall mountain. The only way to the top was by stagecoach. At one point on the road, there was a wall of rock on one side and a cliff with no guardrail on the other. The man needed a driver, so he put an ad in the paper and three men applied. To determine which driver should get the job, the man asked each one to drive the stagecoach up the mountain.

A Point to Ponder

When the first driver got to that dangerous spot, he thought to himself, "To get the job, I have got to prove I can handle this team of horses near the edge of a cliff." So he drove the team within one foot of the precipice.

When the second man got to the same place, he thought to himself, "If I am going to get the job, I have to do better than the first fellow." So he drove within six inches of the edge.

The third man arrived at the infamous test and decided, "Job or no job, I'm not driving anywhere near that edge." He guided the stagecoach as close to the other side near the wall of rock as he could.

Technically, there was nothing wrong with driving within six inches of the edge, but that is certainly not the better part of wisdom.

Which driver would you hire?

A Point to Ponder

ARE BELIEVERS TO REJOICE *ALL* THE TIME?

One of the Bible's most demanding and seemingly impossible verses is in I Thessalonians. "Rejoice evermore" (1 Thess. 5:16). Rejoice *evermore*! Surely, that does not mean rejoice *all the time*. Rejoice in the sunshine, but indeed not in the shadows. After all, even Jesus was a man of sorrows and acquainted with grief.

Maybe a careful study of the Greek text will help. Such an exercise yields to the following observations: 1) "Rejoice" is in the present tense and 2) "evermore" literally means "always, all the time" and, furthermore, it is written in the Greek text in such a way as to be emphatic.

There is no getting around it. This verse means *rejoice all the time*. That includes times of trial and tribulation. When Paul penned this to the Thessalonians, everything was not well. The Thessalonians had plenty of pressure and problems. Some were sorrowing for departed loved ones (1 Thess. 4:13). Some may have had financial problems (1 Thess. 4:11-12). Persecution had been a problem and probably still was (1 Thess. 2:13).

The Bible clearly teaches that we are to rejoice—even when things are not going well. James 1:2 instructs us to count it all joy when we are in trials. Romans 5:3 declares we glory in tribulation. If you don't know how to rejoice during a trial, you don't know how to rejoice.

A Point to Ponder

But how can a person do that? The answer is "before God" (1 Thess. 3:9). Without God, things can look dark and dismal. Before the Lord, I see the light. I see the good hand of God in control and know that all things work together for good; therefore, I can rejoice during a trial. Anyone can sing in the sunshine; only believers can sing in the rain.

Jesus was a man of sorrows and acquainted with grief (Isa. 53:3). He was also the most joyful person who ever lived (Heb. 1:8-9). Paul knew what it was to be amid affliction (1 Thess. 3:7) and yet experience joy (1 Thess. 3:9). So rejoice all the time. You can even have joy amid sorrow—all because of the Lord.

A missionary tells of reaching a small Chinese town shortly after bandits had done their worst. A native Christian showed them the ruins of his house: thatched roof, rafters, rude furniture, all turned to ashes. Then, as though it was the last straw, he said, "They even burned my Bible and hymnbook." He picked up the single page of his Chinese hymnbook from the ruins, which was the only thing that had escaped the flames. The missionary took it and read, "Joy to the world, the Lord has come!" It seemed a mockery, this note of joy in the midst of desolation. But the missionary said, "If you could have gone to the little chapel and seen the light on the face of that Christian and heard him sing, you would know there is joy in the world because the Lord has come."

Picture it: a song of joy amid ashes!

A Point to Ponder

THE AUDIENCE MAKES THE DIFFERENCE

Beware! This truth could change your life. It has altered mine on more than one occasion and in more than one way. I remember well when it affected what I said (and what I did not say) and what I did (and what I did not do). It changed my attitude when I didn't want it changed. What truth does all of that, you ask? Consider a statement from a Psalm. "The Lord looks from heaven and sees all the sons of men" (Ps. 33:13).

THE LORD IS WATCHING! That truth can stop you *from* doing something. A fellow was about to steal something. First, he looked to the right and then to the left to make sure that no one was watching. When his buddy realized what was happening, he said, "There is a direction you forgot." He pointed up. The crime never took place.

That truth cannot only prevent crime, but it can produce cooperation. It can stimulate you to do something. When Louie Little coached football at Georgetown University, he had a player of average ability on his squad. He was a "good boy." He just never made the first team. When the player's father died, Lou was asked to break the news to him. As soon as he did, the student went home for the funeral. Several days later, he was back. "Coach," he pleaded, "Will you start me in the game against Fordham?" Lou was reluctant but finally said, "OK, but only for a play or two."

A Point to Ponder

After the kickoff, when the dust cleared, this player made the tackle on the seven-yard line, so Lou let him stay in the game. For sixty action-packed minutes that inspired youngster ran, blocked and tackled like an All-American. He even won the game because he intercepted a pass.

After the game, Lou praised him. "Son, that was terrific. What got into you?" The student replied, "Do you remember seeing my father?" The coach said, "Yes, I remember seeing you and your father walking arm-in-arm across the campus on several occasions." The student replied, "Well, few people knew it, but my father was blind. I think today was the first time he ever saw me play." The audience makes the difference.

Regardless of what you do or do not do, remember, THE LORD IS WATCHING.

A Point to Ponder

ARE BELIEVERS TO GIVE THANKS IN *EVERY* SITUATION?

Bible-taught believers know that we are to praise God. We are to have an attitude of gratitude. We are to thank God daily. But the apostle Paul made a statement that makes it sound like that even more than that is required. He wrote, "In everything give thanks" (1 Thess. 5:18). In *everything,* give thanks? Certainly, that does not mean thanks in *every* situation. What about circumstances where it would be unreasonable to be thankful, for example, lying on a hospital bed in severe pain?

Technically, 1 Thessalonians 5:18 does not say, "*For* everything give thanks," but "*In* everything give thanks." The idea is that in every circumstance of life, sickness, health, poverty, and wealth, we should give thanks.

Paul taught this truth by example. Listen to him when things were going well. He said, "We give thanks to God always for you all" (1 Thess. 1:2). Again, he explained, "For what thanks can we render to God for you" (1 Thess. 3:9). Now, watch him when things are going wrong. He experienced this truth then as well. In Philippi, he was arrested, beaten, and thrown in jail (Acts 16). The scourging was Roman, not Jewish. The Jews had a limit on the number of stripes a prisoner could receive, namely, forty save one. The Romans had no such restriction. The number of lashes depended on the caprice of the jailer. Luke says it was "*many*

A Point to Ponder

stripes" (Acts 16:23). Paul called it "suffering" (1 Thess. 2:2). Yet, in that painful situation, "Paul and Silas were praying and singing hymns to God" (Acts 16:25).

So, we who know the God of abundant benefits should constantly thank Him in every situation. The next time you are tempted to complain, why not replace griping with gratitude? Thank Him not just when you win but even when you seemingly lose.

During World War II, the Germans bombed England. One morning after a raid, a man stood in the street and gazed at his bomb-wrecked house. Then he told his wife, "This morning someone came to our dugout and told me we had lost everything. It's a lie. Thank God I still have health and strength to carry on my job. I still have you, my dear, and the children. Thank God you are all safe. Hitler hasn't smashed my faith in the love and the wisdom of God or my faith in the ultimate victory over wrong. I still have hope for the future. I can still call my soul my own. I am still alive and ready for action again. So I reckon that you and I ought to thank God that we saved more than we have lost. Houses and buildings may be wrecked and ruined, but you and I still hold on to the things that can never be shaken or destroyed."

In the middle of everything, there is something for which we can thank God.

A Point to Ponder

HOW TO GET YOUR PRAYERS ANSWERED

Imagine a small town with a courthouse in the center of a square. Around the square are shops, stores, and a service station. Nearby is a huge warehouse containing everything everyone in town needs. Everyone has a key. Someone has suggested that that is a picture of us and the warehouse of heaven. God has promised to supply our needs. The key to that divine storehouse is prayer. "Ask," God says, "and you shall receive."

But if you're like me, there have been times you've asked and not received. I have put the key in the lock and it seemed to fit, but the door did not open. So I have asked, what is the key to using the key? What's the key to answered prayer?

Nehemiah 1 contains a prayer that illustrates how we get our prayers answered. Nehemiah prayed in the middle of the prayer, "Remember, I pray, the word that You commanded Your servant Moses, saying" (Neh. 1:8).

Nehemiah heard from his brother that the Jerusalem wall was in ruins and that Jews were being reproached. He remembered that God promised Moses that He would scatter them if they sinned. He also recalled that God promised that if they turned to Him, He would return them. Nehemiah longed to see that promise fulfilled. The burden bowed him before the Lord. In prayer, Nehemiah *reminded God of what He had promised.* Prayer translates promises into performance. Prayer is not to get man's will done in heaven. It is to get God's will done on earth. The key to answered prayer is the will of God as revealed in the Word of God. Prayer reminds God what He said in His Word He wants to do on earth.

Let me illustrate. I have a friend who became concerned about his teenage daughter. She was dating an unsaved fellow. So the fellow prayed that they would break up. The more he prayed, the "thicker" they got. Then, one day, it dawned on him. The will of God in that situation was for the fellow to be saved. So, he prayed that God would save his daughter's boyfriend. Guess what happened? He got saved ... and soon after, they broke up.

The key to answered prayer is to ask what God says He wants to be done in this situation. Then, remind Him of what *He* said *He* wanted and ask Him to do it.

A Point to Ponder

HOW TO GET STARTED

One of evangelism's most challenging tasks is starting an evangelistic conversation. Even trained Christians who know how to present the gospel have difficulty starting the conversation. Personal workers who can lead others to Christ in an evangelistic setting have difficulty getting the conversation started during a coffee break at work. How does one start an evangelistic conversation?

Philip is the only evangelist mentioned in the New Testament. Acts 8 is the only account of him leading someone to Christ. How did he get started? In that chapter, a high-ranking Ethiopian was reading the book of Isaiah aloud. Reading in ancient times was almost inevitably aloud because the words were written together with no space between the words and no punctuation. It was easier to read aloud than to read silently. So, as Philip approached the eunuch, he heard him reading. Luke records, "So Philip ran to him and heard him reading the prophet Isaiah and said, "Do you understand what you are reading?" (Acts 8:30).

Notice Philip started the evangelistic conversation by asking a question. Every evangelistic method I've seen uses this approach. Campus Crusade asks, "Have you heard of the four spiritual laws?" Evangelism Explosion recommends, among other things, that you ask, "Suppose that you were to die tonight and stand before God and He were to say to you, 'Why shall I let you into My heaven?'

A Point to Ponder

Would you say?" A highly evangelistic Baptist pastor recommends you ask, "If you died now, do you know that you would go to heaven?" This approach works with all classes of people. Crusade labors among university students, Evangelism Explosion has been successful among professional people, the Baptist pastor ministers to the working class, yet all use the same basic principle to get an evangelistic conversation going—they ask a question.

If you have not done this before, your reaction might be, "That's a bold approach! Won't it offend people?" If you are genuinely concerned about people and courteous, asking a simple question will not offend them. I have used this approach for over half of a century, and to my knowledge, I do not recall *ever* offending anyone.

A lady was waiting in a shopping mall for her husband. A Christian approached her, gave her a track, and asked if she knew she was going to heaven. As they talked, her husband returned and she had to leave. As they walked away, the husband asked, "What did he want?" The wife replied, "He wanted to know if I was going to heaven." The husband responded, "That's none of his business," to which the wife said, "Funny if you could have seen the expression on his face, you would have thought that it was."

A Point to Ponder

HOW TO BE HAPPY

A national insurance company once conducted a survey that discovered people had three major concerns: happiness, success, and security. Of these, the greatest was happiness. Most, if not all, want to be happy, but how does one find that elusive thing called "happiness?" Some set their sights on a pot of happiness at the end of their rainbow, only to get there and discover the pot is empty. Where is it? What do I have to do to find it?

Psalm 1 has the answer. It says, "Blessed is the man who walks not in the counsel of the ungodly nor stands in the path of sinners nor sits in the seat of the scornful, but his delight is in the law of the Lord and in His law he meditates day and night" (Ps. 1:1-2). The Hebrew word translated "blessed" is not the usual word for blessed. The word used in this passage means "happy." It is written in the Hebrew text in such a way that it should be translated "Oh, how completely is the man." These verses, then, describe the completely happy man from God's point of view.

First, the psalmist tells what the happy man does not do. He rejects the way of the wicked. He rejects the suggestions, the sin, and the scorn of those who do not know God (Ps. 1:1). Second, he receives the way of the Word. He delights in and meditates in the Word of God constantly (Ps. 1:2). The bottom line, then, is the happy man constantly meditates in the Word of God.

A Point to Ponder

What is meditation? The Hebrew word means "to think on, muse." It can also mean "to mourn" or even "to mutter," that is, "to mumble." It is the word used for music. A happy man thinks about the Word all the time and catches himself mumbling it to himself or even singing it to himself. Meditating in the Word results in faith (Isa. 26:3) and obedience (Joshua 1:8). The trusting, obedient man is a happy man. As the songwriter said, "Trust and obey, for there's no other way to be happy in Jesus but to trust and obey." But the key to faith and obedience is meditation.

In Goethe's Egmont, Jetter, a tailor, complains that the spies of the Inquisition listened for every unguarded word. He says that these spies would sometimes push into his house while he was seated at his workbench humming a psalm. "I think nothing about it, humming it just because I got it in my throat. However, right away, they took me off to jail as a heretic."

One wonders what an enemy would find the average Christian "muttering" to himself today while he works. Would it be the Scriptures? Thinking about the Word or your worries is the difference between a happy and an unhappy person.

A Point to Ponder

MINISTERING TO THE MINISTER

During a question and answer session, someone asked me, "How can I minister to my pastor?" (No, it was not a pastor who put someone up to ask the question.) Most believers only think of their pastors ministering to them. They forget that they are to minister to the minister. But how does a "layman" minister to a pastor?

The list of ways a member can minister to the pastor is like a grocery list—long. Certainly, one item that should be at the top of the list is mentioned by the apostle Paul in 1 Thessalonians, "Brethren, pray for us" (1 Thess. 5:25). This is not the only passage in which Paul requested prayer for himself (see 2 Thess. 3:1, Eph. 6:19, Col. 4:3, etc.).

You might ask, "Exactly what do I ask for when I pray for my pastor?" John Welch, a preacher of a bygone day, answered that by saying, "Pray for your pastor. Pray for his body that he might be strong and spared many years. Pray for his soul that he may be kept humble and holy, a burning and shining light. Pray for his ministry that it may be abundantly blessed, that he may be anointed to preach good tidings. Let there be no secret prayer without naming him before God, no family prayer without carrying your pastor in your heart to God."

May I suggest that if the people in a church faithfully prayed for their pastor, that church would experience more of God's blessing? Wilbur Chapman tells of going to Philadelphia to pastor the

A Point to Ponder

Wannamaker's church. After his first sermon, an old man met him in the front of the pulpit and said, "You're pretty young to be the pastor of this great church. We've always had older pastors. I'm afraid you won't succeed. But you preach the gospel and I'm going to help you all that I can."

Dr. Chapman said, "I looked at him and thought to myself, he's a crank." But the old man continued, "I'm going to pray for you that the Holy Spirit's power may be upon you and two others have coveted to join with me." Dr. Chapman continued, "I did not feel so bad when I learned that he would pray. Two became two hundred who met every service to pray. Elders knelt so close around me to pray for me that I could put out my hand and touch them on all sides. I went into the pulpit feeling that I would have God's blessing and answer to the prayers of 218 men. It was easy to preach, a very joy. Anyone could preach with such conditions. And what was the result? We received 1,100 into our church by conversion in three years, and 600 were men. It was the fruit of the Holy Spirit—an answer to the prayers of those men. I do not see how the average pastor preaches under average circumstances."

Brethren, pray for us who are pastors.

A Point to Ponder

A DEED IS WORTH A THOUSAND WORDS

Years ago, a lady who fancied herself a great poet gained admittance to the office of a New York magazine editor. "I would like some of my poems published in your magazine," she said. "About what?" inquired the editor. "All about love," she explained rapturously. "Well, before I look at them, perhaps you ought to give me your definition of that important quality," he replied. Casting her eyes heavenward and putting on an assumed tone, she gushed, "Love is gazing upon a limpid pool at night, as it is bathed in simmering moonbeams, and when the lilies are in full bloom and ..." "Stop! Stop!" cried the editor, "You are wrong—very, very wrong! I'll tell you what love is. It is getting up cheerfully out of a warm bed on a cold winter morning at 2:00 a.m. to give needed affection and tender care to an ailing child."

What is love? Is it a feeling? Is it a poetic expression or a sacrificial deed done in the middle of the night? While it is true that love may be expressed in words, it should also be expressed in works. John the Apostle said, "My little children, let us not love in word or in tongue, but in deed and truth" (1 Jn. 3:18).

The opposite of loving "in word" is to love "in deed" and the opposite of loving "in tongue" is to love "in truth." In other words, a believer should love from the heart and in action instead of professing to love and not having it at all, or saying you love

A Point to Ponder

when you do but going no further.

Would you like to know if you are loving a person? Don't look for just a warm feeling. Don't look at sentimental words. Look at your life and ask, "What am I doing for the person? Am I doing what is best for him or her? Am I seeking that individual's highest good?"

In 1968, Roy Campanella, the famous baseball player, was in a wheelchair because of an automobile accident. He became concerned about the boys on the streets of New York City, so he spent seven weeks of the summer teaching them about baseball. He could have shown his interest by letting his name be used to support the summer program, but instead of just saying something, he did something. That's the kind of love God wants all of us to have.

One deed is worth a thousand words.

A Point to Ponder

TRY THE RESURRECTION

One of the frustrations of trying to win people to Christ is that some who ought to believe don't. When you encounter such individuals, you can't help but scratch your head and ask yourself, "What will it take for some people to believe?" One possible answer is the same thing it took to get James to believe.

James, the half-brother of Jesus, did not believe that Jesus was the Christ (Jn. 7:5). James saw firsthand and close-up the sinless life of Christ. As little boys, they played together. As young men, they worked together in their father's carpenter shop. Yet James did not believe. He also heard the matchless discourses of Christ and even witnessed some of His miracles, yet James did not believe them.

Years later, however, James did believe. In Acts 1, he is in a prayer meeting with the disciples and Mary, the mother of Jesus (Acts 1:14). By Acts 12, he is the leader of the believers at Jerusalem (Acts 12:17; see also Acts 15:13, 21:18, Gal. 2:9, 12). What convinced him?

The answer is in 1 Corinthians 15, which says in part that after that, "He was seen by James and then by all the apostles" (1 Cor. 15:7). Before the resurrection, James did not believe. After the resurrection, he did. What happened in between was that he saw that Christ, indeed, had come back from the dead. Not just seeing the sinless Christ or the miracle-working Christ but coming face-to-face with the resurrected Christ convinced James of who Christ

A Point to Ponder

was. The resurrection changed James from a skeptic to a saint, from a doubter to a disciple.

What the resurrection did for James, it has done for others. A few years ago in England, there was a trial lawyer named Frank Morrison. He was an unbeliever. For years, he promised himself that one day, he would write a book to disprove Christianity, and, finally, he took the time to do just that. He was an honest man and did the necessary work. Starting from the most critical possible approach to the New Testament, he worked his way through the data of the New Testament until he concluded. Christianity was true! What convinced him? The resurrection. If you're interested, you can read his book *Who Moved the Stone?*

The next time you meet someone who is not persuaded of the validity of Christianity, try the resurrection. You might even give him or her a copy of Morrison's book *Who Moved the Stone?* An inexpensive paperback copy can be purchased online. Who knows, the resurrection might convince your friend, too.

A Point to Ponder

DO YOU YEARN TO BE LIKE CHRIST?

Do you yearn to be more and more like Jesus Christ? How do believers become conformed to the image of the Son of God? Paul answers that question in his second letter to the Corinthians. "But we all, with unveiled face beholding as in a mirror the glory of the Lord, are being transformed into the same image from glory to glory, just as by the Spirit of the Lord" (2 Cor. 3:18).

As believers behold the glory of the Lord in the Word of God, they are transformed by the Spirit of God into the same image as the Son of God from glory to glory. This is not a fading glory like the one Moses experienced (cf. 2 Cor. 3:7); it is an ever-growing and greater glory. It is also unveiled, that is, it is on public display. Constantly contemplate Christ and you will be more and more conformed to His image.

Franconia Notch is a famous pass in the White Mountains of New Hampshire. High on one of the rocky walls protruded a granite formation that resembled the profile of an old man looking over the valley. It was called the "Old Mountain of the Mountain." (It collapsed between midnight and 2:00 am on May 3, 2003.) Nathaniel Hawthorne (1804-1864) wrote a story based on that rock formation called "The Legend of the Great Stone Face."

According to the story a boy named Ernest lived in the valley. His mother told him there was an ancient legend that someday a man born in that valley would resemble the great

A Point to Ponder

stone face. From that time in his early years, he spend time concentrating on the face in the mountain. He longed for the day when he could see a real face as kind and as wise as the one that appeared in the rock. He carefully scrutinized individuals within his village but was disappointed. He kept looking at the stone face and searching for the real face. One evening, a man called "the poet" pointed to him and explained, "Look, there's a man who resembles the great stone face." After looking at the image in the mountain and looking for an individual that bore his resemblance, Ernest had become like the great stone face. Whatever we look on with approval, we become like.

A Point to Ponder

THE APPROPRIATE RESPONSE

To those who have trusted Jesus Christ, God has been loving, gracious, and merciful. In light of what God has done for us, what should be our response to Him? In Romans, Paul gives the believer the appropriate response to God's mercy. "I beseech you, therefore, brethren, by the mercies of God, that you present your bodies a living sacrifice, holy, acceptable to God, which is your reasonable service. And do not be conformed to this world, but be transformed by the renewing of your mind, that you may prove what is that good and acceptable and perfect will of God. For I say, through the grace given to me, to everyone who is among you, not to think of himself more highly than he ought to think, but to think soberly, as God has dealt to each one a measure of faith" (Rom. 12:1-3).

Based on the mercy of God, Paul exhorts believers to present their bodies as a living sacrifice (Rom. 12:1). The Greek word translated "present" is the same one used in Romans 6:13, 16, 19. In Romans 6, this word is used to convey the connotation of the use of the body either for sin or for righteousness. Thus, Romans 12:1 does not call for an act of dedication but obedience to God through the body. In short, use your body to obey God.

Paul also exhorts believers to be transformed by renewing their minds (12:2). The present passing age should not continually mold them. They should be remolded from the inside by renewing the mind (see Rom. 8:4). As the mind and heart of believers are fixed on the Word of God in general and on Christ in the Word in particular, they are transformed more and more to Christ's likeness (see 2 Corinthians 3:18, which is the only other place in Paul's writings where the word "transformed" appears). Believers do not need reformation; they need transformation.

Furthermore, Paul exhorts believers to think soberly of themselves, using their gifts in the body of Christ (Rom. 12:3-8). A renewed mind begins with thinking soberly about yourself. Our perception of ourselves should not be overly proud or overly ambitious. We should not overestimate our abilities, especially in our ability in Christian service. Thinking soberly about oneself means understanding how we are uniquely gifted to serve others. Thus, the appropriate response to God's great mercy is for us to present our bodies, minds, and service to Him. Since Christ sacrificed Himself for us, we ought to sacrifice ourselves for Him.

Years ago, a godly teenager named Ron Richardson, who at the time was a senior in high school, told me that he 1) conducted a prayer meeting in his home every Tuesday morning at 6:00, 2) met with other believers at school at 7:45 every morning, Monday through Friday, 3) conducted a Bible Study every Thursday night in his home, and 4) taught five-year-olds in Sunday School. Furthermore, he was captain of the football team and student body president. My response was, "Ron, that's fantastic!" He very calmly looked at me and said, "Oh, I thought it was just my reasonable service." The appropriate response to God's grace to us is our obedience and service to Him.

A Point to Ponder

GREETINGS!

A pastor friend of mine always concludes the service by praying. Then, instead of saying something like, "You are dismissed," he urges the congregation to "Greet one another," and with that, the service is over. The first time I heard him do that, I thought to myself, now there is a new idea. But upon reflection, I realized it's not a new idea at all. It's as old as the New Testament. "Greet all the brethren with a holy kiss" (1 Thess. 5:26).

Paul, Peter, and John concluded some of their epistles with the command to "Greet one another." The word "greet" occurs sixty times in the New Testament and is sometimes translated "salute." We are told to greet all of the brethren (1 Thess. 5:26) and to greet them by name (2 Jn. 14; see also Rom. 16, where Paul practiced what he preached). The Lord Himself, in characteristic fashion, went beyond that and said, "And if you greet your brethren only, what do you do more than others? Do not even the tax collectors do so?" (Mt. 5:47). In other words, according to the Lord greeting the brethren and others is the least we can do.

The implication for evangelism is clear. Greeting one another produces a warm, friendly atmosphere. When done scripturally, this spills over into greeting strangers and saints. If one separated from God comes to the house of God and feels separated from the people, he will not be drawn to the Lord. If there is an outstretched hand at the end of an outstretched heart, he will feel welcome at

A Point to Ponder

God's house and maybe to the Lord Himself.

Let me illustrate. As a teenager separated from God and going my way, I "happened" to attend a church where they practiced greeting people. Now, better than thirty years later, I remember walking up to the church and having two men give me the friendliest greeting I'd ever received. Because of that greeting, I went back. By going back, I was greeted by Jesus Christ Himself. People practicing that old admonition to greet one another was a major factor in my coming to Christ.

So, may I suggest that at the end of the next church service, don't just leave as quickly as possible. Greet one another, greet the saints and greet strangers as well. Who knows, you may even be a factor in causing someone to come back to church and maybe even come to the Lord.

A Point to Ponder

IS BAPTISM NECESSARY FOR SALVATION?

If you've ever witnessed at all, I'm sure you've encountered people who believe that you must be baptized to be saved. One of their favorite verses is Acts 2:38. "Then Peter said to them, 'Repent, and let everyone of you be baptized in the name of Jesus Christ for the remission of sins, and you shall receive the gift of the Holy Spirit'" (Acts 2:38).

Is this verse teaching that one must be baptized to be saved? The answer is no. The Greek word translated "for" in the phrase "for the remission of sins" has at least two different meanings. It can mean "to get" (Lk. 5:4). For example, we say, "I went to the store *for* bread," meaning "I went to the store to get bread." "For" can also mean "because of" (Mt. 12:41), where this same Greek word is translated "at." We say, "He went to jail *for* murder," meaning, "He went to jail *because of* murder."

Now the question is, "Which of these is the meaning in Acts 2:38?" Nothing in the verse or context conclusively proves which rendering is correct. All must go to other passages. Those who believe in salvation by faith will go to verses that say one must believe and those who believe baptism is necessary for salvation will go to verses on baptism. How can such a conflict be solved?

Acts 2:38 was spoken by Peter and recorded by Luke. What is needed is a verse that bears on this issue, in which Peter is speaking

A Point to Ponder

and Luke is reporting. Is there such a verse? Yes! In Acts 10, Peter is preaching at Cornelius' house. In the middle of the sermon, he says, "Whoever believes in Him will receive remission of sins" (Acts 10:43). Notice carefully: 1) As in Acts 2:38, Peter is preaching and Luke is wiring. 2) Peter says faith results in the remission of sins. So, based on Acts 10:43, the weight of evidence is that Acts 2:38 means "be baptized *because of* the remission of sins," that is, believe and at that point, you are saved. Then, because you have been forgiven, be baptized.

Let me suggest one other thing. The rest of Acts 10 clearly demonstrates salvation comes before baptism. Consider Acts 10:47, where Peter says, "Can anyone forbid water that these should not be baptized who have received the Holy Spirit just as we have." Peter recognized they received the Holy Spirit *before* they received baptism.

So, next time someone takes you to what Peter said in Acts 2, you should take them to what Peter said in Acts 10. The whole story is this. Peter taught: 1) Believe. At that point, you are forgiven (Acts 10:43) and you will receive the Holy Spirit (Acts 10:47). 2) Then be baptized because you have received the remission of sins (Acts 2:38).

A Point to Ponder

SHOULD YOU SEEK THE BAPTISM OF THE HOLY SPIRIT?

Some teach that after conversion, believers should seek the baptism of the Holy Spirit. They often point to Acts 19. "Did you receive the Holy Spirit when you believed?" (Acts 19:2). To answer this question, let's look at every reference to the baptism of the Holy Spirit in the New Testament.

First, spiritual baptism was *predicted*. In the gospels, it is referred to four times, but, these are four accounts of the same event (Mt. 3:11; Mak. 1:8; Lk. 3:16; Jn. 1:33). In Acts 1:5, Jesus repeated that promise. So, in these five references, the baptism of the Spirit is *still future*.

Secondly, spiritual baptism then *occurred*. In Acts, it occurs four times: 1) In Acts 2, it happened to the Jews. This is the only time anyone was told to tarry for it (Acts 1:4). The coming of the Holy Spirit was to fulfill the Feast of Pentecost like the crucifixion was to fulfill the Feast of Passover. Hence, they had to wait until the feast day arrived. 2) In Acts 8, the Samaritans received the baptism. This is the first of only two times when the baptism of the Holy Spirit was received due to the laying on of hands. If the Holy Spirit had come upon the Samaritans without Peter having laid hands on them, there would have forever been two mother churches. 3) In Acts 10, it happened to the Gentiles without tarrying and without the laying on of hands. 4) In Acts 19, some disciples of John the

A Point to Ponder

Baptist receive the baptism. The baptism was received due to the laying on of hands to demonstrate that Paul had the same power as Peter. Conclusion: since the spiritual baptism only happened four times in Acts and on four such distinct groups, it would appear that Acts is describing a *transitional period* when Christianity was spread from the Jews to the Gentiles.

Thirdly, spiritual baptism is *explained*. In the epistles, only five verses refer to it (Rom. 6:3; 1 Cor. 12:13; Gal. 3:27; Eph. 4:4, and Col. 2:12). These references, especially 1 Corinthians 12:13, make it clear that spiritual baptism places believers into the body of Christ. Furthermore, the epistles explain that every Christian has it. First Corinthians 12:13 says, "all." (See also Eph. 1:3 and Col. 2:10.) *Therefore, after the transition period described in Acts, every believer who trusts Christ receives the baptism of the Holy Spirit at conversion.* Without the Holy Spirit, you are not a Christian (Rom. 8:9).

Should you seek the baptism of the Holy Spirit? No! How can you seek what you already have? No one in the New Testament ever asked for or sought after the baptism of the Holy Spirit, nor was anyone ever told to do so. No requirements for it are ever given. The one person seeking something connected with the Holy Spirit was rebuked sharply (Acts 8:18-24).

Luther said of Carlstadt, "He wants to teach you *not* how the Spirit comes to you, but how you come to the Spirit." Carlstadt had it backward, as many do today. You do not need to pray to receive the power of the Holy Spirit; you need to pray for an understanding of your power (Eph. 1:18-19).

A Point to Ponder

TONGUES THEN AND NOW

Those who practice speaking in tongues point out that it occurred on the day of Pentecost and they claim that they are doing the same today. Is that true? Peter says, "And they were filled with the Holy Spirit and began to speak with other tongues as the Spirit gave them utterance" (Acts 2:4). What was the nature of tongues in the New Testament? Is tongues speaking today the same as was practiced in New Testament times?

To answer those questions, consider all the references to tongues in the New Testament (Mk. 16:17; Acts 2:4-10, 10:46, 19:6; and 1 Cor. 12-14). From these passages, the following is clear.

1. Tongues were a language (Acts 2:6-10).
2. Tongues were not for every believer (1 Cor. 12:28-30).
3. Tongues were for a sign to unbelieving Jews (1 Cor. 14:21, 22).
   Note: "This people" is a reference to the Jews. This is the only place where the purpose of tongues is given.
4. No more than three were to speak in a meeting. (1 Cor. 14:27)
5. They were to speak one at a time and not simultaneously (1 Cor. 14:27).
6. There was to always be an interpreter (1 Cor. 14:27, 28).
7. No women were to speak in tongues (1 Corn. 14:34).

A Point to Ponder

How does the modern practice of speaking in tongues compare with that?

1. Tongues today are *not* a language. When tongues-speaking was recorded and analyzed by objective linguistic experts, those speaking in tongues were not speaking a known language, nor could they be because what they were saying did not contain enough different sounds to be a language.
2. The tongues movement often claims tongues are for every believer.
3. The movement claims tongues are for believers, not Jews.
4. In meetings, more than three often speak.
5. Frequently, all in a meeting speak in tongues simultaneously.
6. There is very often no interpreter.
7. Women speak in tongues today.

The modern practice of speaking in tongues is not the same as the practice in the New Testament mainly because it is not a known language, and the movement often violates the regulations in 1 Corinthians 14. Don't worry about speaking to God in a language you don't understand. Use the one language you know to talk to and for Him.

A Point to Ponder

THE PERFECT STORM

In 2000, *The Perfect Storm* was a popular movie based on a true story. In October of 1991, three storm systems merged in the Atlantic Ocean off the New England coast to create a storm that had never been seen before in the history of weather watching. Since the Weather Bureau did not foresee the merger, it was called the "No Name Storm" at first. Then, a reporter dubbed it the "Perfect Storm."

Waves were 100 feet high. Ships sank. Buildings were destroyed. People died. One ship named the *Andrea Gail,* with six aboard, sank. All aboard were lost. An author wrote a book about it, and Hollywood made a movie. Hence, the blockbuster, *The Perfect Storm.*

Was the 1991 storm off the Atlantic coast the perfect storm? Is there such a thing? A perfect storm accomplishes God's intended purpose. As Nahum reminds us, "The Lord has His way in the whirlwind and in the storm" (Nahum 1:3).

When God told Jonah, "Arise, go to Nineveh, that great city, and cry out against it (Jonah 1:2), Jonah fled in the opposite direction toward Tarshish "from the presence of the Lord" (Jonah 1:3). The Lord then prepared the perfect storm. He "sent out a great wind on the sea, and there was a mighty tempest on the sea so that the ship was about to be broken up" (Jonah 1:4). The storm accomplished its Divine design. It got the attention of the sailors as well as Jonah (Jonah 1:5-17).

The Heavenly Father disciplines His children. The writer to the

A Point to Ponder

Hebrews says, "For whom the Lord loves He chastens (child trains), and scourges every son whom He receives (Heb. 12:6). The nature of this child training discipline can be any kind of "storm" that God allows to come into our lives to mature us. More specifically, Paul says these "storms" will be in the form of weakness and sickness and, for some who don't get the message of the storm, it can even be premature physical death (1 Cor 11:30).

The problem with a perfect storm is that sometimes, we do not realize what is happening. In the 1991 storm, the people on shore did not take it very seriously. The Weather Bureau did not see this unusual storm system coming ahead of time. Consequently, people were unaware of what was happening. Oh, they knew it was a storm, but they had no idea what was really going on because the storm had no name. One man who experienced the storm said, "If it had been called 'Hurricane Bob,' we would have taken it more seriously." No one took it seriously. Children played in the waves. Adults took pictures.

Not all the "storms" in our lives are God's punishment for sin, but God uses "storms" to "discipline" us. If we understood what He was doing and called it by its proper name, then maybe we would not be so hurt by it but would learn from it. If you let the Lord have His way in your storms, that is, learn from them, they will be your perfect storms.

A Point to Ponder

WHY SO MUCH JUDGMENT?

Why is there so much judgment in the Bible? Judgment is all over the place!

The first book of the Bible no sooner opens than there is the judgment on the human race, which is still in effect (Gen. 3). Several chapters later, God judges the whole world (Gen. 6-9). The entire Pentateuch is filled with pronouncements of judgments and curses for disobedience.

The next section of the Scripture, the historical books, is the history of judgment! Joshua is filled with God's judgment on Canaan's inhabitance. Judges records God's judgment on His children in Canaan. Then, there is God's judgment on the Northern and Southern Kingdoms.

The poetical books are not exactly judgment-free. Read Proverbs.

The subject, or a major subject, of virtually all the prophetical books, is the judgment of God. The subject of Jeremiah is the judgment. Lamentations laments God's judgment of Jerusalem. Daniel is about God's judgment of the Gentiles. The subject of Joel and Zephaniah is the Day of the Lord. Amos, Micah, and Malachi pertain to judgment on Israel. The subject of four other Minor Prophets is judgment on other nations, Obadiah on Edom, Jonah and Nahum on Nineveh, and Habakkuk on the Chaldeans.

Granted, grace came through Jesus Christ (Jn. 1:17), but if you

A Point to Ponder

think the New Testament is without judgment, remember such passages as Matthew 23, Acts 5, and Romans 1, not to mention the references to the chastening of believers in this life and the Judgment Seat of Christ in the next life. The subject of Revelation is Jesus Christ as Judge. He judges the churches (Rev. 2-3), the world (Rev. 4-18), and then unbelieving humanity at the Great White Throne Judgment (Rev. 20:11-15). No wonder the psalmist says, "He has prepared His throne for judgment" (Ps. 9:7). Why so much about judgment? Judgment assumes responsibility and accountability. Granted, we are influenced by our biological predisposition (Gen. 25:23-27), childhood experience (Prov. 22:6), and environment (Rom 12:2), but ultimately, we are personally responsible and accountable for our thoughts, emotions, words, and actions. There are over factors, such as God is just (1 Jn. 1:9) and He wants to give us time to repentance (2 Pet 3:9; Rev. 2:21), but a major reason God says so much about judgment in the Bible is to remind us of our responsibility as well as our accountable. Human nature is bent toward not facing responsibility, denying guilt, and blaming others (Gen. 3:12-13). God wants us to face responsibility. In *The Road Less Traveled*, Scott Peck says we either accept too much responsibility or not enough. God desires that we look realistically at ourselves and face squarely our responsibility. Being aware that we will be judged helps us do that. So, God constantly reminds us of judgment. When I taught at Dallas Seminary, an older, wiser professor said to me, "Students do not do what is expected; they do what is inspected."

A Point to Ponder

GLASSES COME IN PAIRS

We think of people as individuals, but people usually come in pairs—like glass. Just as some glasses only have a single lens, some individuals may function as a single unit, but the overwhelming majority operate as part of a pair. I have observed this in at least three different settings.

One of the first times I detected this phenomenon was as a young pastor dealing with couples. I discovered that unchurched couples often decided to attend church *as a couple*. She said, "I have to talk to my husband." Or I saw him respond with, "I will talk it over with my wife."

I have also observed this among church board members. I noticed that sometimes, board members did not want to decide until the next board meeting. At first, I attributed it to an unwillingness to "bite the bullet" and make the tough decisions. Then, one day, what was happening dawned on me. On some issues, they simply want to talk to their wives! After I said that to them, they readily admitted it. In fact, it became a joke. In the middle of a decision, one would say, "Let's make this decision after we have talked to our wives," and that is what we did.

In the case of one board member, I perceived that sometimes he said things that did not sound like him. I began thinking, "That is not him talking." Then, I realized it wasn't him at all. We were

A Point to Ponder

hearing from the last person who had talked to him about that subject.

I have seen it in selling. When I first became a stock broker, I worked for a financial planning firm that had us making financial presentations to couples. We were warned about making a "one-legged pre," which is a presentation to just the husband or wife alone. We were told that it was virtually impossible to sell our program if only one spouse was present. We were advised that if we arrived to find only one spouse present, we should reschedule the appointment. It did not take long to discover that they were right.

When you look at a human being, remember you are not dealing with one person. You are dealing with a pair of people and maybe more than two. Individuals do not function in isolation. They form opinions, make decisions, and adopt attitudes in conjunction with one or more other people. "For none of us lives to himself, and no one dies to himself" (Rom. 14:7).

I was once told that when a pastor candidates at a church, he should ask, "Who are the five most influential people in this church? Who are the decision-makers?" Likewise, when you deal with individuals, especially if you want to change their minds, ask, "Who are the influential people in this person's life? Who helps them with decisions?"

When you look at one, make sure you see two (or more). To think people make up their minds solely by themselves is to look at people through rose-colored glasses. If you don't see people in pairs, your vision is not 20/20.

A Point to Ponder

WHY SO MUCH ABOUT THE CHURCH?

For decades, I have studied the Bible methodically and meticulously. The more I study the New Testament, the more I am impressed with its emphasis on the church. It's everywhere! In the middle of His ministry, Jesus said, "I will build my church" (Mt. 16:18). At the end of His earthly ministry, He gave the Great Commission (Mt. 28:19-20). According to the Acts, that was done by establishing churches.

That is only the beginning. Paul addressed most of his epistles to churches. The subject of 1 Corinthians is "disorders in the church." Galatians deals with an error in churches. The theme of Ephesians is "our calling to the church." The subject of 1 Timothy is "conduct in the church." The point of Titus is to put things in order in churches. Hebrews exhorts believers not to "forsake the assembling of yourselves together" (Heb. 10:25). First Peter, 2 Peter, 1 John, 2 John, and Revelation are addressed to churches. Does God put a premium on the church? Well, Christ died for the church (Eph 5:25).

Why all the emphasis on the church? Among other things, Paul told the Colossians the purpose of his understanding" (Col. 2:2-3).

Being knit together in love produces a "full understanding," the confidence that one comprehends the truth. The expression "knit together" suggests that God's revelation cannot be understood

A Point to Ponder

"in isolation from the fellowship of other Christians" (Vaughan), that the revelation of God cannot be known apart from the "brotherly love within the community" (Bruce). According to Paul, a believer cannot be spiritually mature or wise apart from being part of a loving community called a church (Eph. 4:11-16).

Robert D. Putnam, a Harvard professor, wrote Bowling Alone. According to the Los Angeles Times, this political scientist believes he has "identified a central crisis of our times, the decline of group activity." Since 1977, the proportion of married Americans who usually eat dinner with their families has dropped from 50% to 34%. "Picnics per capita" have plummeted by 60%. The consequences are an increasingly disconnected society, increasing individual malaise, physical illness, and even suicide. He claims that American life has become too disconnected, making us less happy, healthy, and wise. He urges us all to join something. Robert sounds like Paul.

You cannot believe in the New Testament and not believe in the church. You cannot practice what it teaches and not belong to or be active in a church. You cannot be spiritually mature apart from a loving church. Hence, the emphasis on the church.

PS This article was originally written in 2000. Today, the situation is worse because of the mobile phone.

A Point to Ponder

REFLECTIONS ON AN ELECTION

As I gaze from afar at my home state, a portion of a verse comes to mind, "the nations rage" (Ps. 2:1).

Last month, Patricia and I went to Florida, where I saw my mother in Pensacola and preached in evangelistic meetings in two churches in Tallahassee. My message was, "Jesus saves" (and some got saved). After returning to California and seeing what has happened this month [concerning the debate over the presidential election], I think my message to Florida should have been, "RELAX!"

At least wait until the absentee ballots are counted. This is not (nor will there be) a constitutional crisis. Just relax. Have a little patience. Cool it, or as they say today, "chill out." Who knows, the absentee ballots may just solve the problem. If it doesn't, let's go from there, but taking to the streets and all this rhetoric now is premature.

There is a little Florida in all of us. We are impatient. We rage. "He who sits in the heavens shall laugh" (Ps 2:4).

Well, what should we do? The psalmist says, "Now therefore, be wise, O kings; Be instructed, you judges of the earth. Serve the LORD with fear, and rejoice with trembling. Kiss the Son, lest *He be angry*, And you perish in the way when His wrath is kindled but a little. Blessed are all those who put their trust in Him" (Ps. 2:10-12). In other words:

A Point to Ponder

1. Be Smart (Ps. 2:10). Mankind is denouncing God's rule (Ps. 2:1-2), but God decrees His anointed will rule (Ps. 2:4-6) and the Anointed discloses His rule (Ps. 2:7-9). You cannot escape from the dominion of the God-appointed king. If you persist in your rebellion, you will be destroyed. So, get smart. Be wise, O kings. Be instructed, you judges of the earth.

2. Be Serving (Ps. 2:11). More specifically, start serving the Sovereign. Do it with awe and respect (cf. fear and trembling).

3. Be Submissive (Ps. 2:12). Kiss the Son was an ancient mode of showing allegiance to a king (1 Sam 10:1). Don't perform the external sign without the internal reality, for it will not work nor do you any benefit. That's what happened to Judas. He kissed the Son but only had the external act, not the internal reality. He perished.

In light of the fact that God is going to establish His Son as king of the earth, everyone should trust the Son to be blessed now and not perish later (Ps. 2:12). Someone has written,

It is better to bow than to be broken.
Either kiss the Son or be laughed at by the Father.
God's anointed has been appointed and will not be disappointed.

Come to think about it, in light of eternity, my message in Florida, Jesus saves, is the one that is needed during any chaos and confusion, rage and rebellion.

A Point to Ponder

FOR ME TO LIVE IS MAINTENANCE

We spend our lives in maintenance. For starters, we depleted one-third of our life, maintaining our bodies by sleeping. That is only the beginning. We actually use much more of our life to maintain our bodies. We feed our bodies. We bathe our bodies. We comb our hair. We brush our teeth. We exercise. (Well, some do.) On top of that, there are visits to the dentist and doctors, one for a general check-up, another for eyes, and if the body develops any problem, a specialist. All this maintenance takes a lot of time.

Our lives must be maintained financially. So, we exhaust (an appropriate word) another third of our lives working. That does not include counting the time going to and coming home from work, going to the bank, paying the bills, and balancing the checkbook, all of which eats up more of our lives.

Everything we own demands maintenance. The house must be cleaned and repaired. Even calling a repairman (whoops, repair person. Must maintain political correctness.) takes time. They will not tell you exactly when they will be there, only that they will arrive in the morning or the afternoon. There went the day or at least half of it because if you say morning, which they define as from nine to noon, they show up at 11:45! Then, there is the lawn. It must be mowed, raked, etc. (I solved this one. We live in a condo.)

We must maintain our car (cars) by putting gas in the tank, oil in the engine, water in the radiator, and air in the tires. We wash,

A Point to Ponder

wax, and watch it wear out no matter how much we try to care for it. Oh yes, we take it to get repaired or to have parts, like tires, replaced. That is always a killer, a time killer. Hey, that's my life, spent again in maintenance mode.

That is just the house and the car. Every possession takes time for maintenance. What possessions do you have that possess you? I have a desk. No, I have three desks: one at home, one at the church I pastor, and a third at another church where I am the chairman of the board and chief administrator until they get through ... well, a transition. The paper on the top of a desk (not to mention the drawers in the desk) takes maintenance. Just the mail ... oh well, you know the drill.

The computer has to be defragmented. The silver has to be polished. We haven't got to relationships, the most important part of our lives that also demands, you guessed it, maintenance.

The simple reality is that it is all about maintenance. Maintenance demands time, but the consequences of not maintaining are worse (no oil equals a blown engine). So, contrary to popular opinion, sweat the small stuff so you don't suffer the larger consequences. Besides, according to Jesus, if you master the small stuff, the bigger consequences are all good. Jesus said, "He who *is* faithful in *what is* least is faithful also in much" (Lk. 16:10; see also "His lord said to him, 'Well *done,* good and faithful servant; you were faithful over a few things, I will make you ruler over many things. Enter into the joy of your lord;'" Mt. 25:21). So, sweat the small stuff. Be faithful in the little things.

A Point to Ponder

FROM COMMON SENSE TO NONSENSE

Common sense has never been universally common, but it sure seems less common now than at any time I can remember. As I survey the current scene, it seems that we have gone from common sense to nonsense.

Item: A six-year-old boy in Lexington, NC, was suspended for a day, banned from attending an ice cream party, and sent home. His crime? Sexual harassment. He kissed a female classmate on the cheek.

Item: A six-year-old boy in California was red-carded for playing tag during recess. The explanation? Tag involves touching, which is groping and foreplaying.

Item: A sixty-two-year-old grandma in Cincinnati committed an act of random kindness by feeding money into parking meters to save a motorist she never met from getting a ticket. She was charged with disorderly conduct and obstruction of official business. She was arraigned and released on $1500 bail.

You have heard of these kinds of goings on. What is going on? We have lost our moral compass. True right and wrong are in line with God's plumb line. Once right and wrong were set in stone. Even when the standard drifted into man-made mandates, right was still right, wrong was still wrong, and everyone knew where the line was.

Not anymore. We have replaced right and wrong with legal and illegal, divine morality with political correctness. The consequences have been devastating.

In our desire to perform acceptably (and avoid litigation), we no longer have reasonable judgment by reasoning individuals. We pursue rules and correctness. We have abandoned personal responsibility and have become moral cowards. As someone has so well said, "It takes guts to make decisions that stray from the black and white of rigid written rules into the gray of judgment calls," as seen in the above items. We've lost courage. We're cowards who hide behind correctness, conformity and comfort.

Without a moral compass, we don't know where we are and we don't know which way to turn. Recently, a lady whose compass needle is broken came to see me. She told me exactly what she intended to do, which was all wrong. Soo ... I gently but firmly and plainly told her what the biblical thing was to do. She looked puzzled, deeply disturbed, and said, "Now I'm totally confused." I thought to myself, "How could you possibly be confused? I just told you precisely what God Himself told you to do." The truth was, she was really confused! When your compass is broken, you are confused.

We need a moral compass so we can be "sensible." There is a Greek word in the New Testament that means "sane, sensible, self-controlled." Elders must have it (cf. "sober-minded" in Titus 1:8). Older men should have it ("temperate" in Titus 2:2). Older women should use it ("admonish" in Titus 2:4). Younger women ("discreet" in Titus 2:5), younger men ("sober-minded" in Titus 2:6), and everybody ("soberly" in Titus 2:12) needs it!

A Point to Ponder

LEFT BEHIND

Several years ago, two men, Tim La Hay and Jerry Jenkins, wrote a novel entitled *Left Behind*. It was an imaginary story of what will happen to those left behind when believers disappear. The book sold millions. More novels followed and more are to come. In the meantime, they sold the movie rights, and a film called Left Behind: The Movie was released. It opened in about 900 theaters across the country.

A film critic named Glenn Whipp wrote that it is "poorly made" and "theologically shaky." He went on to say that it is "so awful that even true believers will have difficulty staying awake" and "the end times (are) about as scary as a church bake sale. It all plays like a bad B-movie: cheesy, one-dimensional, and unconvincing. In the midst of personal dramas, the movie tries to develop a back story for the Antichrist, but he ends up being about as frightening and charismatic as Al Gore."

Apparently, he was not impressed. He gave the film 0 stars.

Those of us who know the Lord and His word know that believers will disappear (1 Thess. 4:13-18) and all unbelievers will be left behind. Jesus said, "One will be taken and the other left" (Mt. 24:40-41). There is a debate as to whether or not the words of Jesus are referring to the rapture. Older pre-trib expositors said that they do. More recently, some say that they don't. While that text may be debated, the truth is that at the rapture, "one will be taken and the other left" cannot. The film critic may know films, but he does not know the facts of Scripture. This is not "theologically shaky." It is theological solid ground.

Unfortunately, he may be correct that this theme moves us like a B-rated movie. During sermons on such topics, some believers have difficulty staying awake. Paul reminds us that "The night is far spent, the day is at hand" (Rom. 13:12), "it is high time to awake out of sleep; for now our salvation is nearer than when we first believed" (Rom. 13:11).

Soooo, may I suggest that the title of the novel and the text of Scripture on this point contain two great spiritual reminders? One is, "Don't be left behind. I trust that you have trusted Christ for the gift of eternal life (Jn. 3:36). The other is don't leave others behind. Share the gospel with them so they may share the rapture with you and not be left behind.

During his Presidential campaign, George W. Bush said that education would be his number one priority and added, "No child should be left behind." As the President of the United States says, his number one priority is that no child should be left behind, so we should make our number one priority that no one we know be left behind.

A Point to Ponder

OWNERS OR GUARDIANS?

The city council of the city of West Hollywood, the homosexual epicenter of Southern California, voted 3 to 0 to amend the city's municipal code to remove all references to "pet owner." From henceforth and evermore, pet owners in the two-square-mile city will be officially called "pet guardians." Boulder, Colorado, is the only other city in the United States with such a code.

According to the Mayor, Jeffrey Prang, "There's a tremendous amount of power in words. Choosing the term 'pet guardianship' connotes a much greater sense of responsibility and care for your pets. The resolution has a symbolic purpose" aimed at reminding those with pets that animals have rights.

The ordinance has more bark than bite. Violators who slip up and use the 0 word won't land in the doghouse.

Reaction was mixed. According to the *Los Angeles Times*, "Many in the city's large gay population have dogs and cats they consider members of their families." One man, who is not a resident of West Hollywood, said, "To me, I think it's kind of silly. If you have a pet, you are the owner."

When I heard about this, two thoughts came to mind. First, if what they are doing is expressing compassion toward animals, then they have a point. God is compassionate and uses His compassion toward animals as an illustration. When Jonah was angry that God spared Nineveh (Jonah 4:1-3), God had compassion on a very uncompassionate Jonah, giving him a plant to shade him from the burning sun (Jonah 4:6). Then, to teach Jonah a lesson on compassion, God prepared a worm and an East wind (Jonah 4:7-9) and pointed out "You have had pity on the plant for which you have not labored, nor made it grow, which came up in a night and perished in a night. And should I not pity Nineveh, that great city, in which are more than one hundred and twenty thousand persons who cannot discern between their right hand and their left, *and also much livestock?*" (Jonah 4:10-11).

God's point is simply this: "Jonah, if you could pity one small shrub which you neither planted, labored over, nor caused to grow, can I not have compassion on creatures I created, innocent creatures, that is, the children? Besides, look at all the livestock. Are not sheep superior to shrubs? If you can grieve over the loss of one plant, can I not be concerned over hundreds and thousands of animals and humans?"

Secondly, they are right. We are not owners; we are "guardians." From a biblical point of view, we are stewards, not just of pets, but of everything. The problem with the unjust steward in the parable Jesus told (Lk. 16:1-13) is that he forgot that he was a steward and thought he was an owner. Thanks, West Hollywood, for the reminder.

A Point to Ponder

FROM HONEYMOON HARMONY TO DIVORCE

Ideally, a married couple should live in harmony. After all, they are "companions" (Malachi 2:14), and hopefully, they are headed in the same direction. Unfortunately, many marriages end in divorce. There is a road between the harmony of the honeymoon and the dissolution of the marriage in a divorce court. Where on that road is your marriage?

Differences. Even couples with honeymoon harmony have differences of opinion, even disagreements. As has been said, "If the two of you agreed on everything, one of you would be unnecessary." Differences and disagreements are not a problem, provided both individuals understand, accept, and learn to live with them. Of course, if there are too many differences or the disagreements are too serious, the honeymoon harmony will become more and more difficult to maintain.

Discussion. Discussion is constructive conversation. Married people should be able to discuss their disagreements amicably. They should be willing to work out a solution, usually a compromise that is acceptable to both. The solution may be either he gets his wish, she gets her want, or some compromise in between.

Dispute. To dispute is to debate (from the Latin *dispultare* < *dis*, apart + *pultare*, to think). Instead of compromise, there is controversy. Debate is not necessarily bad, provided that the

A Point to Ponder

fighting is fair.

Argue, that is, present your case without being argumentative. Be careful. Marriage enters the danger zone at this point.

Dissention. Dissention (from the Latin *dissentire* < *dis*, apart + *sentire*, to feel, think) indicates that the two are not thinking alike and it usually involves verbal strife. Strife is the struggle to win. At this point, one (or both) is no longer looking for a solution. Defending a position is the concern. Beware of defensiveness.

Discord. Discord is a lack of concord (concord comes from the Latin word *concordis* < *com*, together + *cordis*, heart). Now, the hearts are not together. People can disagree, discuss, debate, and even temporarily strive but still have their hearts together. With discord, there is an emotional division. Now, fighting for a position is the posture.

In music, discord is a lack of harmony in tones simultaneously sounded. In marriage, both talk but do not hear each other. It is as if they are each playing different tunes simultaneously. Watch out for anger and attack. You are entering the war zone. Wise people choose their battles carefully.

Dysfunction. Dysfunction is a lack of intimacy. The difference has not developed into such a division that there is no longer the sharing of the deepest feelings with each other. There is anger, guilt, fear, bitterness, resentment, a feeling of abandonment, contempt, etc.

Divorce. Divorce is separation, disunion. It is to "disunite." Before there is a legal divorce, there is a mental divorce, an emotional divorce, and a physical divorce. God hates it when that happens (Malachi 2:16). Make a U-turn long before the end of the road.

A Point to Ponder

FOR GOODNESS SAKE

Believe it or not, we Americans have an obsession with goodness! We have a fixation with feeling good and looking good.

We all want to feel good. There is certainly nothing wrong with that. I, for one, do not want to feel bad! On the other hand, we must admit that many of us have made a religion out of doing whatever it takes to feel good.

Most of us also want to look good. Again, that is not evil. Who wants to look bad or be embarrassed? So, we lose weight, buy flattering clothes, fix our hair, wear make-up, etc.

Should we be obsessed with goodness? Absolutely! It is just that we should, in the words of another, "Hold thou the good; define it well (*In Memoriam*, Alfred Lord Tennyson).

We should be good. Jesus spoke of people being "good" and of those who hear the Word "with a good heart" (Lk. 8:15). There are several different Greek words translated "good" in the New Testament. In these verses, the one rendered "good" means "that which is morally good, beneficial, acceptable to God." Jesus thought that we should be good.

We should do good. Paul wrote, "Therefore, as we have opportunity, let us do good to all, especially to those who are of the household of faith" (Gal. 6:10). Every believer should seize every opportunity to do good to everybody. Any time we can do anything beneficial to anybody, we should do it, especially if the

A Point to Ponder

person is a fellow believer.

John Wesley's rule was, "Do all the good you can, by all the means you can, in all the way you can, in all the places you can, at all the times you can, to all the people you can, as long as ever you can."

We should talk about the good news. The Greek word translated "gospel" means "good news." The good news is that Jesus Christ died for our sins and rose from the dead (1 Cor. 15:3-4). The greatest good news I've ever heard is that eternal life is a gift (Rom. 6:23) and that all I have to do is trust Jesus Christ for eternal life (Jn. 3:16). Needless to say, we should talk about the good news (Mk. 16:15). I will not labor this point. I did that in my book *Evangelism: A Biblical Approach.*

If we are good, do good, and talk about the good news down here, we will look good (1 Jn. 2:28) and feel real good (Mt 24:21) up there.

As Shakespeare asked in *As You Like It*, "Can one desire too much of a good thing?"

A Point to Ponder

A PERFECT PRAYER

My favorite prayer is "Lord, help." It is not too much to suggest that it may be the perfect prayer.

In the first place, it is short. Jesus said, "When you pray, do not use vain repetitions as the heathen do. For they think that they will be heard for their many words" (Mt. 6:7). According to Jesus, when it comes to prayer, it is not the quantity of the words, but the quality of the words that matter.

Secondly, it recognizes who God is. He is the Lord. To say the same thing another way, He is the Master: I am the servant. It is easy to get our roles reversed, isn't it? We can pray as if we are trying to get our will done in heaven. That is backward. Prayer is to get God's will done on earth. Jesus taught us to pray, "Our Father in heaven, Hallowed be Your name. Your kingdom come. Your will be done on earth as it is in heaven" (Mt. 6:9-10).

Thirdly, it acknowledges who I am. I need God's help. I am dependent on Him to save me from the mess which I'm in at the moment.

Listen to the Psalmist.

"Arise, O LORD; save me" (Ps. 3:7).
"Return, O LORD, deliver me! Oh, save me for Your mercies' sake! (Ps. 6:4).
"O LORD my God, in You I put my trust; save me from all

A Point to Ponder

those who persecute me; and deliver me" (Ps. 7:1).

"Save, LORD!" (Ps. 20:9).

"Save Me from the lion's mouth and from the horns of the wild oxen!" (Ps. 22:21).

"Make Your face shine upon Your servant; save me for Your mercies' sake" (Ps. 31:16).

"Save me, O God, by Your name, and vindicate me by Your strength" (Ps. 54:1).

"You are my God; Save Your servant who trusts in You!" (Ps. 86:2).

"Help me, O LORD my God! Oh, save me according to Your mercy" (Ps. 109:26).

"Save now, I pray, O LORD" (Ps. 118:25).

My favorite is "Save me, O God! For the waters have come up to my neck" (Ps. 69:1). There are more, but I think I should keep this short. The point is we should pray. It doesn't take long.

A Point to Ponder

NO IS NOT A NEGATIVE

Most of the Ten Commandments are stated in the negative (7 out of 10). That has bothered me so much that I once attempted to state them positively. However, I have realized that one of life's keys is learning to say "no."

Nutritionally. I have learned (the hard way) that if I am to lose weight, I must say "no" to the wrong kinds of food and even to the amount of right food. Forget weight loss. Just to eat healthy, the same principle applies: I must say "no" to the wrong stuff and "no' to too much of the right stuff.

Administratively. I have always had difficulty saying "no" to some activities, such as being invited to speak. Years ago, I realized I could not do everything I was asked to do. The only way to "administer" my life was to say "no." At one point, I resigned from several boards on which I had served. Each was an excellent opportunity to serve, but I could not do everything I was supposed to do and do a good job.

Spiritually. I have discovered that saying "no" is a significant key to the spiritual life. The Bible is filled with negatives. Psalm 1 teaches that the blessed person rejects the way of the wicked (Ps. 1:1) and receives the way of the Word (Ps. 1:2). The negative is before the positive. The New Testament repeatedly states that the way to grow spiritually is to "put off" vices and "put on" virtues (Rom. 13:13-14; Eph. 4:22-24; Col. 3:8-14; Jas. 1:21-22; Heb. 12:1-

A Point to Ponder

2; 1 Pet. 2:1-3). This includes weights as well as sin (Heb. 12:1).

I am not suggesting that it is always as easy as "just say no." Sometimes, it is not just difficult but impossible to "just say no" and *not do* something. Paul confessed, "For I know that in me (that is, in my flesh) nothing good dwells; for to will is present with me, but how to perform what is good I do not find. For the good that I will to do, I do not do; but the evil I will not to do, that I practice" (Rom. 7:18-19). How many times have we all said to ourselves, "I am going to say "no," but "yes" came out of our mouths?

We all need the *strength* to say "no" and we might not have it now. At the same time, it is possible for a believer to find the power, either suddenly or slowly) to say "no" and "yes." Paul declared, "O wretched man that I am! Who will deliver me from this body of death? I thank God; through Jesus Christ our Lord!" (Rom. 7:24-25). Paul learned, "I can do all things through Christ who strengthens me" (Phil. 3:13). The simple reality is that however it happens, at some point, there must be a "no" if we are to grow.

At any rate, no is not a negative. It is very much a positive. When we learn to say "no" to things that hinder us from reaching a positive goal, saying "no" may be one of the most positive things we do.

A Point to Ponder

WHAT MY SHOES HAVE TAUGHT ME

One morning, while I was getting dressed, it occurred to me that my shoes could teach a lot about life. Here are a few lessons.

Comfortable shoes may need to be discarded. My favorite pair of shoes is one I bought more than ten years ago and still own. I have had them resoled more times than I can remember. If I had my way, I would wear them every day; they would be the only shoes I would ever wear. Now, why would I do that? Answer—because they are comfortable. Those shoes have taught me that I do what is comfortable. The truth is, even though these shoes are comfortable, I need to discard them.

Hurtful shoes must be dumped. I have another pair of shoes that, under certain circumstances, hurt my feet. Yet, I keep them and wear them anyway. My shoes have taught me that I sometimes do what hurts me. Harmful shoes need to be dumped.

New shoes need to be displayed. Paul speaks of "having shod your feet with the preparation of the gospel of peace" (Eph. 6:15). When He penned these words, a Roman soldier was standing near him. Roman soldiers wore something similar to heavy boots. What are the boots of preparation of the gospel of peace?

The answer is protection. We need the shoes of the gospel to protect us. The gospel tells us that we are sinners, that Christ died for our sins and that we must trust Him for peace with God. You can't buy these shoes. The only way you can get them is as a gift.

A Point to Ponder

It is possible that the word "preparation" could be translated "foundation" (this Greek word is so translated in the Septuagint. See Ps. 88:14, Ezra 2:68, etc.). In other words, the foundation of the believer is the gospel. Believers are to stand solidly on the foundation of the good news of peace. They have peace with God through faith in Jesus Christ (Rom. 5:1) and are to let God's peace rule in their heart (Col. 3:15).

It is also possible that this passage says that the believer should be ready to defend and spread the gospel. After all, in Paul's picture, the gospel is on the believer's feet. Whether or not that is Paul's point in this passage, it is a biblical point made in Isaiah 52:7 and Romans 10:15.

So, my shoes have taught me that comfortable customs and harmful habits need to be put off and the gospel needs to be put on and published.

Some don't have the shoes they need. They need a new pair of shoes called the gospel of peace. Some have, but do not use, the shoes they have. If you have gospel shoes, you need to wear them. Many have a pair of shoes called the gospel of peace, but they are wearing old shoes that need to be discarded. One of the problems with shoes is that it is hard to discard them. Ask Amilda Marcos.

A Point to Ponder

FOR MERCY SAKE

Earlier this month, the denomination to which my church belongs held an evangelism conference in Green Lake, Wisconsin. I was invited to attend and chose to drive instead of fly so that Patricia and I could take some time off and travel after the meeting. (We went to Niagara Falls).

As we approached the booming metropolis of York, Nebraska (population 8000), we stopped to eat at a local restaurant instead of some fast food place along the freeway. So, we drove into town, found a delightful place and devoured a delicious meal. The food was fabulous, the ambiance was quaint, and the service was excellent. The cut glass and wood walls, the Tiffany-style lamps, and the decorations reminded us of Marie Callendars, a restaurant chain in Los Angeles.

On the way out of town, we began chattering away about our delightful dining experience, oblivious to everything else—including the speed limit sign and highway patrolman. He said I was going 75 miles per hour in a 55 miles per hour zone.

I was crushed. Until this point in the trip, the speed limit on the freeways had been a generous 75 mph. I had consistently set the speed control at about 78 and meticulously slowed when the speed was less.

After what seemed like two hours of writing a ticket, the officer explained that the penalty for my crime of breaking the speed limit was $225.00. However, he said he would only issue me a warning ticket.

What an illustration of mercy. Justice was $225.00. Mercy was $0.

As a result of that act of mercy, I decided that I would go back to driving dependent on cruise control. I pulled onto the freeway, set the cruise control and Patricia and I picked up our conversation. Only now were we not talking about the meal we had just had. We were overwhelmed at the mercy I had just experienced.

Because of the mercy I experienced, I obeyed the speed laws for the rest of the trip, which was well over 5000 miles. That is the kind of response my Heavenly Father wants out of me.

Paul put it like this, "I beseech you therefore, brethren, by the mercies of God, that you present your bodies a living sacrifice" (Rom. 12:1). That famous verse is the conclusion (see "therefore") of the discussion on mercy at the end of chapter 11. The meaning of "present your body" is to use your body to obey (Rom. 6:12-13). Paul's point is that the proper response to mercy is obedience.

As my experience with the mercy of the patrolman prompted me to obey the speed limit, the Lord wants my encounter with His mercy to provoke me to obey Him.

A Point to Ponder

THE 9/11 ATTACK ON AMERICA

What happened on September 11, 2001, is incomprehensible! Unimaginable! Unpredictable! Unparallel! Unbelievable!

The whole nation has talked nonstop for a week. I, too, have looked at the pictures in stunted disbelief. I have listened to the chatter. I have read, read, and read some more. I have felt grief for the victims and their families and friends, fear for the country, and anger at the barbarians who did this.

What do you say? After listening and saying a few things myself, I have one question? If He were here as He was before the ascension, "What would Jesus say?" What would He say about foreigners shedding blood on our shores? What would He say about towers collapsing and killing innocent people?

We do not have to guess what Jesus would say because something similar happened while He was here and we know what He said and did.

There were present at that season some who told Him about the Galileans whose blood Pilate had mingled with their sacrifices. And Jesus answered and said to them, "Do you suppose that these Galileans were worse sinners than all other Galileans, because they suffered such things? I tell you, no; but unless you repent you will all likewise perish. Or those eighteen on whom the tower in Siloam fell and killed them, do you think that they were worse sinners than all other men who dwelt in Jerusalem? I tell you, no; but unless

A Point to Ponder

you repent you will all likewise perish" (Lk. 13:1-5)

The parallels between what happened when Jesus walked on the earth and what happened in New York on September 11, 2001, are unmistakable. A foreigner, Pilate (Lk. 13:1), killed people on Israel's soil in a violent act (Lk. 13:1). In another case, a tower in Siloam fell, killing eighteen innocent people (Lk. 13:4).

In the first century, the people thought that in both of these cases, the ones who died were killed because of their sin and that their sin was worse than their own. Jesus took what they thought and turned it into a discussion of their salvation (Repent! Lk. 13:3, 5). In other words, Jesus used a travesty and a violent attack as an opportunity to evangelize. Be Christ-like; use the tragedy to proclaim the gospel.

Be like Christ, who came to seek and save the lost (Lk. 19:10). Which picture lingers in your mind? The planes hitting the towers? The building becoming a bomb? The towers burning? The towers crumbling to the ground? The searching through the rubble? The image that should be burned in our brains is of so many seeking to save people.

A Point to Ponder

THE MOTIVATION OF A SUICIDE TERRORIST

On September 11, when it dawned on me that what had happened was men had deliberately slammed planes into the World Trade Center towers and the Pentagon, I immediately had one burning question, "What would so motivate someone to want to kill innocent people that they would kill themselves to do it?" It didn't take long to figure it out. The following Sunday, I included this question in my message. Since then, notes left by the terrorist have been found that prove my suspicion was correct.

What inspired this unspeakable evil was *religion*! Not all Arabs or all Muslims are guilty, but an extreme form of militant Islam teaches martyrs go to heaven. A letter the suicide terrorist left behind reveals their motivation. It says, "You are embarking upon a mission that God is pleased with and you will be rewarded by living with the inhabitants of heaven. Smile to hardship, O youth, because you are on your way to Paradise!"

The half has not been told. According to some Muslims, a faithful martyr can expect to be *greatly* rewarded. In 1999, Sheik Abd Al-Salam Skheidm said,

> "From the moment his first drop of blood spills, he feels no pain and he is absolved of all his sins; he sees his seat in heaven; he is spared the tortures of the grave; he is spared

A Point to Ponder

the horrors of the Day of judgment; he is married to 70 blacked-eyed women; he can vouch for 70 of his family members to enter paradise; he earns the crown of glory, whose precious stone is worth all of this world" ("Palestinians' Sheer hatred Blocks Peace." Mona Charen. *Daily News* August 20, 2001, p. 13).

That is the *religious* teaching that motivated the suicide attack on America. Religion kills! Some religions kill physically (Extreme Islam, Heaven's Gate, Jim Jones, etc); all religion kills spiritually. Jesus said, "Woe to you, scribes and Pharisees, hypocrites! For you travel land and sea to win one proselyte, and when he is won, you make him twice as much a son of hell as yourselves" (Mt. 23:15).

Speaking of Religionist, Paul wrote, "Beware of Dogs" (Phil. 3:2). As for his own religion, he said that he had "no confidence in the flesh" (Phil. 3:3), so he counted his religion as "rubbish" (Phil. 3:8). The Greek word translated "rubbish" was used of leftover food, which was thrown away, and of excrement (Lightfoot). Religion is garbage; dump it!

Biblical Christianity is not religion; it's a relationship with Jesus Christ. Religion is death; a relationship with Jesus Christ is life (Jn. 17:3). Paul dumped religion for a relationship with Christ (Phil. 3:8-10), an advisable move for all.

A Point to Ponder

HOW TO HANDLE THE ANTHRAX SCARE

When planes slammed into buildings, for me, it was a continent away. "Just stay away from large crowds for a while," I thought. Now, the attack is through the mail! That is not only closer to home; it is in my house! One reporter said there is a "riptide of anxiety" in America. A medical director said, "It's boarding on mass hysteria." Have the events of this last week made you feel afraid? What should be our response?

Rely on God's protection. The Bible is filled with promises that God will protect us. For example, the psalmist says, "The Lord is my light and my salvation (that is, deliverance); whom shall I fear? (Ps. 21:1). The statistical failure of September 11th demonstrates that even in a direct attack, not all are hurt or killed. If the buildings hit and the planes lost had been filled and all died, 74,280 people would have been killed. Of that number, 93% survived or avoided the attacks. God protects us, even amid an attack.

Remember, be practical. During a storm at sea, Paul said God told him, "There will be no loss of life among you" (Acts 27:22). So, "Do not be afraid" (Acts 27:24). Later, he said, "Unless these men stay in the ship, you cannot be saved" (Acts 27:31). God promises to protect, but our part is to be practical. The Post Office gives guidelines for opening the mail: isolate suspicious mail and notify authorities immediately.

A Point to Ponder

Rest in the grace of God. Does that mean that God will protect us in every case? Obviously not. Believers get disease, are disabled, and die. Two truths need to be kept in mind. 1.) Nothing can happen to believers who walk with the Lord except God allows it. Of no fault of his own, Job, who was walking with the Lord, lost his servants, his livestock, and his children, but only because God allowed it (Job 1:8-12). 2. If God allows it, He will give grace for it. In a painful situation, God told Paul, "My grace is sufficient for you, for My strength is made perfect in weakness" (2 Cor. 12:9).

God protects those who walk with Him and those who walk wisely, and if He permits problems, He will provide grace. The issue, then, is our relationship with the Lord.

Paul's response to the problem God allowed in his life was, "I will rather boast in my infirmities, that the power of Christ may rest upon me" (2 Cor. 12:9).

David said the Lord will protect me (Ps. 27:1-3), but "One thing I have desired of the Lord, that will I seek: that I may dwell in the house of the Lord all the days of my life, to behold the beauty of the Lord, and to inquire in His temple (Ps. 27:4).

When Job lost all, even his children, He worshipped (Job 1:20).

As the writer to the Hebrews said, "Be content with such things as you have. For He Himself has said, 'I will never leave you nor forsake you'" (Heb. 13:5).

A Point to Ponder

REAL THANKSGIVING

In an attempt to develop better eating habits, a family began eating "turkey franks," "turkey ham," "turkey bacon," and "turkey burgers." When Thanksgiving came, the mother made a beautiful traditional dinner with all the trimmings. As the father began carving the bird, their ten-year-old daughter asked, "Mom, is this real turkey or turkey turkey?" Good point. There is a "turkey Thanksgiving" and a "real Thanksgiving."

Turkey thanksgiving is a national holiday that occurs once a year. On that day, we give thanks for our blessings. It is done out of custom or based on circumstances. That is not all bad, but is it real thanksgiving?

Real thanksgiving is giving thanks all the time. Paul instructs us to give thanks "always" (Eph. 5:20). Giving thanks one day a year is better than never being grateful, but it is at least 364 days short.

Real thanksgiving is giving thanks in all things. Paul admonishes believers to "In everything give thanks" (1 Thess. 5:18). Believers are to give thanks in every circumstance of life, sickness and health, poverty and wealth.

After being robbed, Matthew Henry wrote in his diary: "Let me be thankful. First, I was never robbed before. Second, although they took my purse, they didn't take my life. Third, although they took my all, it was not much. Fourth, let me be thankful because it was I who was robbed and not I who did the robbing."

A Point to Ponder

Real thanksgiving is giving thanks for all things. Technically, 1 Thessalonians 5:18 does not say "*for* everything give thanks," but "*in* everything." Another passage, however, speaks of giving thanks "for all things" (Eph. 5:20). Perhaps in can be argued that in the context of Ephesians, "all things" is a reference to "all blessings" (Eph. 1:3). At any rate, I get the impression from the Scripture that we should be thankful for more than we are. Real thanksgiving is a constant attitude of gratitude to God, realizing that all things work together for good (Rom. 8:28).

The lone survivor of a shipwreck washed up on a small, uninhabited island. He cried out to God to save him. Every day, he scanned the horizon, searching for help. Finally, he managed to build a rough hut and put his few articles in it. One day, coming home from hunting for food, he was stung with grief to see his little hut in flames. Early the next day, a ship rescued him. When asked, "How did you know I was here?" They replied, "We saw your smoke signal." When he saw that the fire worked with other events for his own good, he was thankful for the fire.

In the Wednesday night prayer meeting before Thanksgiving, a lady in the church I pastor said, "I thank God for the hard times because they have made my heart soft." That is the real thing.

A Point to Ponder

I HAVE BEEN ROBBED!

On Saturday, November 24, 2001, I sent an article entitled "Real Thanksgiving." In it, I said, "Paul admonishes believers: 'In everything give thanks' (1 Thess. 5:18). Believers are to give thanks in every circumstance of life, in sickness and health; in poverty and wealth."

I also quoted one of my favorite examples on this subject. After being robbed, Matthew Henry wrote in his diary: "Let me be thankful. First, I was never robbed before. Second, although they took my purse, they didn't take my life. Third, although they took my all, it was not much. Fourth, let me be thankful because it was I who was robbed and not I who did the robbing."

On Sunday, November 25, 2001, I was given an opportunity to practice what I wrote. While preaching, someone entered my church office and took my laptop computer. I have been robbed! With all due respect to Matthew Henry, I would like to edit his diary entry.

First, I can't say that I have not been robbed before because I have been. Years ago, one afternoon, when no one was home, thieves robbed my house in broad daylight. On more than one occasion over the years, things in my car have been stolen.

Second, I am grateful that no one was hurt. Thanks, Matthew, that's a good reminder.

Third, in my case, the thief did not take all; he (or, to be politically correct, he or she) did not take all he or she could have.

A Point to Ponder

I used the laptop carrying case as a briefcase. In one pocket were several folders containing some very important papers, including financial documents. In another compartment was my checkbook, Palm Pilot, two complete sets of keys to two locations, etc. For some reason, the thief lifted the folders out of the pocket and placed them on the seat. As far as I know, nothing else was taken from my office. I am grateful the thief left the folders.

Fourth, with Matthew, I am thankful I was robbed and not I who did the robbery. I did not lose any sleep because of guilt.

Fifth, something else occurred to me when I thought about Matthew's comment on his loss. Jesus said, "Do not lay up for yourselves treasures on earth, where moth and rust destroy and where thieves break in and steal; but lay up for yourselves treasures in heaven, where neither moth nor rust destroys and where thieves do not break in and steal" (Mt. 6:19-20).

I am reminded that, in the words of the old spiritual, "This world is not my home, I'm justa passin through." All things can be stolen here, but I have treasure hidden out of sight "where thieves do not break in and steal!"

A Point to Ponder

ChURCH MATH

Early in my ministerial experience, I was introduced to "church math." A pastor told me, "I count nickels and noses. If the numbers are down on Sunday, I'm down on Monday." I was not impressed, but I soon learned there is a "numbers" side to church.

It has been suggested that 90% of a pastor's counseling is crisis counseling. I believe it! When most people see a pastor for counseling, it is not for a spiritual check-up but for ER stuff. Not a few are ready for ICU.

The 80/20 rule is that 80% of the work is done by 20% of the people and another version of the same adage says that 20% of the people do 80% of the giving. It does not take long to figure out that most people in the church do little and give little.

Over the years, I have concluded that there is a 30/30/30/ rule. No matter what I do or what I say, 30% of the people will agree, 30% will disagree, and 30% won't care one way or the other. (Before someone informs me that 10% are missing, technically, the numbers are thirty-three and a third each.) If the 30% who do not care begin to side with the 30% who disagree, the pastor is in trouble.

If you want to see how low the number can get, call a business meeting or, better yet, go to the prayer meeting. Back in the days when churches had three services a week, I once decided that in the average church, 50% of the morning crowd returned Sunday evening, and 25% of the Sunday morning attendance went to

A Point to Ponder

prayer meeting on Wednesday night (also the larger the church, the smaller the numbers). When I shared my calculations with pastors, I was often told they wished their numbers were that good! W. A. Criswell, the famous Pastor of the First Baptist Church in Dallas for fifty years (and one of my favorite preachers), who just went to be with the Lord, used to say that those who love the pastor attend on Sunday morning, those who love the church attend on Sunday night, and those who love the Lord attend on Wednesday night.

Is it biblical to think like this? What Jesus taught in the parable of the Sower (Mt 13:3-9) could be called the 25/25/25/25 rule. Only 25% of the people who hear the Word produce fruit! Of those who produce fruit, not all produce a hundredfold. Jesus said that only some produced a hundredfold and the other fruit bearers produced sixty and thirtyfold (Mt. 13:8).

Hum? If only twenty-five percent produce fruit and only a third of the twenty-five percent produce one hundred percent, only eight and a third percent produce a hundredfold. In the words of the old spiritual, "Lord, I want to be in that number."

A Point to Ponder

MARRIAGE MATH

Marriage is a give-and-take that can be expressed in mathematical terms. Many mates feel that their marriage is 60/40, meaning they give 60% and get 40%. Of course, others would say that their marriage adds up differently, more like 70/30, 80/20, 90/10, or worse. As the second number slides down, the marriage's state slips further from the ideal.

Most couples with whom I have talked in marriage counseling seem to figure that what is fair is 50/50. Please note: couples *in marriage counseling* think that 50/50 is fair!

Over the years, I have told couples that marriage is a 100/0 proposition, meaning each should give 100% without expecting anything in return. As they say, it looks good on paper. In real life, it rarely adds up. Frankly, barring some extreme circumstances, such as one being bedridden, to expect nothing in a marriage is idealism in the extreme. At best, it is an excellent attitude toward which to strive. Under normal circumstances, if it came down to giving 100% and getting nothing, it would take a masochistic or an unbelievable saint to stay in the marriage. I don't doubt that both happens.

How does God compute marriage math? In the words of Genesis, "Therefore a man shall leave his father and mother and be joined to his wife, and they shall become one flesh" (Gen. 2:24). "One flesh" is the physical consummation. However, expositors

A Point to Ponder

from ancient rabbis have understood it to include other aspects of the relationship. Assuming that "one flesh" is more than just the physical side of marriage, the divine math of marriage is $1 + 1 = 1$.

Two becoming one does not mean that they become identical. The two keep their identity and some of their tastes, preferences, and opinions. At the same time, they slowly become more and more one. In the case of some couples who have lived together harmoniously for many decades, they are said to even look alike in their old age.

In many ways, Patricia and I have experienced divine marriage math in our marriage. For us, one of the greatest expressions of the fact that we were becoming one happened on our seventh wedding anniversary. As was our custom, we bought each other an anniversary card. To our amazement, we picked out cards for each other with identical text. The cards were different in design, but the text was the same!

If your marriage is not adding up, the solution is not subtraction or division. Use higher math, and your intimacy will multiply.

Happy Valentine's Day!

A Point to Ponder

HOW SAD

What a sad sight! A grown man is eating out of a garbage bin. I see it often.

I live in Santa Monica, CA, which is located on the Pacific Ocean. The weather is about as ideal as it gets on this planet. Consequently, it attracts homeless people. The people of Santa Monica are, for the most part, sympathetic. It is a very liberal town, affectionately known as "The People's Republic of Santa Monica." The government, as well as non-profit organizations, provide beds and meals. No one in Santa Monica needs to lack a good meal or a clean bed. Nevertheless, people sleep on the beach or in the parks every night and rummage through garbage bins. Many are collecting bottles and cans to sell so they can buy booze, but some are looking for food. With so many other options, it's really sad to see people choose to eat garbage.

What I have just described happens every day. It is also an allegory of me and you. We don't eat out of garbage bins; we watch TV and listen to talk radio. I gave up TV years ago, except for a few select programs, not because I felt it was sinful to watch TV, but because I have better things to do with my time. Living in LA, however, I have a lot of car time and, for years, I have listened to the radio, especially talk radio. Is it me, or is it getting worse?

On occasion, I have mentioned that someday, I would love to read, or at least know something of, the one hundred greatest books. To my surprise and delight, my wife gave me "The World's Greatest Books" on tape for Christmas. Since then, I have listened to tapes in the car. Some days, I don't listen to the news, a departure from my norm.

One of the things that has jolted me is the level of food I have allowed my mind to feed on in my own car! What a difference it is to listen to something more educational.

Some will suggest that I listen to Christian radio. I have, and sometimes I do, but not all on Christian radio is health cuisine. Some will say that I should listen to Christian tapes. I do. I recommend that you do as well. A friend got the Bible on tape for Christmas. He listens as he commutes to work and back.

That is not my point. My point is that we allow ourselves to do all of that while still feeding on garbage. Perhaps there is so much of it in the world, some of it is unavoidable. Maybe I just feel like the old spiritual, "This world is not my home; I'm just a passin through." Whatever, this much I know, we should follow Paul's advice. "Finally, brethren, whatever things are true, whatever things are noble, whatever things are just, whatever things are pure, whatever things are lovely, whatever things are of good report, if there is any virtue and if there is anything praiseworthy; meditate on these things" (Phil. 4:8).

A Point to Ponder

THE ANATOMY OF AN AFFAIR

For an affair to occur, there must be a push and a pull. The push is from within the marriage; the pull is an attraction outside the marriage. An affair is not likely if there is a push but no pull or a pull but no push. When, however, something is pushing the married partners away from each other and a third party attracts one of them, the married person is vulnerable.

To be more specific, the martial connection is volitional, mental, physical, and emotional. Married people share choices, intellectual ideas, and sex. The deepest level of connection, however, is emotional. Married people should be able to express their deepest emotions on any subject with their mate and feel they are being heard.

Many marriages lack emotional intimacy. In some cases, one or both never learned to express emotion. Or, one tries, and the other gets defensive or attempts to "fix it." When there is no emotional connection, differences are not dealt with properly. The simplest decision becomes divisive. Anger, resentment, and open hostility quickly follow.

If there is no emotional connection, married people do not *feel* connected. When they do not feel connected to each other, a push is present. It may be only a slight nudge or develop into a shove. They feel disconnected, alienated, and "pushed" away.

The pull is an attraction to another person. The attraction may be physical ("Wow! Is she ever good-looking.") or intellectual

A Point to Ponder

("Working together, we discovered that we think alike."). At this point, it could get physical, but the real danger is when they begin to share their emotions and feel that they "understand" and are being "understood," things missing in their marriage. Everything else is like a pile of dry timber. The emotional element is the spark that sets it ablaze.

Once the physical affair has begun, it is extremely difficult to repair the damage. To do so, the issues that must be dealt with are 1) the guilty person's feelings for the third party, 2) the guilty person's feelings for his or her mate, 3) the "innocent" person's feelings and willingness to forgive and continue with the marriage, and 4) the emotional connection between the married couple. The situation is so serious that Jesus said it was grounds for divorce (Mt. 19:9).

What about prevention? First, stay in touch with the Lord. The believer who has an affair is not walking in the Spirit because those who walk in the Spirit do not fulfill the lust of the flesh (Gal. 5:16). Even when there is a push and a pull if the tempted person is rightly related to the Lord, the temptation can be overcome (1 Cor. 10:13). Second, stay emotionally and sexually connected with your mate (1 Cor. 7:1-5). Third, guard your heart. Out of it, "spring the issues of life" (Prov. 4:23). Share the deepest feelings of your heart *with your mate.*

A Point to Ponder

"I HAVE A PROBLEM"

People have problems. Granted, some problems are slight and others are severe, but everyone, without exception, has problems. No one has arrived.

So, you would think it would be easy to say, "I have a problem." Or "It is my fault." Or "I have sinned." Is such the case? Not even close!

After over forty (now fifty-plus) years of talking to people, it seems that people will do just about anything rather than face the reality about themselves.

People deceive themselves. John says, "If we say that we have no sin, we deceive ourselves" (1 Jn. 1:8). According to James, it is even possible to look in the Word, see ourselves, and then deceive ourselves (Jas. 1:22-24). Jeremiah says, "The heart is deceitful above all things and desperately wicked; who can know it?" (Jer. 17:9). Commenting on that verse, Paul Meier, the Christian psychiatrist, once said to me, "and we deceive ourselves more than anyone else." Psychologists call this "denial."

People shift the blame. This maneuver is as old as Adam. He told God, "The woman whom You gave to be with me, she gave me of the tree, and I ate" (Gen. 3:12). Caught red-handed, Adam was forced to admit the truth, but first, he subtly blamed his wife and even God! We blame our genes, our early environment, our circumstances, our mates, our children, our job, etc. We're pros at it. Psychologists call this "rationalization."

A Point to Ponder

In denying accountability and shifting the blame away from responsibility, some conclude, "I am a problem." They play the "woe is me" game. Rather than simply saying, "I have a problem," they go to the extreme of "I am a problem." Psychologists call this low self-esteem. If you are a believer, you are a new person in Christ. You have a new divine nature and the Holy Spirit. *You* are not a problem, but you also still have the flesh. So, you *have* a problem.

The first step in solving a problem is identifying it. I have often told people that 50% of solving a problem is finding out what it is. Jesus put it this way, "You shall know the truth, and the truth shall make you free" (Jn. 8:32). The Greek word translated "truth" means, "reality." To be free from a problem, we must first face reality and the reality is that "I have a problem." It is not, "Someone else (my mother, my brother, my mate, my boss) has a problem." Or "I am a problem," but "I have a problem. I need to identify it so that I can solve it.

Several things need to be clarified. This is not to say that others do not have a problem. They do. They are human too. Nevertheless, in the midst of the mess, I have a problem, which may be that I need to forgive. Also, by saying that you need to solve it, I do not mean to imply that you can do that alone. You may need the help of others (Phil. 4:3) and the Lord (Jn 15:5, Phil. 4:13), but the process begins with, "I have a problem."

A Point to Ponder

SPORTS HISTORY

On the eve of the fourth and final (?) game of the 2002 NBA finals, Bill Plaschke, the talented sports writer for the *Los Angeles Times,* wrote, "So tonight the suspense begins, tick by tick, dribble by dribble, a town and its team counting down the most anticipated sight in the Los Angeles sports landscape. The Fourth game of the NBA Finals could produce it. Emotion will rule it. History will judge it. Millions might never forget it" (*Los Angeles Times*, June 12, 2002, p. D-1).

Well written. Eloquently stated. I wish I could write like that, but give me a break.

Before I give you a piece of my mind, a confession or two is in order. 1) Throughout my life, I have been a baseball fan of sorts (Dodgers), an on-again, off-again football fan (Dallas Cowboys), but I have never been much of a basketball fan. 2) In the last two years, I have gotten interested enough in the Lakers to at least keep up with the finals. 3) Although I have not seen much, I have probably watched more basketball in the last thirty days than in all the rest of my life put together. 4) I want Shaq to win tonight.

With that off my chest, back to the break (Pardon the pun). Obviously, emotion will rule the post-game celebration. Surely, for millions, tonight will be a memorable moment. No doubt, the 2001-2002 Lakers will get in the record books.

A Point to Ponder

BUT in the overall scheme of things, is this all that significant? Granted, it is of momentary importance to the Lakers, their fans, and many others who will profit financially from what happens, but if the Lord tarries, will this game make it to the history books? In all the years that the Roman Coliseum stood, can anyone name a single gladiator who fought there? Did any gladiator ever win a victory that affected the world?

A few years before the Coliseum was built, Paul was imprisoned in Rome. During that imprisonment, he wrote four letters: Ephesians, Philippians, Colossians, and Philemon. From prison, Paul wrote four letters that affected millions for almost two thousand years, not to mention eternity. As he wrote, "Therefore we do not lose heart. Even though our outward man is perishing, yet the inward man is being renewed day by day. For our light affliction, which is but for a moment, is working for us a far more exceeding and eternal weight of glory, while we do not look at the things, which are seen, but at the things which are not seen. For the things which are seen are temporary, but the things which are not seen are eternal" (2 Cor. 4:16-18).

So, if you are a sports fan (or whatever your thing is), enjoy. Just remember, all of this is temporary. Don't forget the eternal.

A Point to Ponder

UNDER GOD

Because of the phrase "under God," on June 26, 2002, the 9th Circuit Court of Appeals declared the Pledge of Allegiance unconstitutional!

Reaction was swift and strong. President Bush called it "ridiculous." By a vote of 99-0, the US Senate approved a bill reaffirming support for both the pledge and the national motto, "In God we Trust." The US House of Representatives passed a resolution, 416 to 3, protecting the ruling (The three votes were Democrats, two of which are from California). The next day, Judge T. Goodwin, a Republican appointed by Richard Nixon and the one who wrote the ruling, issued an unusual order blocking its enforcement until petitions for a rehearing are resolved.

The reality is that no matter what the President, the Senate, the House, or federal judges think, say, or write, the United States of America is one nation under god—the god of this world! Satan is the god of this world who has blinded the minds of unbelievers to the light of the glorious gospel of the grace of God (2 Cor. 4:4). As a result, unbelievers live "according to the prince of the power of the air" (Eph. 2:2).

Actually, the Lord is over all. The Scripture, the real Supreme Court, declares,

Yours, O LORD, is the greatness, The power and the glory, The victory and the majesty; For all that is in heaven and

A Point to Ponder

in earth is Yours; Yours is the kingdom, O LORD, And You are exalted as head over all. Both riches and honor come from You, And You reign over all. In Your hand is power and might; In Your hand it is to make great And to give strength to all" (1 Chron. 29:11-12).

The Lord is "head over all." He reigns "over all." So aware of it or not, like it or not, we are all under God. The Sovereign Lord God of heaven and earth is over all nature ("all that is in heaven and in earth), all nations ("Yours is the kingdom;" see Dan. 2:21), and all the natives on this planet ("You reign over all").

The Lord rules over all, but in the final analysis, He wants to personally rule in the individual heart (Gal. 4:19, Eph. 3:17, Col. 3:15). For God to personally rule over you, you must place yourself under Him daily.

The issue is not just whether the phrase "under God" is in the pledge we say before the flag, but is the reality of "under God" in our heart before the Father daily. After the court decision, the students at one Elementary school recited the Pledge of Allegiance and when they got to the disputed phrase, they screamed, "UNDER GOD."

May my heart shout "under God" daily.

A Point to Ponder

AN "HONEST" THIEF

Many years ago, a fairly wealthy man gave me an expensive designer wallet as a gift of appreciation. It lasted for years but eventually went the way of all wallets; it began to come apart. Knowing how much I liked that wallet, my wife gave me one like it as an anniversary gift.

I had only had the new wallet for about six months when last Saturday, dressed in a pair of shorts with a very shallow rear pocket, I went to Staples to purchase paper for my printer. Apparently, after I paid for the supplies with a credit card from my wallet, I did not put it firmly in that shallow pocket. It probably fell out in the parking lot of Staples. At any rate, a short time later, I discovered it was missing. I returned to Staples only to discover that no one had returned my wallet. I immediately canceled the credit cards and grieved the loss.

Yesterday, when I returned home from church, I found an envelope with the contents of my wallet in it! Someone had gone to the trouble of copying my address from my driver's license, taping it to the front of the envelope, wrapping the contents of the wallet in a plain white piece of 8½ x 11 paper, putting it in an envelope and bring it to my house. All that was missing was the expensive wallet and a spare 20-dollar bill I carry in my wallet. (My spendable money is always in a money clip, which I always keep in my front pocket.) Unbelievable!

A Point to Ponder

Frankly, I appreciated it. Whoever did that obviously did not have to do it and it saved me a lot of time today (Monday) in that I did not have to take the time to replace my driver's license, car insurance card, health insurance card, etc.

I immediately thanked the Lord. This may sound silly to some, but I had asked Abba if He would be so kind as to see to it that the stuff was returned. He at least answered most of the prayer.

Now, may I ask a question? Assuming that the one who returned the wallet's contents, minus the money, was the thief, what was he (or she) thinking? I can only imagine. Let me speculate. Could that individual have thought, "I am an honest person. I will return the contents of the wallet and keep the money and the wallet as a small token for my trouble. The owner will be glad to get the contents back and would probably reward me for finding the wallet, anyway." Such self-justification would, no doubt, make the thief feel better, at least not as bad, and maybe even feel a little honest.

We all rationalize our sins, don't we? The problem, of course, is that in the final analysis, "the judgment of God is according to truth" (Rom. 2:2), not according to what we think or feel. Moreover, even when we think we are justified, that does not mean we are (1 Cor. 4:3-5). So, we need to beware of the self-justification of our sin.

A Point to Ponder

WHY DOES LIFE HAVE TO BE SO DIFFICULT?

A young lady I led to Christ several years ago attends the church I pastor. She told me about a difficult situation and punctuated the conversation with, "Why does life have to be so difficult?" I borrowed her expression when describing my difficult days to my wife.

I take comfort in the fact that Job felt the same way. He said. "Man is born to trouble, as the sparks fly upward" (Job 5:7) and "Man who is born of woman is of few days and full of trouble" (Job 14: 1). As someone has said, "Life is filled with trouble and then we die." Life is filled with problems. Why?

From a biblical point of view, there are many reasons, one of which is that "tribulation produces perseverance" (Rom. 5:3). The Greek word translated "tribulations" means "pressure" and is used figuratively for distress, affliction, physical hardship, and sufferings. The Greek word rendered "perseverance" means "endurance." Does tribulation always produce endurance? Obviously not. Tribulation produces endurance when "it is met by faith in God which receives it as God's fatherly discipline" (Cranfield; Jas. 1:2-3, says that the approved part of faith produces endurance).

From a practical perspective, we would never mature if life were easy and not difficult. People born with a silver spoon in their mouths grow up thinking that others are to serve them and they don't have to serve others. Some people are born on third base and they think they hit a triple. Years ago, A lady told me she was a cashier in a market when scanners began to be used. She said, "I could process groceries faster using a scanner than I could punch in each item with my figures." Then, she added, "The faster the process, the more impatient people became." Isn't that true of all of us? The easier life becomes, the more impatient we become.

On the other hand, I recently talked to a man I had not seen in several years. He struck me as much more calm and patient than I remembered. After he told me what he had been through, I understood why. In his case, tribulation had worked.

If problems, pressure, and tribulation are for my benefit, then maybe I should be grateful instead of griping. In fact, the full text of what Paul said is, "We also glory in tribulations, knowing that tribulation produces perseverance" (Rom. 5:3). The Greek word translated "glory" in verse 3 is the same Greek word translated "rejoice" in verse 2. We can rejoice, glory, boast, and be jubilant in future hope (Rom. 5:2) and present troubles (Rom. 5:3) because tribulation benefits believers.

The young lady who rhetorically asked, "Why is life so difficult?" answers her own question by saying, "I know, 'Trials are for your training,'" quoting a line she heard me use in a sermon. Some days, I must remind myself to listen to my sermons.

A Point to Ponder

WHAT JESUS' WORDS HAVE TAUGHT ME

I have asked myself, "If I am to be a disciple (that is, a learner) of Christ, what have I learned from Him?" I decided to make a list. I stopped at twenty because I did not have much time at the moment. Before you read my list, create your own. In one sitting, list all the things the Lord has taught you in His own words. You know, the ones that are printed in red. Here is my initial offering.

1. The gift of eternal life is received by trusting Him (Jn. 3:16; 4:10).
2. The gift of eternal life can never be lost (Jn. 3:16; 5:24).
3. Believers who wish to learn from Him must abide in His Word (Jn. 8:30-31).
4. truth shall make you free (Jn. 8:32). Lies bind.
5. Some tragedies happen in life, not because the victims did anything wrong, but so the works of God can be revealed (Jn. 9:1-3).
6. Believers need constant cleansing (Jn. 13:1-17).
7. Believers should love others as Jesus loved them (Jn. 13:34).
8. God wants fruit (Jn. 15:1-11).

A Point to Ponder

9. To be like Him, Believers will have to be betrayed, denied, and deserted (Jn. 13:21, 13:37; Mt. 26:31
10. People should be approached differently (Jn. 3:1-21; 4:726; 20:26-29).
11. When talking to people about their problems, ask them if they want to be well (Jn. 5:6).
12. If you love the Lord, then, even when you have failed Him, you should return to tend to His business (Jn. 21:15-17).
13. We are not here to be served but to serve (Mk. 10:45). Righteousness is not just an external action but an internal attitude (Mt. 5-7).
14. The goal of learning from Him is to be like Him (Lk. 6:40).
15. After you have presented the truth and have answered people's questions, if they choose to walk away, let them (Mk. 10:17-23).
16. In fact, if people will not receive you or hear you, shake the dust off your feet (Mt. 10:14).
17. The gospel is to be given to every person on the planet (Mk. 16:15).
18. Be merciful; be compassionate (Mt. 5:7).
19. Be a peacemaker (Mt. 5:9).

I wish I could say I have mastered all of this. PBPWMGINFWMY (Please be patient with me; God is not finished with me yet.)

A Point to Ponder

WHO MINISTERS TO THE MINISTER?

For thirteen years, I traveled around the country, conducting evangelistic meetings and Bible conferences in churches. I spent a lot of time with pastors. I have personally served as a pastor in three churches for at least twenty years. Currently, I am the president of the Los Angeles Minister's Council for American Baptist Churches USA. From being a pastor and rubbing shoulders with hundreds of pastors for decades, I have learned something about pastors; namely, being a pastor is a discouraging job.

The sources of the discouragement are many. People do not respond as they ought. People do not keep the promises they make. People get offended over things they should not. There is never enough money to do what needs to be done. There is more work than week; the job is never done.

People in the church often don't tell the pastor what is happening until there is a problem. While that is not the total picture, this much is: most don't talk to the pastor until there is a problem. From the pastor's point of view, there is bad news, bad news, and bad news, and every once in a while, there is a little bit of good news. After a while, it gets to pastors, especially if they care about people and most pastors I know do.

Then, there is the reality that will not change. People treat pastors like they do their dentist. Most do not brush their teeth three times a day, or they do not floss. They do not go see their dentist for regular checkups. Oh, no, they wait until they get a toothache. With pastors, people don't come for counsel until there is an abscess! Regarding counseling, pastors are like doctors who work in ER.

Who ministers to the minister? Again, there are many sources, but one of them should be YOU. Yes, you, the "lowly layman," should minister to your pastor. That is what the Bible teaches. Paul told the Romans, "For I long to see you, that I may impart to you some spiritual gift, so that you may be established; that is, that I may be encouraged together with you by the mutual faith both of you and me" (Rom. 1:11-12). Paul the Apostle taught that believers could and should "encourage" him.

There are numerous ways for you to minister to your minister. One significant way is to tell him how he has ministered to you. Don't just tell him that it was a good sermon or that he is a good speaker. Get specific about how what he said changed your life. Nothing encourages me more than to know someone has trusted Christ or has grown due to the ministry of the Word.

So, remember when you go to church next Sunday. You are not there just to be ministered to; you are there to minister (Mk. 10:45) and one of the individuals you are to minister to is your pastor. In fact, according to the writer to the Hebrews, all of us are to be encouraging each other daily (Heb. 10:25).

A Point to Ponder

THE WHINER

In my lifetime, I have known several people who were whiners. Being in the ministry and wanting to help, I would listen and offer suggestions. I learned the hard way that is not what they want. I then learned to just listen.

The whiners I have encountered moan and groan (on and on) about all their problems, sighing, "I just don't know what to do." They will say, "I've tried thus and so, but nothing seems to work out." If they are Christians, they will say, "I have prayed, Lord, show me what you want me to do." Or "If you want me to do something, show me what it is." To hear them tell it, they would have no luck if they did not have bad luck.

I have to confess that listening to a whiner irritates me. After listening to the same thing or type of thing, over and over wears me out! I was comforted (only slightly) by the fact that, according to one dictionary, a whiner complains annoyingly. (Another says a whiner complains in a childish, undignified way.) A whiner, by definition, annoys people.

What whiners do is focus on the problems and whine. When they attempt to do something to solve some of their problems, they often do the wrong thing, and they do it with the halfhearted attitude: certain this, too, will fail.

No matter what happens, they complain. They complain when they win. As an elderly lady entered a department store, a band

A Point to Ponder

began to play, an orchid was pinned on her dress, and a $100 bill was placed in her hand. With a TV camera focused on her, a man said, "You're the one-millionth customer. Can you tell us why you came to our store today?" Yes," said the little old lady. "I'm on my way to the complaint department." Whiners are always on their way to the complaint department.

They need to stop concentrating on the past and complaining about the present and construct a course of action for the future. If that plan does not work, they should decide not to whine about it. Instead, they should use their time and energy to design another plan and take action.

Please don't take my word for it. Try God's, especially the book of Philippians. "Do all things without complaining and disputing" (Phil. 2:14)."Brethren, I do not count myself to have apprehended; but one thing I do, forgetting those things which are behind and reaching forward to those things which are ahead (Phil. 3:13). "I can do all things through Christ who strengthens me" (Phil. 4:13).

If you are a whiner, read Philippians repeatedly. If you know a whiner, tell'm what I just told you. Or give them this piece of God's mind.

Martin Luther said, "The devil is a chronic grumbler. A Christian ought to be a living doxology."

A Point to Ponder

RECKONED RIGHTEOUS BY WORKS

Abraham had faith, and that faith was accounted for by him for righteousness (Gen. 15:6). This is one of the most important teachings in the Bible. It is called "justification (to be declared righteous) by faith." Paul explains it in detail (Rom. 3:21-5:1), insisting that justification is by faith and not by works (Rom. 4:2-3, 5).

It is surprising to discover that the Bible says man's *work* was accounted for righteousness. "Phinehas stood up and intervened, and the plague was stopped. And that was accounted to him for righteousness to all generations forevermore" (Ps. 106:30-31).

In the wilderness, some committed "harlotry" with the women of Moab (Num. 25:1). Then, they "bowed" to the gods of Moab (Num. 25:2). When the Lord told Moses to kill the offenders, Phinehas killed two of them with a javelin (Num. 25:3-15). The Lord gave Phinehas a "covenant of peace" (Num. 25:12), saying, "It shall be to him and his descendants after him a covenant of an everlasting priesthood" (Num. 25:13). Phinehas' work of killing two people was "accounted to him for righteousness!" (Ps. 106:31).

Admittedly, as J. A. Alexander, the Bible scholar, says, "The form of expression is borrowed from Genesis 15:6." Indeed, it has been called a "striking instance of the fearlessness of expression which is to be found in the Scriptures as compared with dogmatic forms of modern controversial theology" (Perowne), but what does it mean? Does the Bible teach justification by

A Point to Ponder

faith, or does it teach justification by works?

The answer is "both." There is clearly a justification by faith (Gen. 15:6; Rom. 4:3; 5:1; Gal. 3:6; Jas. 2:23). There is also a justification by works (Jas. 2:21, 24-25). Justification by faith is before God (Rom. 4:5). Justification by works is before people ("*you* see" in Jas. 2:24).

So, both Abraham and Phinehas were justified by faith and both were justified by works. Abraham was "justified by works when he offered Isaac his son on the altar" (Jas. 2:21) and Phinehas was justified by works when he obeyed God's command to kill people worth of capital punishment (Ps. 106:31). God sees faith and declares the believer righteous (Phil. 3:9), assured of heaven. God sees obedience and declares the believing worker righteous (Jas. 2:21, Ps. 106:31), worthy of reward. We cannot see the faith, but we can see the work.

Commentators concur. One calls what Phinehas received a "reward" and says it was "not a justifying act by which Phinehas was saved, but a praiseworthy act for which he, a justified or righteous man already, received the divine commendation and perpetual memorial of his faithfulness" (Alexander). Another says, that what he did was "looked upon as a righteous act and rewarded accordingly" (Perowne).

The question is, "Are you justified?"

A Point to Ponder

NEW YEAR'S RESOLUTIONS BIBLICAL?

At the end of every year, I evaluate the last year and set some goals for the next year. It's my version of a New Year's resolution. I have not always succeeded in meeting the goals, but overall, I would say that it has been a beneficial practice.

Are New Year's Resolutions biblical? Is there any biblical basis for such a practice? Obviously, the practice we call "New Year's resolutions" is not mentioned in the Bible. Moreover, it could be argued that every day is like every other day. One day should not necessarily be more highly regarded than another. Paul says, "One person esteems one day above another; another esteems every day alike. Let each be fully convinced in his own mind" (see Rom. 14:5).

On the other hand, the Scripture speaks of "new beginnings." At least the Old Testament reflects such an idea. Each week ended with the Sabbath (Ex. 20:8-11) and the day after the Sabbath began a new week. All inheritances were restored at the beginning of the Jubilee year (Lev. 25:10, 13, 23-28), and all slaves were freed (Lev. 25:39-40). They obtained a new beginning. Every year on the Day of Atonement (Lev. 23:27-28), everyone could "start over again," freed from sin until the following year."

The New Testament repeatedly admonishes believers to put off vices and put on virtues (for example, Eph. 4:20-32). In a sense, any day is a day to start over again. Any time is a good time to put off the sins of the past (year) and set your sights on spiritual accomplishments for now and in the future. So, why not at the beginning of the year? It is as good a time as any. Or maybe I should say, "It's about time!"

A word of caution: if there is a problem with our practice of New Year's Resolutions, it is that we are going to make a resolution and, therefore, we will change. While that may work for some people in some areas of life, it doesn't work for most. Hence, all the broken New Year's Resolutions. If your resolutions include spiritual issues (and they should), then remember, you can't change spiritually without the Lord (Jn. 15:5).

In one of those "put off/put on" passages, the writer to the Hebrews says believers are to "lay aside every weight, and the sin which so easily ensnares us, and let us run with endurance the race that is set before us" (Heb. 12:1). Then He adds, "looking unto Jesus, the author and finisher of our faith, who for the joy that was set before Him endured the cross, despising the shame, and has sat down at the right hand of the throne of God. For consider Him who endured such hostility from sinners against Himself, lest you become weary and discouraged in your souls (Heb. 12:2-3). Look to Jesus. He is the supreme example of an enduring faith. Also implied in the word "look" is the idea of "trust."

So, make New Year's resolutions. Make a few spiritual ones too, but remember, you will need the Lord's help and grace to make spiritual resolutions a reality.

A Point to Ponder

ONE OF THE GREATEST NEEDS IN AMERICA

What would you say are the greatest needs in America? Like the country's diversity, various answers exist, including evangelism, education, equality, and economic justice. A much longer list could be assembled. A case could be made for evangelists and educators, prophets and politicians, revivalists and reformers.

May I suggest that one of the greatest needs in America is for shepherds? When Jesus looked at "a great multitude" of people, He was moved with compassion by the great need. Obviously, in a great number of people, there would be a number of different needs, yet the Scripture focuses on one great need. It says, "And Jesus, when He came out, saw a great multitude and was moved with compassion for them because they were like sheep not having a shepherd (Mk. 6:43a). One of the greatest needs in America today is for godly shepherds to feed and lead people.

Good shepherds do the work of an evangelist (2 Tim. 4:5). Jesus said, "O Jerusalem, Jerusalem, the one who kills the prophets and stones those who are sent to her! How often I wanted to gather your children together, as a hen gathers her chicks under her wings, but you were not willing!" (Mt. 23:37). That deeply felt emotional expression certainly includes evangelism.

Godly shepherds teach. When Jesus saw the "great multitude" and was moved with compassion, thinking they needed a shepherd,

A Point to Ponder

"He began to teach" (Mk. 6:34b). Jesus told Peter, a shepherd (1 Pet. 5:1-2), to "Feed My sheep" (Jn. 21:17).

Great shepherds sacrifice themselves to meet the needs of the sheep. Jesus, the "good Shepherd (Jn. 10:11a), "that great Shepherd of the sheep" (Heb. 13:20), "did not come to be served, but to serve" (Mk. 10:45b), to "gives His life for the sheep (Jn. 10:11b), to "give His life a ransom for many" (Mk. 10:45b). Shepherd not only watch sheep give birth and see to it that the sheep are fed, they "tend" the flock (Jn. 21:16), helping heal the hurts (Lk. 4:18), etc.

When shepherds do what they are supposed to, there is evangelism, education, equality, and even economic justice. One of the outstanding examples is John Newton, ex-slave trader, author of *Amazing Grace* and pastor who shepherded William Wilberforce. In the year Newton died (1807), Parliament passed Wilberforce's bill abolishing the slave trade on British ships.

Pray that the Lord will rise up shepherds to minister to the flock (Lk. 10:2) and pray for the shepherds who are ministering to their flocks now (Heb. 13:17-18). They are meeting one of the greatest needs in the world, one sheep at a time. Shepherds receive little recognition now, but when the chief shepherd (1 Pet. 5:4) appears, shepherds who have done their job well will "receive the crown of glory" (1 Pet. 5:4).

A Point to Ponder

YOUR MEMORIAL TABLE

For years, I was "on call" for Forest Lawn Mortuary. If someone needs a minister to officiate at a funeral but doesn't have one, Forest Lawn selects one from their approved list. As a result of being on their list, I conducted nearly 200 funerals in ten years. It was an excellent opportunity to share the gospel with people who usually never darken the door of a church.

On one occasion, I was assigned to conduct a funeral in a small chapel at Forest Lawn. As I walked into the chapel, I was immediately struck by the fact that no casket was present. That was not necessarily unusual. I have conducted services where an erne was in place of a casket. In this case, however, there was no erne, only a small table. To the right of the table stood a life-sized picture of Elvis Presley.

On the small table, there were a number of objects. At the back was a group of pictures. In front of the photographs was a fresh hamburger and an order of French fries that smelled like they had just come off the grill, a can of beer, a pack of cigarettes and a lighter, a package of sunflower seeds, and a large pile of keys, all on the same ring.

Shortly after entering the chapel, I met the widow. I learned that her husband, who was only 55 years old, had died suddenly of a heart attack. She then began to describe her husband to me. Looking affectionately at the objects on the table, she said, "That's

A Point to Ponder

him." She explained that he loved hamburgers; he could eat them three times a day. He liked eating hamburgers and fries, drinking beer, and smoking cigarettes while watching the Dodgers and the Angels on TV or listening to Elvis. Everything on the table symbolized who he was.

On the way home, I couldn't help but think about that table. Beside Paul's table would probably be a full-size picture of Christ, for he said, "For me to live is Christ" (Phil. 1:21 him). I wondered, if there is a Memorial Table instead of a casket at my funeral, what would the people near and dear to me put on it? I decided what I would put on it if I were choosing the contents of the table, but I wondered what others might do.

Later, when I told Patricia, my wife, about what happened. I asked what she thought my Memorial Table would look like. I was pleased to hear her say that she would put a Bible on the table and I was surprised to hear her say that she would put a highlighter on the table. After a moment's reflection, I understood why. I am constantly reading and have often said that I can't read without a highlighter. Putting a highlighter on my Memorial Table would be appropriate. She listed some other objects, such as my PDA, etc. I am sure that others would put a different set of items on my table, some of which might not be as complementary to the ones Patricia chose.

What would you put on your Memorial Table? What do you think others might put on your Memorial Table? What objects symbolize who you are?

A Point to Ponder

THE PROBLEM WITH GAMBLING

William J. Bennett, the author of *The Book of Virtues,* has admitted to gambling. He denies he has lost $8 million but concedes that he has gambled "large sums of money." In his defense, he pointed out that the kind of gambling he did was legal, that he always paid taxes on his winnings, that he never put his family in danger, and that he pretty much "always broke even." Although Bennett never addressed the morality of gambling in his books or speaking engagements, his critics charged him with hypocrisy.

What is the problem with gambling? Isn't gambling just taking a risk and don't we all take risks daily? Therefore, we all gamble, right?

As with most words, the word "gamble" has several definitions. It means: 1) to risk, to expose to hazard. 2) to take a risk to gain some advantage. 3) to play games of chance for money. 4) to speculate. Thus, in one sense of the word, everyone gambles every day. The act of getting out of bed exposes us to hazards. It's risky! It could be called "gambling" in the simplest sense.

The ethical issue is not about the risk of everyday living. It is about playing a game of chance for money. Traditionally, Christians have vilified gambling as a sin against the Protestant work ethic. There is another issue.

In his book *Something for Nothing: Luck in America*, Jackson Lear, a Rutgers history professor, looks at gambling less as a vice

A Point to Ponder

and more as a worldview. He calls it a "culture of chance." He says, "This country has always been fascinated by the 'breaks.' The risk-taking entrepreneur is a cultural hero; look at the day trader—they are nothing but compulsive gamblers and they become an icon of the age." He also says, "Gamblers rarely pass by someone who is tapped out. They know how quickly things can turn. And in helping each other, they rarely ask questions, rarely ask if someone deserves the help."

May I suggest that the problem with game gambling is worldview? While not many would question spending a few bucks on a game and all agree, even those within the gambling industry, that compulsive gambling can cause great damage to people, families, and even society, the basic issue is worldview.

Imagine Bennett, or anyone else, as the solitary, obsessed slot player standing in front of a slot machine, pulling the lever for hours and hours. What does that say about the gambler's use of time and money, not to mention relationships? The issue is worldview, isn't it?

While the opponents of virtues and morality delight (without moderation) in Bennett's blunder, perhaps, before we cast stones, we should ask, "How am I spending *my* time and money?" "See then that you walk circumspectly, not as fools but as wise, redeeming the time, because the days are evil" (Eph. 5:15-16).

A Point to Ponder

LEARNING TO LISTEN

On occasions, people have thanked me for "listening." Some have also said, "Are you listening to me?" What do I do that makes some people think I am genuinely listening? What do I do that makes some feel that I am not listening? How can we develop listening skills? Here are a few suggestions.

Attitude Listening begins with a loving attitude. It is the attitude of, "I care about you and I am genuinely interested in what you have to say."

Body Language Experts contend that most of communication is body language. When listening, you are not speaking, but your body is sending signals and speaking more loudly than you might be aware. The body has a language that communicates. Make sure that your body is sending the message you want to convey.

Some body posture sends a negative message, for example, crossing your arms. Sitting behind a desk conveys a power position and less personal warmth. To communicate a caring attitude with your body, focus on the one speaking. Eye contact is critical. Look the speaker in the eye. There are times when what really communicates is learning forward. On many occasions, when people came to see me as a pastor, I removed my tie as a symbol of wanting to relate as a person and not just in the formal role of a pastor.

Talking Listening involves speaking! What the listener *says* lets the speaker know that he or she was actually being heard. Ask

A Point to Ponder

questions. After hearing someone speak, one of the first things you need to do is ask questions. Avoid "shut down" questions," such as, "Were you really that mad?" Ask "open up" questions, such as, "What happened when you said that? You might even ask, "You seem to be saying ____. Do I hear you correctly?

Practice appropriate and limited self-disclosure. Nothing communicates that you have heard, that you care, and that you identify like self-disclosure. Just make sure that it is appropriate. Disclosure about you that includes information about others may be inappropriate disclosure. Also, in most situations, it needs to be limited. Reveal enough detail to let the other person know you understand without dumping all the details. This is about listening to them, not about them listening to you. When you practice appropriate self-disclosure, you are more like a tour guide than a travel agent.

Hurting people want to be heard. "Hear, O Lord, when I cry" (Ps. 27:7). Listening is God-like. "I have called upon You, for You will hear me, O God" (Ps. 17:6). Let's be Godly. Let's listen.

A Point to Ponder

GEORGE W. BUSH VERSUS SADDAM HUSSEIN

Every time I watch the war in Iraq on TV, I am reminded of a great contrast between George W. Bush and Saddam Hussein. It is not just that one is committed to democracy and the other is a practicing dictator, or that one is a committed Christian and the other is a practicing Muslim. It is more fundamental than that.

A former church member recently invited my wife and me to spend a few days with them near Mammoth. While there, we wandered into a bookstore with a "sale table." The price got my attention—one dollar each! As I browsed through the bargain books, I found one entitled *Out of the Ashes, the Resurrection of Saddam Hussein* by Andrew Cockburn and Patrick Cockburn (HarperCollins Publishers, 1999). Given all the books I would like to read, I would not normally have bought such a book, especially at the retail price of $26, but the price and the titles of a few chapters overwhelmed me.

The book is about what happened to Saddam Hussein after the Gulf War. It also gives background material on Hussein. For example, it claims that in September 1979, soon after he seized power in Iraq, he said, "What is politics? Politics is when you say you are going to do one thing while intending to do another. Then you do neither what you said or what you intended. That way, no one could predict what you were going to do" (p. 7).

A Point to Ponder

That is the way some politicians practice politics and that is the way some people live their lives. Their words and actions do not match their intentions.

Contrast that with George W. Bush. Whatever else can be said about his political views, policies, and decisions, he is at least attempting to tell us his intentions and then do what he says.

When I see the war on TV, I see war, but I also see something else. I am reminded that it is real time TV of a war! I see embedded reporters with the troops. That practice must have been approved at the highest levels of the administration. It is hard to imagine that the man at the top did not approve of it. It has never been done before in the history of warfare!

What a contrast! On the world stage at this moment are two figures bigger than life. Out of the mouth of one spills who knows what and out of the mouth of the other pours his truthful intentions.

Actually, we all struggle with intending to do one thing and doing another (Rom. 7:15, 19). As a result of the battle that is within us, we are not just guilty, we are wretched (Rom. 7:24). Thank God, there is deliverance "through Jesus Christ our Lord" (Rom. 7:25). "To be spiritually minded is life and peace" (Rom. 8:6). So let us set our minds on the things of the Spirit (Rom. 8:5), that is, the Word of God (1 Cor. 2:10-13) and walk according to the Spirit and not the flesh (Rom. 8:1, 4).

A Point to Ponder

THE PROBLEM WITH GAMBLING

William J. Bennett, the author of *The Book of Virtues,* has admitted to gambling. He denies he has lost $8 million but concedes that he has gambled "large sums of money." In his defense, he pointed out that the kind of gambling he did was legal, that he always paid taxes on his winnings, that he never put his family in danger, and that he pretty much "always broke even." Although Bennett never addressed the morality of gambling in his books or speaking engagements, his critics charged him with hypocrisy.

What is the problem with gambling? Isn't gambling just taking a risk and don't we all take risks daily? Therefore, we all gamble, right?

As with most words, the word "gamble" has several definitions. It means: 1) to risk, to expose to hazard. 2) to take a risk to gain some advantage. 3) to play games of chance for money. 4) to speculate. Thus, in one sense of the word, everyone gambles every day. The act of getting out of bed exposes us to hazards. It's risky! It could be called "gambling" in the simplest sense.

The ethical issue is not about the risk of everyday living. It is about playing a game of chance for money. Traditionally, Christians have vilified gambling as a sin against the Protestant work ethic. There is another issue.

In his book *Something for Nothing: Luck in America*, Jackson Lear, a Rutgers history professor, looks at gambling less as a vice

A Point to Ponder

and more as a worldview. He calls it a "culture of chance." He says, "This country has always been fascinated by the 'breaks.' The risk-taking entrepreneur is a cultural hero; look at the day trader—they are nothing but compulsive gamblers and they become an icon of the age." He also says, "Gamblers rarely pass by someone who is tapped out. They know how quickly things can turn. And in helping each other, they rarely ask questions, rarely ask if someone deserves the help."

May I suggest that the problem with game gambling is worldview? While not many would question spending a few bucks on a game and all agree, even those within the gambling industry, that compulsive gambling can cause great damage to people, families, and even society, the basic issue is worldview.

Imagine Bennett, or anyone else, as the solitary, obsessed slot player standing in front of a slot machine, pulling the lever for hours and hours. What does that say about the gambler's use of time and money, not to mention relationships? The issue is worldview, isn't it?

While the opponents of virtues and morality delight (without moderation) in Bennett's blunder, perhaps, before we cast stones, we should ask, "How am I spending *my* time and money?" "See then that you walk circumspectly, not as fools but as wise, redeeming the time, because the days are evil" (Eph. 5:15-16).

A Point to Ponder

MEMORIAL DAY

Paul instructs us to "Render therefore to all their due ... honor to whom honor" (Rom. 13:7). Memorial Day is when we remember the millions who have given life, limb, and liberty so that we might enjoy the land of the free. Here is one of the finest tributes I've seen. Unfortunately, I do not know who wrote it. If you do, please let me know.

"I want you to close your eyes and picture in your mind the soldier at Valley Forge as he holds his musket in his bloody hands. He stands barefoot in the snow, starved from lack of food, wounded from months of battle, and emotionally scarred from the eternity away from his family, surrounded by nothing but death and carnage of war. He stands, though, with fire in his eyes and victory on his breath. He looks at us now in anger and disgust and tells us this...

I gave you a birthright of freedom born in the Constitution and now your children graduate too illiterate to read it.

I fought in the snow barefoot to give you the freedom to vote and you stay at home because it rains.

I left my family destitute to give you the freedom of speech and you remain silent on critical issues because it might be bad for business.

A Point to Ponder

I orphaned my children to give you a government to serve you and it has stolen democracy from the people.

It's the soldier not the reporter, who gives you the freedom of the press.

It's the soldier, not the poet who gives you the freedom of speech.

It's the soldier not the campus organizer, who allows you to demonstrate.

It's the soldier who salutes the flag, serves the flag, whose coffin is draped with the flag that allows the protester to burn the flag!"

Perhaps soldiers who have died or just faded away could be upset with us (and justly so) because of the way we have treated the freedom they sacrificially secured for us, but let us honor them by remembering that: "It is the soldier who has given…."

A Point to Ponder

MY ENCOUNTER WITH AN ORTHODOX JEW

For years, I have known of the practices of Orthodox Jews. Recently, I had the experience of seeing one practice his religion up close and personal. Here's what happened.

Carleen Glasser, the wife of Dr. William Glasser, the founder of Reality Therapy and Choice Theory, teaches a seminar on Choice Theory in their home. Their home is located high in the hills in West Los Angeles, not too far from where Patricia and I live in Santa Monica. When we learned that on one of the days of the four-day seminar, Dr. Glasser himself met with the class, Patricia and I enrolled.

On the first day of class, we discovered that several Orthodox Jews had signed up for the course. On Saturday, the second day of class, we passed four of them walking up a steep hill as we drove to class. I knew that practicing Orthodox Jews could not drive on Saturday, but I thought that, perhaps, if I were driving, they might be able to ride in a car. So, I stopped to ask if they would like a ride. They explained that they could not do that, but they would be happy for me to take several small bags that they were carrying, which I did.

All five Orthodox Jews in the class, including the four we passed, made it to class on time. One of them walked seven miles, one way, to get there. As class began, we discovered that they couldn't take

A Point to Ponder

notes! When asked why they couldn't take notes on the Sabbath, they told us that writing was creative. The logic behind this prohibition has to do with the work. The Jewish Law forbids working on the Sabbath. Creating is work and, therefore, it is prohibited.

In the days after my encounter with those Orthodox Jews, I couldn't help but reflect on what I had seen. In the first place, it made me grateful that as a believer in Jesus Christ, I am not under the Law but under grace. The apostle Paul states clearly, "You are not under law but under grace" (Rom. 6:14). That does not mean believers are without any law whatsoever. Believers are under the Law of Christ (Gal. 6:2), which is the law of love and love fulfills the Law (Rom. 13:8-10). It does mean believers are not under the Mosaic Law, which is why Christians worship on Sunday, the day of the resurrection, and not Saturday. (Nine of the Ten Commandments are repeated in the New Testament. Keeping the Sabbath day holy is conspicuous by its absence.)

My second reaction was respect for their commitment. I had to ask myself, "Would I be willing to walk fourteen miles to attend a seminar where I couldn't take notes?" If I wanted to attend something badly enough, I might be talked into doing that once. Orthodox Jews do something similar every week! Should not we who are so blessed under grace do more than those who are less blessed under the Law?

A Point to Ponder

SCOTT FREE

The story you are about to read is true. The names have NOT been changed for reasons that will become clear.

Scott and Sara (their real names) had radically different religious backgrounds, but that did not affect their relationship because they did not attend church, any church of any kind. Scott came from a Mormon family but was not a practicing Mormon. One side of Sara's family was Unitarian and the other side was Catholic. When she was a teenager, she attended a youth group several times at a Bible Church but never attended their church services.

As a result of a brief encounter I had with them, they agreed to meet with me to discuss "religion." We met at a restaurant. As we began, Scott said very little. Sara said, "I'm confused. Religion does not make sense to me."

I no sooner got started on my presentation than Sara brought up the Trinity. Admitting that no human fully understands the Trinity, I explained the doctrine using the illustrations of the egg (one egg has three parts, but the problem is the three parts are made of different substances) and water (water, steam, and ice are all h2o, but they do not exist in one place at the same time). No doubt, as a result of her Unitarian influence, Sara said, "I'm confused. That does not make sense to me."

As the conversation continued, it became apparent that Scott believed the "stuff" about Jesus and that salvation was obtained by

A Point to Ponder

living a good life. When I showed him that the Bible says salvation is a gift received by faith and not by works (Eph. 2:8-9), he said, "Yeah, that's what a Baptist at work keeps telling me, but I believe you have to live right. How can just believing without living right get you to heaven?" Sara said, "I'm confused. That does not make sense to me."

At that point, I said, "Let me explain this as simply as I can: 1) The Bible says that we are all sinners (both readily admitted that they had sinned). 2) The penalty of sin is death. 3) Jesus died in our place to pay for our sin. I used illustrations on each of these points.

I said, "Since the penalty of sin is death and Jesus died to pay that penalty, there is nothing we can *do* to earn salvation; all we can do is *trust* Christ (and His payment) for the gift of eternal life." As if I had slapped them awake, Scott said, "You mean, it's Scott free!" and Sara said, "Oh my God! That makes sense. Nobody has ever explained that to me before like that. That makes sense."

Yes, Scott, it's Scott-free!

Yes, Sara, it makes sense!

Yes, Mike, it's not your brilliant explanations of theology; it's the work of the Holy Spirit that opens the eyes of the blind so that they cry, "Now I see; it's free!" Scott-free!

A Point to Ponder

WHAT MY AUTO ACCIDENT TAUGHT ME

On a pleasant Sunday morning, my wife and I left for church. I stopped at a red light within a mile or so of the church. As usual, the light seemed longer than necessary. At last, it changed, and I stepped on the pedal of my diesel and began to move slowly through the intersection.

In the meantime, an elderly lady was also on her way to church. Unfortunately, she did not see that her light was red. The next thing I knew, she had rammed into the rear tire on the driver's side of my car and spun us around 180°. She ricocheted off my car and plowed into a car waiting in the left-hand lane to make a turn.

My first concern was the safety of all involved. My wife and I had our seat belts on and could at least walk. (Later, I learned from experience about soft tissue injury that I have heard about all my life.) The car that hit us contained two elderly ladies. I asked them if they were OK, and they said, "Yes," but one was complaining of chest pains. So, I immediately called 911 on my cell phone for paramedics. The lady with the chest pains was taken to the hospital.

Having done everything I could at the moment, the thought struck me that this accident was not my fault, but this could end up being my word against hers. At that point, I went to several people standing around to ask if they had seen the accident. Several said they had and that it was the elderly lady who ran the red light.

A Point to Ponder

Needless to say, we got their names, addresses, and phone numbers.

After giving the police a report, I had some church members who had come upon the scene take us to church. Arriving just at service time, I was able to speak.

After it was all over, I began to feel sore. Later, I learned that they wanted to total my car. The elderly lady did not admit it was her fault. I then heard about a case where there were no witnesses, just two drivers, each claiming they had the green light. The jury was deadlocked, with six on each side.

I, however, was confident. I had four witnesses who saw the accident. It was then that it hit me. What if they would not give a statement? What if they would not testify? This could get ugly. I know they saw what happened; they said so at the time of the accident, but what if, for some reason, they changed their minds later and didn't tell what they knew? They would be *worthless witnesses.*

From my accident, I learned that it is possible to have worthless witnesses! Fortunately, in my case, they told what they knew and the insurance company fixed my car, but for a moment, I had a small glimpse of what the Lord must think. We who know the Lord have witnessed firsthand the grace of God, and He wants us to be witnesses to Him (Acts 1:8). Unfortunately, too many of His witnesses are worthless. It must make Him sad.

A Point to Ponder

THE DECLINE IN FAMILY LIVING

God intended for parents and children to live together as a family (Deut. 6:7-9). When America was founded, immigrants with a Judeo-Christian heritage poured onto American soil. Living as a family on a farm was the norm. Then, family living began to decline.

1. The Industrial Revolution made America more urban. Urban fathers worked outside the home.

2. The automobile made the family more mobile, taking them outside the home, but they still lived in neighborhoods. There was a sense of community. People knew their neighbors and their neighbors knew them.

3. When World War II came, the men left home to go to war and the women left home to go to the factories. When the war ended, the men came home and the women didn't. The extra income was for extra things. There were more things to buy. Neighborhoods changed. Homes built before 1974 had sidewalks, which gave people an opportunity to meet their neighbors. Newer communities lack sidewalks. ("Where you live affects your life," Parade Magazine, August 3, 2003, p. 9).

4. In the 1950s, TV replaced the radio as the activity of choice in the evening.

5. In the meantime, the car, the Sexual Revolution, birth control, and abortion took teens more and more out of the house and away from the influence and ideals of the home.

A Point to Ponder

6. As cities expanded, America became more suburban. In suburbia, there were fewer sidewalks and more driveways. There was less sense of family and community.

7. By the end of the twentieth century, the very nature of the family was being redefined. One parent had reared many. In 1960, every state had a law against homosexuality. Now, homosexuals can be legally married! The definition of "family" has changed.

There is more. In many places in America today, once children enter the public school system, they are taught tolerance is a great virtue, not something that can be a great vice as well, that homosexuality is simply an alternative, not an abomination, and that sex outside of marriage is permissible, provided that you use a condom to prevent disease and/or unwanted pregnancy. Then, there are the movies, music, and monstrous computer games.

Family living is no longer the norm. What is a family to do? The pattern for family living is in Deuteronomy 6. Parents are to love the Lord (Deut. 6:5), know the Word (Deut. 6:6), and teach the Word diligently to their children, which means spending time with them (Deut. 6:7). It takes a great deal of thought, planning, energy, and discipline to establish and maintain family living in the American culture of the 21st century. We need to pray for the families we know.

A Point to Ponder

GIVE ME A PROBLEM

To put it mildly, things had not been going well for her at work. Eve (not her real name) had about had it with her job. So, one day, she quit her job and to find a new one. For several reasons, that was a radical decision. At any rate, she decided to quit her job.

So, she called her husband and, without any explanation, said, "I am going to quit my job and go to work for another company." Later that day, she talked to me. Without any introduction or small talk, she announced that she was quitting her job. Knowing how that would impact her husband, her family, and even her, I wasn't just surprised, I was stunned.

She and I talked through the complexities of the situation. Later, when her husband joined us, we mapped out a plan to address the problem. This particular situation did not provoke a crisis, but I have seen this very kind of thing get very volatile quickly.

As I thought about this episode with this couple, it occurred to me that what happened in this situation is what often happens in marriages and board meetings that cause problems that could be easily avoided. Let me explain.

Because of several legitimate problems, this wife concluded and then announced that *conclusion* to her husband, along with a number of reasons why she should change jobs. Some of her reasons were sound and others sounded like the emotion of the moment. How she handled this situation left no room for her

A Point to Ponder

husband, or anyone else, to think about the best possible solutions to a difficult problem or to reason with her about her conclusion. She had reached her conclusion and announced it for everyone in her life to accept. Needless to say, that kind of approach does not nurture relationships; it creates a crisis that divides and does not unite people to each other.

Later, I suggested that she alter her approach. I suggested that she: 1) Present the problem(s). 2) Offer options. 3) Then, argue for her alternative. In other words, *begin with the problem*, not the solution.

Will following such a simple formula solve all the problems between couples and board meetings? Of course not. What it will do is prevent other people from becoming adversarial. It will allow for reasonable discussion. It will also allow others to have input *before* a conclusion is reached.

Personally, I would say, "Give me a problem." Don't just give me a conclusion. To say the same thing another way, if you want unity and harmony, begin with the problem so that "as much as depends on you, live peaceably with all men" (Rom. 12:18). If you want confrontation and division, start with the conclusion.

A Point to Ponder

DECODING THE DA VINCI CODE

In 2003, ABC aired a program entitled "Jesus, Mary and Da Vinci." It was a documentary-type program on the novel *The Da Vinci Code* by Dan Brown.

The novel opens with the murder of Jacques Saunirer, the curator of the Louvre. A baffling cipher is found near the body. Police call Robert Langdon, "professor of religious symbology" at Harvard, to help solve the riddle. Langdon discovers that it leads to clues hidden in the works of Da Vinci. He joins forces with Sophie Neveu, the victim's granddaughter, a cryptologist. They learn the curator was involved in the Priory of Sion, a secret society whose members included Isaac Newton, Victor Hugo, and Da Vinci. They eventually decided that Mary Magdalene was married to Jesus and that Jesus and Mary had a daughter. Moreover, the Holy Grail, the cup that Jesus used at the Last Supper, was actually Mary Magdalene, who held the blood of Jesus in her womb while carrying his child. Da Vinci knew about all of this because he was a member of the Priory and in his painting of the Last Supper, he placed Mary on the left side of Christ!

The novel has been criticized for its "characters thin as plastic wrap, undistinguished prose, and improbable action" (Miesel). Yet a writer has accused Brown of plagiarism! The *New York Daily News* book reviewer said Brown's "research is impeccable." Yet another reviewer said, "So error-laden is *The Da Vinci Code* that

A Point to Ponder

the educated reader actually applauds those rare occasions where Brown stumbles (despite himself) into the truth" (Miesel). For example, The Priory is an organization officially registered with the French government in 1956. It does make claims of antiquity, but it most likely originated after World War II. Except for filmmaker Jean Cocteau, its illustrious list of Grand Masters, including Da Vinci, Newton, and Hugo, is not credible (Miesel). Novelist Mark Lawson (*Going Out Live*) says, "There are probably a couple of verses in Nostradamus predicting the triumph of *The Da Vinci Code*. Certainly, the novel's success can be attributed to those who read Nostradamus and believe that the smoke from the blazing Twin Towers formed the face of the devil or Osama Bin Laden." In her review, Miesel concludes, "In the end, Dan Brown has penned a poorly written, atrociously researched mess" (see her excellent, detailed review at crisismagazine.com).

"Was Jesus married?" The answer is, "not yet." He was not married to Mary. ABC asked several biblical scholars, "Is there any proof in the Bible that Jesus was not married? Of course not! The Bible does not give any proof that Jesus was not married for the same reason that it does not provide any proof that He had six fingers on His left hand.

But Jesus is engaged. All who have trusted Him are His Bride (2 Cor. 11:2) waiting for the Marriage Supper of the Lamb (Rev. 19:7, 9). "Even so, come Lord Jesus!" (Rev. 22:20).

A Point to Ponder

THANKSGIVING IS NOT A HOLIDAY

As a nation, we set aside one day a year we call "Thanksgiving." On that day, many, at least, think about why they are thankful. Some give thanks on that day when they say grace over the turkey. Some even have each one at the table tell for what he or she is thankful.

Those are good things, but as far as God is concerned, thanksgiving was never intended to be a holiday! From His point of view, thanksgiving is to be a constant attitude of gratitude every day. Paul instructs believers to "Rejoice always, pray without ceasing, in everything give thanks; for this is the will of God in Christ Jesus for you" (1 Thessalonians 5:16-18).

The last phrase in verse 18, "this is the will of God in Christ Jesus for you," could go with the previous command or refer to all three commands. Most expositors would say that it goes with all three. Thus, the will of God is for believers to rejoice *always*, pray *without ceasing,* and give thanks *in everything*. That certainly sounds like a constant attitude of gratitude all day, every day, in everything. Paul taught this truth by example. Throughout 1 Thessalonians, he constantly expressed thanksgiving for the believers at Thessalonica. In 1 Thessalonians 1:2, he said, "We give thanks to God always for you all" and in 3:9, he exclaimed, "What thanks can we render to God for you?"

Technically, 1 Thessalonians 5:18 does not say "*for* everything give thanks," but "*in* everything" (however, see Eph. 5:20). The

A Point to Ponder

concept here is that believers are to give thanks in every circumstance of life, in sickness and in health; in poverty and in wealth. In every situation of life, there are those things for which a believer can be genuinely thankful.

One morning during World War II, after a German raid, an Englishman stood in the street and gazed at his bomb-wrecked home. Then he told his wife, "This morning someone came to our dugout and told me we had lost everything. It's a lie. Thank God I still have health and strength to do my job. I still have you, my dear, and the children. Thank God you're all safe. Hitler hasn't squashed my faith in the love and wisdom of God or my faith in the ultimate victory over wrong. I still have hope for the future. I can still call my soul my own. I'm still alive and ready for action again. So, I reckon that you and I ought to thank God that we have saved more than we have lost. Houses and buildings may be wrecked and ruined, but you and I can still hold on to the things that can never be shaken or destroyed." He did not thank God for the bomb-wrecked house, but in that situation, he could still thank God.

G. K. Chesterton said that the most important lesson he learned was to take things with gratitude and not for granted. Every day ought to be a thanksgiving day.

A Point to Ponder

WHAT A CHRISTMAS PRESENT!

Giving families a *source* of food rather than short-term relief is now the ministry of Heifer International, a nonprofit organization founded in 1944. You can provide chicks, ducks, or geese for $20, trees for $60, a buffalo for $250, and an ark full of animals for $5000. There are other possible gifts, including giving seedlings for $10. Each gift helps impoverished families become self-reliant by providing food, income, and training. Since 1944, Heifer has helped more than 4.5 million families in 128 countries. No wonder *Forbes* magazine named Heifer International one of the 10 "Gold Star Charities" for 2004. (The Gold Star Charities list is Forbes' annual list of organizations that achieve the highest impact from donors' gifts.)

This Christmas, someone gave a Heifer International gift animal (Bees) to someone in the world *in our name*. We received a fold-out card with fourteen folds explaining the program in twelve simple, short, colorful panels.

What an idea! What a gift! "Heifer animals (and training in their care) offer hungry families around the world a way to feed themselves and become self-reliant. Children receive nutritious milk or eggs; families earn income for school, health care, and better housing; communities go beyond meeting immediate needs to fulfilling dreams. Farmers learn sustainable, environmentally sound agricultural techniques" (Quoted from Heifer's website

A Point to Ponder

(www.heifer.org. You can call them at 800-422-0474).

In a passage on giving, Paul wrote, "Therefore, as we have opportunity, let us do good to all, especially to those who are of the household of faith" (Gal. 6:10). So, put this idea on your Christmas list for next year.

Years ago, my brother and I gave to the Lord's work the money we planned to spend on each for Christmas. Don't just curse the commercialism of Christmas; give gifts that last and last and last, eternally.

A Point to Ponder

WHAT DO YOU MEAN BY THAT?

This is a parable. It is not about church. I have often heard people say, "This is my church." As a pastor, I can't help but wonder what they mean by that. It doesn't take reflection to figure out that there are all kinds of options.

For some, it means nothing more than, "If I went to church, that is where I would go." There is a story that has floated around for years about a pastor who was shopping in a department store. As he was talking to a clerk, the subject of church came up in the conversation. When he asked her which church she attended, she named a church and spoke of it in glowing terms. It sounded as if she were a regular attendee. The minister to whom she was speaking had been the pastor of that church for years, but he had never seen her in church once. By the expression "my church," she meant "The church I would go to if I went to church."

Others use the expression "my church" and they actually go. Well, they attend the Christmas and Easter services. On Easter Sunday, Dr. Louis Talbot, the famous pastor of the Church of the Open Door, used to wish his congregation "Merry Christmas" because, as he explained, he would not see some of them again until Christmas.

Of course, some say, "my church" and attend more than on Christmas and Easter. They may even darken the door once a month or so.

A Point to Ponder

Then, some call their church "my church" and don't just attend periodically; they attend faithfully, but only on Sunday morning. Moreover, all they do is attend.

The ultimate goal is for someone to say "my church" and mean, "I faithfully attend. I am involved. I serve. I give—faithfully."

At the beginning, I said this was a parable. While it is true that it could serve as a sermon, I have in mind something different.

Recently, Patricia and I were counseling with a married couple. During the conversation, they both used the expression "my marriage." As Patricia and I listened, it became apparent that what she meant by "my marriage" radically differed from what he meant. Conflict was created between them because each tried to get the other to conform to their meaning of "marriage."

I told them that the object of marriage was companionship, not combat and that it was a process of two becoming one (Gen. 2:24). I suggested that they were using the same words but different dictionaries and I used the expression "my church" to illustrate." They got it, and they are doing very well.

May I ask you, "What do you mean by 'my marriage?'" Perhaps you and your mate should ensure that you are using the same dictionary.

A Point to Ponder

WHAT ARE PARENTS TO DO?

Apparently, the only requirement for being a parent these days is a sex drive. You don't have to have a license, as in a marriage license, and no one requires instruction on performing one of the world's most important jobs. One of the greatest needs in our society is for someone to write a job description for being a parent.

In His Word, God has done just that. The major passages in the Bible on how to be a parent are in the books of Deuteronomy, Proverbs, Ephesians, and Colossians. These passages indicate that parents must love, teach, and discipline.

Love Moses wrote, "You shall love the LORD your God with all your heart, with all your soul, and with all your strength. And these words which I command you today shall be in your heart. You shall teach them diligently to your children, and shall talk of them when you sit in your house, when you walk by the way, when you lie down, and when you rise up" (Deut. 6:5-7). Before parents teach their children, they must be lovers. They should love the Lord and each other (Eph. 5:25; Titus 2:4). As has often been said, 'The greatest thing a father can do for his children is to love their mother." Obviously, parents should love their children. Parents are to be, first and foremost, lovers.

Teach Moses also mentions that parents are to teach their children diligently. Both parents are teachers. The children are students and the Word of God is the curriculum. While others, such as pastors

A Point to Ponder

and school teachers, may supplement the information given by parents, there is no substitute for parental example, education, and exhortation. God's philosophy of education begins with parents.

Discipline Solomon says, "Train up a child in the way he should go, and when he is old, he will not depart from it" (Prov. 22:6). Parents are not only to teach, they are to train their children. Training includes discipline. Solomon says,

- "He who spares his rod hates his son, but he who loves him disciplines him promptly" (Prov. 13:24).
- "Foolishness *is* bound up in the heart of a child; the rod of correction will drive it far from him" (Prov 22:15).
- "The rod and rebuke give wisdom, but a child left *to himself* brings shame to his mother" (Prov 29:15).

Paul concurs (Eph. 6:4; Col. 3:21). Solomon and Paul's instruction are sorely needed.

Oh, by the way, the Word from God assumes that it takes two, a male and a female, who are married to each other.

A Point to Ponder

"THE PASSION OF THE CHRIST"

People have asked me about my opinion of the film "The Passion of The Christ." So, here it is. First of all, Mel Gibson did what he set out to do and he did it well. The word "passion" comes from the Latin word for "suffering." As applied to Christ, it refers to the period following the Last Supper and includes the crucifixion. Gibson intended to tell the story of the Passion as recorded in the New Testament in graphic detail and he did.

Second, the film emphasizes the details of Christ's sufferings more than the New Testament. Jeff Jacoby wrote that it "has to be the most graphic and brutal death ever portrayed on film." Years ago, after hearing an evangelist graphically describe the crucifixion of Christ, someone said to me that the New Testament never does that. From a New Testament point of view, the film is too graphic.

Third, it makes Mary more prominent in the Passion than the gospels. Bill Murchison says Mary is "a mother rent by pain almost equal to her son's." That's going too far.

My opinions aside, the question is, "Who is responsible for the death of Jesus?"

The Romans Jesus was "condemned by Pontius Pilate" (Lk. 23:13-25). The Romans actually killed Jesus, but the question is not, "Who killed Jesus?" The question is, "Who is responsible?" A "hit man" may pull the trigger; the question is, "Who hired him?

The Jews of the Day Are the Jews responsible? Yes, at least

A Point to Ponder

the leaders and crowd there that day (Acts 2:23; 3:14-15; 1 Thess. 2:14-16).

Should that be the basis for anti-Semitism? No, not more than the fact that the Romans were responsible, which should not make us anti-Italian. The Japanese leaders and their followers of the 1940s bombed Pearl Harbor, but that does not mean we should be anti-Japanese. The German leaders and their followers of the 1940s killed millions of Jews and others, but that does not mean we should be anti-German. Some Arab leaders and their followers flew planes into the World Trade Center, but that does not mean we should be anti-Arab.

God I understand Jesus died for the sin of the world, but I am not aware of any passage of Scripture that says we all killed Him and I know of several passages that specifically say who is responsible and it is not us. Jesus voluntarily laid down His life (Jn. 10:18) and God the Father planned it (Isa. 53:10; Jn. 3:16; Acts 2:23; Rev. 13:8). God did it to demonstrate His love (Rom. 5:8), to provide a sacrifice for sin (1 Pet. 3:18) and an example of suffering (1 Pet. 3:18 in the context of 1 Pet. 3; see also Phil. 3:10; Heb 12:1-4). God so loved the world that He gave His only begotten Son so that we might have forgiveness and an example of suffering.

See the film, but remember this is what *God* did, not the Romans, the Jews, nor just us.

A Point to Ponder

MARTHA STEWART'S GREATEST LESSON

Martha Stewart has taught millions about food, decorating, and entertaining. That is nothing compared to the greatest lesson of her life. Here is the story.

Samuel D. Waksal, the founder of Imclone Systems Inc., and Stewart were friends. Waksal's company developed a drug to treat cancer. While waiting for the Food and Drug Administration's approval, Stewart bought 3,928 shares of ImClone stock.

In December of 2001, believing that the Food and Drug Administration was about to decline approval of their new drug, Waksal and his family began selling their ImClone shares. Peter E. Bacanovic, Stewart's stockbroker, called to tell her that Waksal was selling his stock. Apparently, based on that information, Martha Stewart sold her shares on December 27, 2001. Sure enough, the Food and Drug Administration did not approve the new drug. By selling when she did, Martha made about $50,000.

There was just one problem. Selling a stock because of an inside tip before it is public knowledge is illegal. It is called insider trading. Waksal was eventually sentenced to seven years for it. The SEC investigation of Waksal spilled over to Stewart.

The plot thickens. Evidently, Stewart and Bacanovic concocted a story that they had a prior agreement to sell the stock if it fell to $60 a share, which it did do that day. Then, they repeatedly lied to investigators. So, instead of being charged with insider trading, Martha was charged with conspiracy, obstruction of justice, and two counts of lying to investigators. On Friday, March 6, 2004, Martha was found guilty on all four counts. The maximum penalty is 20 years in jail and $1 million in fines.

Why did the US Attorney's office "throw the book" at Martha Stewart? As compared to the billions of dollars worth of financial damage done by Enron and WorldCom, there was a relatively small amount of money involved in the Stewart case. David N. Kelley, the Interim US Attorney, said he hoped that this case would send a message that we will not tolerate dishonesty and corruption. He added that lying to investigators strikes at the judicial system's integrity.

That is the lesson. Don't lie. In Colossians 3, Paul says, "Put to death your members which are on the earth: fornication, uncleanness, passion, evil desire, and covetousness, which is idolatry" (Col. 3:5) and "Put off all these: anger, wrath, malice, blasphemy, filthy language out of your mouth" (Col. 3:8). Then he adds, "Do not lie to one another" (Col. 3:9). Instead of giving another list of sins, Paul singles out the one sin of lying, making his command dramatic and emphatic.

On Friday, March 5, 2004, the stock of Martha Stewart Living Omnimedia Inc. plunged $3.17 from $14.03 to $10.86 (23%). Martha, who owns 61% of the stock, lost 95 million dollars. She also spent five months in a minimum-security prison and, after that, five months in home confinement. Had she not lied, none of this would have happened.

A Point to Ponder

SAME-SEX MARRIAGE

Same-sex marriage? Unbelievable! Who would have believed a year ago that same-sex marriage would be a subject of public debate and—a constitutional amendment? (This was written on April 21, 2004.)

Have you listened to the arguments for homosexuality and same-sex marriage? Religious, natural, and legal issues are being used. The Episcopal Church has a practicing homosexual Bishop and the Methodist Church has decided that a practicing lesbian can be a pastor. Homosexuals say it is natural ("I was born this way."). Is it not right for gay couples to have equal rights under the law? If religion, nature, and the law are for it, who can say anything against it? Confused yet?

From God's point of view, it is ungodly. God calls it an abomination (Lev. 18:22). In fairness, it should be pointed out that He also calls other sins an abomination (Deut. 12:31) and He is willing to save homosexuals as well as other sinners (1 Cor. 6:9-11). The Bible is not anti-homosexual; it is anti-sin and pro-compassionate toward sinners. Some "religious" people are for it; God is against it.

From nature's point of view, it is unnatural. The Bible says that homosexuality is "against nature" (Rom. 1:26) and "shameful" (Rom. 1:27). To say anything against homosexuality is considered by some to be homophobic, gay-bashing, or, worse yet, hate-mongering.

A Point to Ponder

To say that homosexuality is unnatural is natural; it has nothing whatsoever to do with hating or bashing. God hates sin, but He loves sinners. He loves them so much He sent His Son to die for them (Jn. 3:16, Rom. 5:8). By the way, all of us are born with a sin nature. Sin is "natural" to us, but being natural does not make it right.

From history's point of view, it is unprecedented. In all of history, there has never been a civilized society that has had same-sex marriage. A homosexual man I know tells me that there is a case where it has occurred. If so, that would be an exception and an exception should not determine the rule. An exception is an *exception* to the rule.

From a legal point of view, it is unpredictable. If we redefine marriage, where do we draw the line? Polygamy? Group marriage? Incestuous marriage? Marriage to an animal? Don't laugh. Paul Harvey reported that there was a marriage between two trees in India to appease the God of rain (3/22/04). Once the natural line of marriage between a man and a woman is crossed, there is no other natural, logical place to put the line.

Why do homosexuals want to be *married*? If equality under the law is the issue, why not crusade for civil unions or demonstrate for domestic partnerships? Why marriage? Could it be that what they really want is acceptance? Is it that they want society to say it is O. K.?

Well, it is not O. K. Same-sex marriage is unacceptable because it is ungodly, unnatural, unprecedented, and unpredictable.

A Point to Ponder

TRIBUTE TO A SERVANT

As a teenager in Pensacola, Florida, I was a Brooklyn Dodger fan. I think I was the only Dodger fan in a town filled with Yankee fans. At any rate, my heroes were giants, such as Duke Snyder, Pewee Reece, Roy Campanella, Don Drysdale, Don Newcombe, etc. Since those days, long ago, I have become a believer in Jesus Christ. I am still a fair-weather Dodger fan, but these days, I have a different standard for a "hero" or, better yet, a "role model." Here is a classic example.

As the result of an automobile accident, Roy Campanella was paralyzed from the shoulders down. In 1963, a lady named Roxie married him anyway. Thirty years later, Roy died. Roxie spent 30 years in devotion to her husband, who was bound to a wheelchair!

When she died in 2004, Bill Plaschke, a *Los Angeles Times* Sports writer, said, "She loved him not for his ability to throw out a runner, steal a base, or even pick up a cup of coffee. She loved him not because he could win her a championship, make her a million, or even pick her a flower. She loved him for, well, him. It was a love that endured countless attendants, numerous obstacles, a painful existence in days before disability access." She rolled his wheelchair down the steps and over grass to the batter's cage. She pushed his wheelchair across thick carpet and through narrow doorways. Roxie carried the famous fifties Dodger catcher.

There's more. Plaschke wrote, "For the duration of their marriage, he sat front and center while she labored behind him. He was the one everyone sought for autographs. She was the one who helped put his quivering hand to the paper. He was the famous one who posed. She was the unknown one who pushed."

Roy died in 1993. A week after he died, Don Drysdale died. Don's widow, Anne, said, "Roxie helped me through many hard times. She was my rock."

Years later, Anne said she could not help but wonder if, perhaps, Roxie was relieved that Roy had left this world. Roxie began to cry. She replied, "Of course not. I miss him. I miss him every day. He was never a burden, never once. How can anyone you love ever be a burden?" Anne confessed, "I, too, was crying, morning my pathetic ignorance."

Bill Plaschke concluded his tribute with these words, "How much Roxie Campanella taught us. How much she could teach us still."

I read the story of Roxie, not as a Dodger fan but as a disciple of Jesus Christ. He said, "For even the Son of Man did not come to be served, but to serve, and to give His life a ransom for many" (Mk. 10:45). As Anne said, "Roxie was a role model for us all."

Roxie was an example of a behind-the-scenes servant who served out of love. We who know the Great Lover and Servant should love Him enough to sacrificially serve Him by serving others. Lovingly pushing a wheelchair for thirty years is a good example.

A Point to Ponder

ELEMENTS OF A HAPPY MARRIAGE

What is the secret to a happy marriage? An old adage says, "Opposites attract." Most social scientists say that, as general rule, opposites might initially attract, but over time, they tend to repel. What is essential is shared goals, values, and what they want out of the relationship.

After being happily married for 45 years and having counseled thousands of couples for 35 years, psychologist Neil Clark Warren, founder of eharmony.com, an internet matchmaking service, concluded that the happiest couples were those who tend to be of similar intelligence, energy, ambition, and industriousness, with many common interests and things they enjoy doing together. Some things, such as religion or wanting or not wanting to have children, are critical depending on how important those factors are to each individual. One particularly significant measure of compatibility seems to be whether or not two people share a passion for the arts. If neither does, it's fine, but if one does and the other doesn't, it could be a big problem (*Los Angeles Times*, 4/26/04, p. F8).

There are other factors. Claiming he knows "all the pitfalls" of marriage, Patrick A. Winning, a divorce attorney, says the primary factors he sees in his clients seeking a divorce are the inability to communicate and manage conflict. Granted, one might expect that from couples seeking a divorce, but at the same time, common sense would say that couples who do not communicate or manage

A Point to Ponder

conflict are headed for trouble, if not a divorce.

Then, there is chemistry. To my knowledge, no one has yet figured out why one is drawn to one person and not another, but that is a reality of life. Warren says he does not understand attraction, adding, "I don't care how compatible you are, if there's no chemistry, don't seal the thing: Love minus chemistry equals friendship. Don't try to turn it into love."

This much I know. The happiest couples I know, including my wife Patricia and I, have chemistry. Such couples just seemed to be very much in love with each other. They enjoy each other's company. They like to do things together, even simple things. They touch each other. They finish each other's sentences. They brag about being "soulmates."

According to the Scripture, believers should marry a believer (1 Cor. 7:39). If you know the Lord and a potential partner doesn't, compatibility is a huge problem.

If you are not yet married, compatibility, communication, and chemistry should be major criteria in your search for a soulmate.

If you're already married, focus on what you have in common. Improve your compatibility. Communicate. Work on developing the relationship. In the final analysis, a happy marriage takes hard work.

A Point to Ponder

INDEPENDENCE

Today is Sunday, July 4th, Independence Day. On this day, we celebrate our nation's independence. May I suggest that we take a moment to reflect on personal independence?

Independence Every human being needs to be independent, at least to some degree. Those who are too dependent on others are children, regardless of age. Having said that, it is imperative to note that it is possible to be too independent! We also need to be dependent too. Perhaps we need a national holiday to recognize and remember our dependence.

Dependence Every human being needs to be dependent. We need to be dependent on the Lord for eternal life. Some think, "I'll be good," or "I'll do good things." If you are so independent that you think you can make it without Him, you are too independent.

According to the Bible, all have sinned (Rom. 3:23) and the penalty for sin is death (Rom. 6:23), that is, separation from God. The glorious Good News is that Jesus Christ died in our place to pay the penalty for our sins (Rom, 5:8). The simple spiritual reality is that people cannot work their way to heaven (Rom. 4:2). All they can do is trust Jesus Christ for the gift of eternal life (Jn. 3:16). The only way anyone can make it to heaven is by being dependent on Jesus Christ for the gift of eternal life.

Some ingenious soul decided to enter an important game by printing his ticket. He did not make it. Likewise, some think they will get to heaven by creating their own ticket. They will not make it. You must have a ticket printed by God. It says, "Jesus died for me, and I trust Him to get me to heaven."

We also need to be dependent on the Lord to live life (Gal. 2:20). As I often say, "The Lord is never going to let you get to the place where you don't need Him." We need a Statue of Dependence on the West Coast to balance the Statue of "Independence" on the East Coast.

Interdependence We also need to be interdependent on each other. God never intended for individuals to live on an island by themselves. In fact, when God Himself created a paradise called the Garden of Eden and put a single soul in it, His own estimation was, "This is not good" (Gen. 2:18). He immediately placed a companion in the Garden so that it could be paradise.

We need each other. We need to be interdependent. "For none of us lives to himself, and no one dies to himself" (Rom. 14:7). If for nothing else, we need to be interdependent on one another for encouragement (Heb. 10:25).

So, on this Independence Day, remember, granted, in a sense, we need to be personally independent, but we also need to be dependent on the Lord and interdependent on each other. By the way, we have a holiday celebrating dependence and interdependence. It is called "Sunday." Did you go to church today?

A Point to Ponder

KERRY'S LOGIC CONCERNING ABORTION

As a Baptist pastor who believes in the separation of church and state, I refrain from making political comments. However, I reserve the right to comment on spiritual and moral issues. That's my turf. When politics invades my turf, I have the right, and even an obligation, to speak.

With that in mind, I would like to speak my mind on an issue. This is not intended to be a political comment; it's about morality.

Roman Catholic John Kerry told an Iowa Caucus that he believed that life began at conception. A short time later, he told Peter Jennings on ABC News that abortion was *not* murder! If I understand him right, Kerry's explanation is that at birth, the fetus is alive, but it is not human! I know a politician's favorite color is plaid, but that is ridiculous.

There are two issues here. First, "When does life begin?" It seems to me that Scripture teaches that a fetus is a human being. When Mary greeted Elizabeth, who was pregnant with John the Baptist, the baby "leaped in her womb" (Lk. 1:41). Elizabeth told Mary, "As soon as the voice of your greeting sounded in my ears, the babe leaped in my womb for joy" (Lk. 1:44). A mass of tissue does not experience joy; humans do.

The second issue is, "Should people's religious conviction affect their decisions in every area of life?" If spiritual

A Point to Ponder

values do not affect our thinking and actions, what value are they? I am not suggesting that politicians force others to submit to their religious convictions. Many politicians have said that they believe that abortion is wrong, but as a government official, they will abide by the law. At the same time, because of their *personal* conviction, they will work within the law to change the law. That is a reasonable position.

Kerry's stand on abortion is illogical and inconsistent. Crispin Sartwell, a Political Science Professor at Dickinson College in Carlisle, Pennsylvania, has written an article entitled "Kerry's Illogical Stand on Abortion" (*Los Angeles Times*, July 28, 2004, p. B13). In it, Professor Sartwell says, "If we could not bring our faith to bear on the law, we would have to separate the state not from the church but from all human values." Concerning Kerry, Sartwell adds, "One can only conclude that there is absolutely no belief of his own that he would not compromise to be president."

Sartwell goes on to say that he can respect the position that the fetus is part of a pregnant woman, the position that the fetus is a human being, or the position that one does not know what to say. He concludes, "What I can't respect is the position that abortion is killing human beings and that is at the same time a political right that must be defended by the state. That position reflects a complete failure either of logic or of ethics; it is a sign of deep stupidity or deep cowardice."

A Point to Ponder

THE OLYMPIC SPIRIT

The earliest precise record of the ancient Olympic Games dates back to 776 B.C. They ended in 393 A.D. The Apostle Paul was not only aware of the games, he used them as an illustration. He described the Olympic spirit that it takes to win a gold medal.

In 1 Corinthians 8-10, Paul discusses Christians eating meat offered to an idol. He says nothing is wrong with it because an idol is nothing, but not everyone is knowledgeable. So, the stronger must be careful not to hurt the weaker brother, who is not as knowledgeable. That takes self-denial. So, Paul launches into a lengthy elaboration of giving up one's rights. He applies that to more than just eating meat offered to idols (1 Cor. 9:19-23) and ends with an illustration from the games.

Paul writes, "Do you not know that those who run in a race all run, but one receives the prize? Run in such a way that you may obtain *it*. And everyone who competes *for the prize* is temperate in all things. Now, they *do it* to obtain a perishable crown, but we *for* an imperishable *crown*. Therefore, I run thus: not with uncertainty. Thus, I fight: not as *one who* beats the air. But I discipline my body and bring *it* into subjection, lest, when I have preached to others, I myself should become disqualified (1 Cor. 9:24-26).

Paul's point is that believers should run the race of life to win the prize. Eternal life is a gift (Rom. 6:23) received simply by trusting Jesus Christ (Jn. 3:16). All who trust Christ will be judged, not to determine their eternal destiny, but their eternal reward (1 Cor.

A Point to Ponder

3:11-15). If we live a loving life, we will be rewarded in heaven (1 Jn. 4:17-18), but that takes discipline, which is Paul's point in 1 Corinthians 9.

Paul adds they do it to obtain a perishable crown, but we do it for an imperishable crown. In the Olympic Games, the crown was made of olive leaves. If they put themselves through such strenuous self-denial for such temporary, fleeting rewards, how much more should we practice self-discipline for an incorruptible crown (1 Tim. 4:7-8)?

The "Olympic Spirit" is not to watch; it is to work. It is not to be a spectator; it is to be a participator. It is not to play; it is to persist. In this passage, Paul puts all the emphasis on human effort. In other passages, he stresses God's grace and power.

In the 1992 Summer Olympics, American sprinter Gail Devers, the clear leader in the 100-meter hurdles, tripped over the last barrier. She agonizingly pulled herself to her knees and crawled the last five meters, finishing fifth—but finishing. In the 400-meter semifinal, British runner Derek Redmond tore a hamstring and fell to the track. He struggled to his feet and began to hobble, determined to complete the race. His father ran from the stands to help him off the track, but the athlete refused to quit. He leaned on his father, and the two limped to the finish line together to deafening applause.

Here is the tragedy: 87% of Americans who own running shoes don't run.

A Point to Ponder

PLAYING CARDS

Several years ago, Patricia decided that we should go on an Alaskan cruise to celebrate our anniversary. So we booked passage, flew to Vancouver, British Columbia, and set sail for Alaska.

The trip was delightful. We saw a whale on the sea, eagles in a tree, and salmon spawning up a river. We heard the history of the Ketchikan, Juneau, Skagway, and Sitka. We lounged, loafed, and laid around. Beyond a doubt, the climax of the trip was on the last day at sea. Our ship sailed up the College Fjord (a fjord is a narrow river) to the face of the Harvard Glacier.

I've had the privilege of traveling virtually all over the world. I have been to London, Paris, Rome, Damascus, Jerusalem, Cairo, Mexico City, Ecuador, Bogotá, Beijing, Hawaii, and Sydney. I've walked on a glacier in Alaska, stood in awe before Niagara Falls, and traveled through a rainforest in the Amazon jungle, but nothing I have ever seen quite compares to standing on a ship looking at the face of a mammoth glacier.

Our ship pulled within three to five hundred yards of the face of the Harvard Glacier, which is a mile and a half wide, three hundred feet high, and six and a half miles deep. It is bright white and Windex blue. Portions are black from the rock the glacier crushed as it moved. It makes sounds like thunder. Sheets of ice crashed into the water. We stood speechless before the magnificent block of ice.

A Point to Ponder

We were so close to the glacier that I could not get it all in one picture, even with a wide-angle lens. So, I decided to go to the back of the ship and get a picture with my wide-angle lens as we pulled away from the glacier. The cruise ship was nine hundred and sixty-three feet long, more than three football fields. As fast as I could move, I made the trip from bow to aft without breaking into a run. The journey took me down several flights of stairs and through a couple of dining halls.

As I passed through the otherwise deserted dining halls, I was stunned to see one lone couple—playing cards! Imagine being in the presence of one of the most spectacular sights on the earth and playing cards!

They may have seen it before, maybe even several times. Even if that were the case, I would have had difficulty not taking another look. Their card playing was not a commentary on the glacier; it was a commentary on them.

Upon reflection, I decided that people do this all the time. On Sunday morning, they stand in the presence of the Word of God and the God of the Word and mentally play cards. How many have sailed through life missing the majesty because they are preoccupied "with cares, riches, and pleasures of life, and bring no fruit to maturity" (Lk. 8:14)?

By the way, I got the picture. Did you?

A Point to Ponder

THE CARDINAL VIRTUES

Anyone who thoughtfully reads the New Testament cannot help but notice that it contains several lists of virtues (Mt. 5:3-12; Gal 5:22-23; 2 Pet, 1:5-7; etc.). Over the years, as I have studied the New Testament, I have noticed that some virtues are repeatedly mentioned in and outside the lists. Obviously, the three great Christian virtues are faith, hope, and love (1 Cor. 13:13). Beyond those, what are the great virtues?

Long ago, I concluded that high on God's list of desirable virtues are: being sensible ("soberly" in Titus 2:12 means "sensible"), having self-control (Gal. 5:22), and endurance ("perseverance" in Rom. 5:4 means "endurance"). To that list could be added justice, gratitude, meekness, and gentleness.

Recently, I read again something C. S. Lewis wrote. In his book *Mere Christianity*, Lewis has a chapter on the cardinal virtues. According to Lewis, there are seven virtues, three theological and four "cardinal." The theological virtues are those "which, as a rule, only Christians know about." They are faith, hope, and love.

The four cardinal virtues are those that all civilized people recognize. The word "cardinal" comes from a Latin word meaning "the hinge of a door." In other words, these four are "pivotal." The cardinal virtues are prudence, temperance, justice, and fortitude.

Prudence is "practiced common sense," taking the trouble to think out what you are doing and what will likely come from it. Quoting Jesus' statement that we are to be "wise as serpent and

A Point to Ponder

harmless as doves," Lewis says that God wants us to have "a child's heart and a grown-up head." Our motto should be "Be good" and "Don't forget this involves being as clever as you can." This "cardinal" virtue is the biblical concept of sensible.

Temperance does not refer to alcohol; it refers to all pleasures. It is not just abstaining but "going the right length and no further." Lewis suggests that a man who makes golf or his motorcycle the center of his life, a woman who devotes all her thoughts to clothes, bridge, or her dog is as intemperate as someone who gets drunk every evening. This is the biblical concept of self-control.

Justice is "fairness." It includes "honesty, give and take, truthfulness, keeping promises, and all that side of life." Justice, of course, is a biblical concept.

Fortitude includes "both kinds of courage—the kind that faces danger as well as the kind that sticks it under pain." "Guts" is perhaps the nearest modern English equivalent. Lewis adds, "You cannot practice any of the other virtues very long without bringing this one into play." This idea of "fortitude" includes the biblical concept of endurance.

We need to add the "theological" virtues (faith, love, and hope), the "cardinal" virtues (prudence [sensible], temperance [self-control], justice, and fortitude [endurance]) as well as gratitude, meekness, gentleness, etc. to our lives. Wow! We have a lot of adding to do.

A Point to Ponder

NOW THAT THE ELECTION IS OVER

Now that the 2004 election is over, I would like to make an observation. This is about more than politics.

I am old enough to remember the days when contenders for the White House entered mortal political combat and the country seemed to come together again when one lost. The attitude was, "I disagree with the politics of the winner, but he is the President and I respect that." Somewhere along the line, we seem to have lost that American tradition. The attitude these days is, "I hate the winner. I am depressed. I feel like moving to another country." That is sad. We need to adopt the attitude of Derek Shearer.

Derek Shearer is a professor in the Interdisciplinary Diplomacy and World Affairs program at Occidental College. He has been a professor at Occidental since 1981. Politically, it would be conservative to say that Schaefer is a liberal. In the 1980s, Santa Monica, California, was so liberal that it was renowned as the "People's Republic of Santa Monica." During that period, Shearer's wife was mayor and he was the Planning Commissioner. President Clinton appointed him to a top Commerce Department post and, later, Ambassador to Finland. He is one of Clinton's dearest FOBs (Friends of Bill). He is so liberal that the Wall Street Journal described him as "miles to the left of the Democratic mainstream" (*LA Times*, 11/17/2004. p. B2). This year, Shearer worked on the Kerry campaign.

A Point to Ponder

These days, Shearer is back from his leave-of-absence at Occidental College, challenging students who criticize George W. Bush unfairly! He talks about the "non-thinking liberal critique" of Bush. When Jane Platt, a political major, said in class that Bush voters were "motivated by fear and hate," Shearer engaged her in a discussion. As a result, Platt concluded that fear and hate were unfair characterizations of legitimate viewpoints. Because of his exposure to Shearer, another student, Bradley Basham, said, "I hate him (Bush) less personally now. I just hate his politics."

What happened to liberal Derek Shearer? It was something that occurred many years ago. At Yale, he was a classmate of George W. Bush. As freshmen, they lived across the hall from each other. Shearer says, "We weren't friends, but we were friendly." Since their Yale days, Shearer and Bush have met on occasion. In 2000, when Shearer's 21-year-old son died suddenly, Bush took time from campaigning to write Shearer a note.

In other words, Shearer has had enough personal exposure to Bush to see him as a person. If we are to live civilly with each other, we need to learn to disagree without being disagreeable. We need to *respectfully* disagree in politics, business, church, and fami*ly*. Peter told believers to honor everybody (1 Pet. 2:17) and added that servants were to "respect all, not only to the good and gentle but also to the unjust" (1 Pet. 2:18, ESV).

As the old saying goes, "agree to disagree agreeably."

A Point to Ponder

A TRIBUTE TO MY MOTHER

At 6:25 p.m. on Christmas Eve, my brother John called from Dallas to tell me Mother had passed away. After her heart operation just several months ago, John and I thought she would live for years. Complaining of pains in her chest and abdomen, she was taken to the hospital several days before Christmas. At first, we expected this to be a routine gallbladder operation. Then, abruptly, she took a turn for the worst and, shortly after that, she passed away. She was 84 years old.

When John and I talked to our mother about the Lord, she would tell us about her conversion at age thirteen. She never got involved in a church, nor was she the spiritual influence in our lives, but my mother enormously impacted us.

My mother loved her two sons. I have rarely met a mother who loved her children as much as our mother loved us. When I was pastor of the Church of the Open Door, we invited J. Vernon McGee, who had pastored the church for 21 years, back to speak. In his closing prayer, he expressed thanks "for the mother love of the Father God." The phrase was so striking, the thought so profound, it made an indelible impression on me. My mother was one of the finest examples of mother love I have ever known. Her unconditional love was like the love of our Father God.

Needless to say, my mother's love has significantly impacted me. It would not be too much to say that her love was the foundation

A Point to Ponder

from which I was launched into life.

My mother was born handicapped. She arrived with one hand. Her left arm was severed at the wrist so that she had a nub instead of a left hand. As far as I know, she never let that bother her. She accepted it as a reality. She had an artificial hand, which she wore to work, but she did not wear it around the house. She did not try to hide, deny, or ignore her handicap.

My mother never would allow me to feel sorry for her. I could be angry with her, but she would not permit me to feel pity. She did not want sympathy because of her handicap—from me or anyone else.

My insistence that we must look the realities of life in the eye, no doubt, began with my mother.

My mother did not let her handicap stop her from anything she wanted to do. As a child, she did not get very far in school. As an adult, she went back to school and got a GED. She was divorced when I was six and my brother was two. She went to work, raised two boys by herself and did it with great gusto. I remember the three of us taking a bike ride to Pensacola Beach. That was a twenty-mile trip! (By the way, in those days, the three-mile bridge across Escambia Bay was made of wood.)

My mother was a dedicated, sacrificial mother. I am grateful. I honor her (Ex. 20:12) with this article and a tree I planted in her memory outside the window of my office at church.

A Point to Ponder

REAL SPIRITUAL GROWTH

Would you like to grow spiritually? Evidently, many in America do not particularly care for religion, but they want to be "spiritual." I suspect many who attend church do so because they desire something spiritual. What does spirituality look like? Is it just being interested in something beyond the material side of life? Is it being religious?

Spirituality includes many factors. From a biblical point of view, it is impossible to be "spiritual" apart from knowing God, who is spirit (Jn. 4:24). The way to know God is by trusting Jesus Christ for the gift of eternal life (Jn. 17:3; Rom. 6:23; 1 Tim. 1:16).

In the New Testament, "spirituality" is spiritual maturity. In 1 Corinthians 2, Paul uses the word "spiritual" (1 Cor. 2:6) to describe the "mature" (1 Cor. 2:13, 15. See also Gal. 6:1). When he says, "comparing spiritual things with spiritual" (1 Cor. 2:13), he means explaining spiritual truth to spiritual-minded people. He has come full circle from the thought expressed in verse 6 and introduces what follows in the passage.

If spirituality is growing to spiritual maturity, what does spiritual maturity look like? Among other things, it is being established in spiritual truth (Rom. 1:11; 16:25; Col. 2:7; 1 Thess. 3:13; 1 Pet. 5:10; 2 Pet. 1:12) and being strong in the Lord (Eph. 6:10).

Being strong in the Lord is tricky because when we hear "strong," we think of self-sufficiency. Spiritual maturity is being strong *in the Lord*, which means that I am only strong *in Him*. Paul said,

A Point to Ponder

"I can do all things through Christ who strengthens me" (Phil. 3:10). To be strong in Him, I must realize that I am a sinner in need of a Savior, a weakling in need of strength.

Spiritual growth can be traced by people's assessment of themselves. In 57 AD, 22 years after his conversion, Paul wrote, "For I am the least of the apostles, who am not worthy to be called an apostle because I persecuted the church of God" (1 Cor 15:9). In 61 AD, Paul called himself, "the least of all the saints" (Eph. 3:8). A year later he claims to be the "chief of sinners" (1 Tim. 1:12). As he grew in the Lord, Paul realized more and more, just how sinful he was. His assessment of himself went from being the least apostle to the least of all saints to the chief of sinners. When we see the holiness of God, we realize our sinfulness (Job 42:5-6; Isa. 6:5; Lk. 5:8). The closer we get to the light, the more we see our darkness and realize we need help.

It is when we see our sin and weakness that we are strong. When God told Paul, "My grace is sufficient for you, for My strength is made perfect in weakness" (1 Cor. 12:9a), Paul responded, "Therefore most gladly I will rather boast in my infirmities, that the power of Christ may rest upon me" (2 Cor. 12:9) and added "when I am weak, then I am strong" (2 Cor. 12:10). That is real spiritual growth.

A Point to Ponder

NO TIME TO THINK

Daniel Arnold is a junior in high school who would like to attend one of the nation's top universities. Being highly motivated, he set out to find out what a high school student has to do to gain admission to such a university. What he discovered is the subject of an article he wrote ("Why Isn't Just Thinking Rewarded?" *The Los Angeles Times*, 11/27/04).

To get into a top university, he takes every honors course available, attends every class, reads every assignment, works on every physics problem, and writes and rewrites every English essay. On top of that, he mentors math students, participates in sports, enters math and science competitions, interns with a civil rights attorney, and gets high scores on the SAT I and II. He also donates hours to help get out the vote, cares for the needy, and nurtures the poor. According to Arnold, universities seem to consider good grades, high SAT scores, and community service to be just par for the course.

Arnold has a complaint. His objection is not that the expectations are too high. He protests that today's high school students are so busy they do not have time to think. He means "deep thinking," "puzzling over a question until a glimmer of the answer appears."

This realization hit him when he was just thinking in front of his computer. He says that he felt guilty that he was thinking and not doing. He also noted that he could put on a college application that he had 500 hours of community service or 50 hours mentoring math students but he would not get credit for just thinking.

This Carlsbad, California high school student asks, "Didn't Einstein have to just think for hours on end?" He also points out, "College professors say their students do not know how to think critically." He then asks, "How can they think critically before they have learned how to formulate good questions and then spend hours trying to answer them?"

Arnold concludes his article by saying, "Good ideas are grown in the garden of the human mind. And thinking is the water that makes that garden grow."

As I read his article, I thought, "You may not get credit for thinking on a university application, but the Scripture puts a premium on meditation, good old thinking!" Consider Joshua 1:8, Psalm 1:2, 63:6, 77:12, 119:15, 119:23, 119:48, 119:78, 119:148, 143:5, Philippians. 4:8.

Like Arnold, our lives are so crowded with things to *do* that we do not have time to *think*. We need to unload some of the baggage to read the Scripture long enough and deep enough until we can "formulate good questions, and then spend hours trying to answer them." Thinking deeply about God's thoughts is the water that grows spiritual life.

A Point to Ponder

THE TEN COMMANDMENTS CONTROVERSY

The debate over whether or not The Ten Commandments should be displayed on government property has reached the Supreme Court. The issue is, "Does the prominent display of The Ten Commandments on government buildings violate the separation of church and state." The court's decision is expected this summer.

What is the problem with The Ten Commandments? It is hard to imagine anyone in America seriously disagrees with five: 1) Honor your father and mother. 2) Do not murder. 3) Do not commit adultery. 4) Do not steal. 5) Do not bear false witness. Certainly, anyone who disagrees with these five prohibitions is on the fringe of American society. No less than Justice Antonin Scalia says that 90% of the American people support having The Ten Commandments on display, even if "85% of them couldn't tell you what they say." Besides, murder, stealing, and lying (called fraud) are illegal! What is the problem with posting laws in a government building?

Is the problem the Constitution? The First Amendment says, "Congress shall make no law respecting an *establishment* of religion, or prohibiting the free exercise and thereof." Is the public display of The Ten Commandments the establishment of religion? As a pastor, I wish it were that easy to establish a church.

Give me a break! Does anyone seriously believe that the posting of The Ten Commandments on government property establishes

A Point to Ponder

a religion? Exactly which religion does it establish? The Ten Commandments are part of both Judaism and Christianity.

No, the objection to posting The Ten Commandments on government property is not the Constitution's First Amendment. Nor is it the last six of The Ten Commandments. The issue is not the First Amendment; it is the first Commandment!

The first Commandment says, "You shall have no other gods before me" (Ex. 20:3). According to the preamble of the Ten Commandments, the One who said that is "the LORD your God" (Ex. 20:2). At least one Supreme Court Justice has figured out the nature of the controversy. Justice Anthony M. Kennedy says the demand to remove The Ten Commandments shows "hostility to religion."

What posting of the Ten Commandments on government property does do is recognize our laws are based on God's laws. As Justice Antonia Scalia says, "It's a symbol that the government derives its authority from God. That's what this is about. Our laws are derived from God."

That is the nature of this controversy. It is not about the establishment, or even the endorsement, of religion. It is about the recognition of God! This is not about the separation of church and state. It is about separating any acknowledgment of the Supreme Sovereign of the universe from American society.

A Point to Ponder

DO WE NEED A POPE?

When Benedict XVI was elected Pope, several TV channels flashed the message across the bottom of the screen, "We have a Pope." As I looked at the message, I thought to myself, "What do you mean, '*We* have a Pope?'" Whose idea was it to have a Pope?

According to the Roman Catholic Church, the answer is "Jesus." When Jesus asked, "Who do you say that I am?" Peter replied, "You are the Christ, the Son of the living God." In response, Jesus said, "You are Peter, and on this rock, I will build My church" (Mt. 16:15-16, 18). Catholicism claims that since the Greek word "Peter" means "rock," Jesus is saying that He will build His church on Peter, the first Pope.

The rock is not Peter. The Greek word translated "rock" means "a mass of rock." The word rendered "Peter" means "stone." Furthermore, in the Greek text, "rock" is feminine and "Peter" is masculine. (That also means the rock is not Christ.)

The rock is Peter's confession of faith. In Matthew 16, Jesus says to Peter, "You are Peter, a stone, but upon the massive rock of your confession of faith I will build My church. As one commentator states, "The faith that he (Peter) expressed was the rock upon which He (Christ) would build His church" (Tasker). Tasker points out that there is no suggestion in this passage that Peter's successor would enjoy the same privileges and have the same spiritual authority as Peter himself.

A Point to Ponder

There is no biblical support for a Pope. According to Catholic doctrine, the Pope must be a priest. Priests cannot be married, but Peter was married (Mt. 8:14). Peter would not allow people to bow down to him (Acts 10:25-26).

Catholics also claim that the Holy Spirit is responsible for selecting a Pope. In talking to reporters, several of the Cardinals spoke of the Holy Spirit guiding them. If true, why did it take *four* votes to elect Benedict XVI? Was there something wrong with the Holy Spirit on the first three votes? Were some of the Cardinals not listening? Or does that not just indicate that the whole process was a political, not a spiritual, exercise?

Where did the idea of a Pope originate? It evolved. After the close of the New Testament, the office of bishop was created. Eventually, all bishops were given the title of "Pope" (Latin for "father"). In 604 AD, the title of "Pope," as the *universal* bishop, was first given to Gregory I, the Bishop of Rome, by the emperor Phocas to spite the Bishop of Constantinople, who had justly excommunicated him. Gregory refused the title. His successor, Boniface III (607 AD), assumed it. The rest, as they say, is history (*Roman Catholicism*, Loraine Boettner, p. 125).

We do not need a Pope. We do need a mediator between us and God. Thank God, He has provided one. "For *there is* one God and one Mediator between God and men, *the* Man Christ Jesus" (1 Tim. 2:5).

A Point to Ponder

EVERYBODY LOVES RAYMOND

After nine seasons and 210 programs, the TV sitcom, "Everybody Loves Raymond" aired its last episode. It was the most popular TV comedy show on the air when it ended. Raymond, the star of the program, was the highest-paid comic in television history. Evidently, a lot of people love Raymond.

A confession is in order. I, too, love Raymond. I do not watch much TV. When I do, I watch the news, business, and history channels. Several years ago, someone introduced my wife and me to Raymond, and we fell (head over heels) in love with Raymond. We even watch reruns!

It is a well-written, funny sitcom. Patricia and I found ourselves laughing aloud in virtually every episode. Some of the one-liners were one of a kind. We love Raymond because we enjoy humor.

The characters of "Raymond" are an interesting lot. Raymond is a clueless husband. Debra, his wife, is a frustrated, under-appreciated wife. Raymond's parents, who live across the street, are classic in-laws. Marie is a noisy, pushy, controlling, opinionated mother and mother-in-law. Frank is a self-centered, blunt fellow who is always eating. All Raymond thinks about is sex and all Frank thinks about is food.

Then, there is Robert, the older brother, who lives in the shadow of his younger brother Raymond. He always feels like the second-fiddle, second-class, last-in-line brother. There are other characters.

A Point to Ponder

Robert is married to Amy, who is upbeat but slightly dingy. She has religious parents, who are "strange" and a brother who is "weird."

When I first saw the show, I wondered how it got its title. I assumed, by the title, that Raymond was a likable, lovable fellow. I soon discovered that Raymond had many foibles and failures plenty. At one time or another, everyone, including his kids, was down on Raymond, especially his wife and his brother. Sometimes, his mother came to his defense, but rarely, if ever, did his wife or brother. I thought they should have named the show "Poor Raymond."

I was wrong! The last episode dramatically portrays that everyone, including his wife and brother, really loves Raymond. In the final program, Raymond had a minor operation, and for about thirty seconds, everyone thought Raymond was not coming out alive. They panicked, even his wife and brother. As a result, it was apparent that they really did love Raymond, warts and all.

We can all learn a great lesson from this otherwise dysfunctional family. We may have problems with people with whom we must live and work. They may be as clueless as Raymond. Nevertheless, we should love them, warts and all. After all, did not God set an example for us by loving us like that? "God demonstrates His own love toward us, in that while we were still sinners, Christ died for us" (Rom. 5:8).

A Point to Ponder

EXAMPLES WORTHY OF NOTE

In our competitive world, position, degrees, and titles are important. How many people do you know who feel that they would feel significant if they just had a higher position in their company? How many want a degree they can wear as a mark of distinction? I know of a Ph.D. who insisted that everyone in his life, in and outside of his professional life, call him "Doctor." How many crave a title because they want recognition?

In this regard, the authors of the New Testament are worthy of note. They had positions, degrees, and titles but did not flaunt them. They either did not use them at all or only when absolutely necessary.

Matthew was an apostle who never bothered to mention his name, much less his position when he penned the first book of the New Testament. Mark was Peter's assistant when he wrote his book, but, like Matthew, his name does not appear in his work. Luke was a medical doctor and Paul's traveling companion, but in his two-volume set (Luke and Acts), his name does not appear. The Gospels are known as the "Gospel according to Matthew," etc., because others later attached their names to their works.

The apostle John wrote four books. In two, his name does not appear at all; in the other two, he identifies himself not as an apostle but as an elder (2 Jn. and 3 Jn.). Even when he needed to speak officially, he used a lesser title.

A Point to Ponder

In his first epistle, Peter does say he is an apostle (1 Pet. 1:1) but later calls himself an elder (1 Pet. 5:1), reminding elders that they are not to lord it over the flock (1 Pet. 5:3). He used his authority because it was necessary, but he did not throw his authority around to feel important or gain the awe of others. In his second epistle, he again calls himself an apostle, but first, he calls himself a "bondslave of Jesus Christ." This apostle took on the position of a slave. He is the example (1 Pet. 5:3).

Like Peter, Paul mentions his apostleship when necessary, but he identified himself as a slave of Jesus Christ (Rom. 1:1, Phil. 1:1, Titus 1:1) and as a prisoner of Jesus Christ (Phlm. 1).

The two authors of the New Testament who were half-brothers of Jesus Christ, James and Jude, never mention that fact. Instead, both call themselves slaves of Jesus Christ (Jas. 1:1, Jude 1)!

Then there is Hebrews. The author of Hebrews not only does not give his name, but he hides himself so that no one today knows for sure who wrote it.

You do not need to have a position, degree, or title to be significant. If you have them, use them when necessary and with humility. In the final analysis, we are servants. It is sufficient and significant enough to be called His servants.

A Point to Ponder

HOW DIFFERENT MEN LEARNED TO GET ALONG

Meet two very different people.

Simon was a Zealot (Lk. 6:15). Josephus, the Jewish historian, records that according to the Zealots, "God is the Ruler and Lord." Consequently, they refused to give the title of king to any man. Furthermore, they had "an inviolable attachment to liberty" (*Antiquities,* 8.1.6.). Zealots were committed to the cause of freeing their country from the rule of Rome and willing to endure any pain to do so. If necessary, they were prepared to die. They were even willing to assassinate people to rid their country of foreign rule. They were patriots *par excellence* and the most nationalist of all nationalists.

Matthew was a tax collector (Mt. 10:3). Everyone hates tax collectors; with the ancient Jews, the hatred was particularly severe. They had a deep religious conviction that God alone was King. They felt that to pay taxes to any mortal man was an infringement of God's rights and an insult to His majesty. To make matters worse, some were serving as tax collectors for their country's conqueror, Rome

According to Jewish law, tax collectors were included in unclean things. Leviticus 20:5 was applied to them. It says, "I will set My face against that man and against his family, and I will cut him off from his people, and all who prostitute themselves with him to

A Point to Ponder

commit harlotry with Molech" (Lev. 20:5 NKJV). Consequently, tax collectors were barred from the synagogue and forbidden to be witnesses in court. They were classed together with robbers and murderers.

It has been suggested that if Simon the Zealot had met Matthew, the tax collector, Simon would have stuck a dagger in Matthew.

These two extremely opposite individuals became disciples of Jesus Christ. On top of that, Jesus called both of them to be apostles (Mt. 10:1-4). How did those two men with such radically different opinions about critical matters learn to get along in a small group of twelve people without killing each other? The answer is, "They became disciples of Jesus Christ." The Greek word translated "disciple" means "learner." They could get along because of the things they learned from Jesus Christ.

They learned to seek first the kingdom of God instead of the kingdoms of this world (Mt. 6:33). They learned that the meek, not the mighty, inherit the earth (Mt. 5:5). They learned to hunger for true righteousness instead of getting hung up on their view of what is right (Mt. 5:6). They learned to be merciful instead of hateful (Mt. 5:7). They learned to be peacemakers instead of troublemakers (Mt. 5:9). They learned not to be so judgmental (Mt. 7:1-5), but to love each other (Mt. 7:12). Barclay observes, "Here is the tremendous truth that men who hate each other can learn to love each other when they both love Jesus Christ."

A Point to Ponder

SOME SAY, "JESUS NEVER LIVED"

If you have not heard, there is a new documentary titled "The God Who Wasn't." Brian Flemming, a former "born-again Christian" who made the hour-long documentary, argues that the biblical Jesus never lived! According to Flemming, Jesus was a mythological figure like Paul Bunyan.

Flemming grew up attending a Methodist church with his parents. They enrolled him in the Sun Valley Christian School when they became concerned about the violencse in the Sylmar, California public schools. There, he came to believe what his teachers taught about the Bible. Those beliefs began to crumble when he attended the University of California at Irvine and began studying philosophy and science, especially evolution. According to Fleming, in college, he "learned" that Christians misrepresented evolution.

Fearing that children are being indoctrinated in the Christian faith, Flemming made the documentary to demonstrate Jesus never lived. To promote his movie, Flemming places it in the company of other exposés anticipating that it will expose religion, like "Bowling for Columbine" did the gun culture and "Supersize Me" did the fast food industry.

I'm amazed that someone can be so ill-informed in the name of intelligence.

The first-century Jewish historian Josephus said that Jesus was a wise man, whom Pilate condemned to the cross and that

A Point to Ponder

he appeared alive again on the third day (*Antiquities of the Jews* 18:3.3). Eusebius (*ca.* 325 AD), a Christian historian cites this passage from Josephus (*Ecclesiastical History* 1.11). In another book, Josephus says that James was "the brother of Jesus, who was called Christ" (*Antiquities of the Jews*, 20.9.1). Tacitus (55-117 AD), the dean of Roman historians, mentions Christ in his writings.

Michael Wilkins and J. P. Moreland conclude that from non-Christian writings such as Josephus, the *Talmud*, Tacitus, and Pliny the Younger, it would be possible to know that 1) Jesus was a Jewish teacher. 2) Many believed that He performed healings and exorcisms. 3) The Jewish leaders rejected him. 4) He was crucified under Pontius Pilate in the reign of Tiberius. 5) His followers believed he was still alive and had spread beyond Palestine, so there were multitudes of them in Rome by 64 AD. 6) By the beginning of the second century, "all kinds of people from the cities and countryside-men and women, slave and free, worshiped Him as God" (Wilkins, Michael J. and Moreland, J. P., eds. *Jesus Under Fire: Modern Scholarship Reinvents the Historical Jesus*. Grand Rapids: Zondervan Publishing House, 1995).

Dr. Thomas Rausch, a professor of Theology at Loyola Marymount University, says, "I don't know any serious scholar who questions the existence of Jesus." Rejecting Jesus as God in the flesh is one thing. To say He never lived is just plain ignorant. Remember, Satan blinds the mind (2 Cor. 4:4).

A Point to Ponder

KATRINA AND NOW RITA!

Hurricane Katrina and now Hurricane Rita! What in the world is happening?

Are the environmentalists correct? Are these hurricanes the result of global warming? Are they the judgment of God? Speaking of God, what is His part in all of this? Isn't He in control?

God allows natural disasters. As the supreme Sovereign of the universe, God is in control. So, we must conclude that God, at least, allows natural disasters.

God does not directly cause natural disasters. When God created the earth, Adam and Eve, and the Garden of Eden, there was no disease, deformity, disaster, or death. When Adam sinned, all creation fell under a curse (Gen. 3:17) and groans for redemption (Rom. 8:18-21). After the fall, the world changed. For the first time, weeds grew in the garden. Nature was out of joint. The world we live in today is a result of the fall.

In other words, natural disasters are *natural* disasters, *not* acts of God. These hurricanes are not the result of global warming. Weather experts inform us that every 25 to 40 years, there is a cycle of severe storms. Nor are these storms judgments of God (Lk. 13:1-5). Natural disasters *naturally* happen.

On November 1, 1755, an earthquake flattened the Portuguese city of Lisbon, killing thousands of its inhabitants. At the time, Lisbon brazenly called itself a "party town." John Wesley attributed the earthquake to "the curse that was brought upon the earth by the original transgression of Adam and Eve." But as Pastor Doug Giles wrote, "If you build a big city below sea level in the middle of hurricane highway, then the chances are you're eventually going to take a hit. It doesn't mean God hates you. It just means there is a cost to living on the coast."

God wants us to learn from trials (Jas. 1:2-4). Here are several possible lessons.

1. Life does not consist in the abundance of our possessions (Lk. 12:15).

2. Life is about relationships (Mt. 22:37-39). Rick Warren said, "If you measure your life by the things you've accumulated (car, clothes, toys) and one day those things are all taken away, it forces you to reevaluate what life is really all about! If your definition of family is tied to your house, yard, or neighborhood and suddenly it's completely destroyed, it forces you to re-think the true meaning of a family. If your concept of church is a building with stained glass and a steeple and it is instantly reduced to a heap of rubble, it forces you to realize that church is people, not a building!"

3. Life is about helping others (Jas. 1:27). James begins his first chapter with you having a trial (Jas. 1:2) and ends it with you helping others in trouble (Jas. 1:27).

Conclusion: A sovereign God allows natural disasters; we should learn spiritual lessons from them (Lk. 13:1-5).

A Point to Ponder

WOULD YOU SAY "NO" TO $4 MILLION?

Last year, Cadillac® dangled $15 million in front of the rock group The Doors for permission to use their song "Break on Through (to the Other Side)" to hawk its luxury SUVs. John Densmore, the drummer, said, "No thanks!" Here is the story.

The rock group The Doors was formed in 1965. It consisted of Jim Morrison, the lead singer, John Densmore, the drummer, and two other band members, Ray Manzarek and Robbie Krieger.

As the decade of the 60s was ending, The Doors was offered $50,000 to allow their biggest hit, "Light My Fire," to be used as a commercial for the Buick Opal. At the time, Morrison was in Europe. In his absence, the other three agreed to the deal, but when Morrison returned, he was furious. As a result, the deal was never consummated. In 1970, The Doors entered a written agreement that any licensing would require a unanimous vote. Jim Morrison died in 1971.

Armed with the power of a legal contract, John Densmore has repeatedly said "No" to offers to use their songs in commercials. He says such use of their music would trample their legacy. He is unalterably opposed to such commercialization.

Using popular rock music in commercials is now common and profitable. Led Zeppelin pitches Cadillacs, the Rolling Stones—Ameriquest Mortgage, Paul McCartney—Fidelity Investments, and

A Point to Ponder

Bob Dylan—Kaiser Permanente. Nevertheless, there are holdouts, including Bruce Springsteen, Neil Young, Carlos Santana, and, of course, much to the chagrin of the rest of The Doors, John Densmore.

When Apple Computer offered $4 million for commercial use of one of their songs, Densmore vetoed the idea and when Cadillac came with $15 million in hand, it was thumbs down again. Densmore will not even allow the remaining Doors to use the name "Doors" for a reorganized group that does concerts. That conflict landed in court, and Densmore won in August of this year [2005]!

His reasoning borders on the sacred. He says, "On stage when we played these songs, they felt mysterious and magic. That's not for rent." The remaining Doors have opened the door for Densmore to team up with them again for a concert tour. He refuses to do that! He explains, "I would love to play with The Doors and play those songs again. I would. And I will play again as The Doors. Just as soon as Jim shows up." That is going to take a while. Jim's heart gave out in 1971.

If I understand the math correctly, Densmore says "No" to almost $4 million ($15 million split four ways). Now, *there* is a drummer who marches to a different drum beat. It makes me want to ask myself, "What are my convictions? How much are they worth? Would I compromise a conviction for $4 million?" When offered millions for the message of grace, Elisha said, "*As* the LORD lives, before whom I stand, I will receive nothing" (2 Kings 5:16).

A Point to Ponder

"IN GOD WE TRUST"

Recently, in the name of the First Amendment, The Ten Commandments have been removed from a courthouse. A lawsuit was filed to remove the phrase "under God" from the Pledge of Allegiance, and now, there is a lawsuit to remove "in God we trust" from our money. Does the First Amendment prohibit government references to God?

The First Amendment of the Constitution of the United States says, "Congress shall make no law respecting an establishment of religion, or prohibiting the free exercise thereof." It contains two clauses. The first clause is known as the Establishment Clause and the second is known as the Free Exercise Clause.

When the Constitution was written, England and Europe had (and still have) state churches. Against that backdrop, the Founding Fathers, on the one hand, wanted to prevent the federal government from establishing a state religion, and on the other, they wanted to promote religion. Hence, the Establishment Clause and the Free Exercise Clause of the First Amendment were put into the Constitution.

Many today believe the Constitution mandates a "wall of separation" between church and state. There is no such phrase in the Constitution. That phrase was written years after the Constitution and the Bill of Rights were adopted. It comes from a letter written in 1802 by Thomas Jefferson to the Danbury Baptist Church,

A Point to Ponder

assuring them that he believed the First Amendment built "a wall of separation between church and state." What he meant by that was no more than what the First Amendment states, namely, that the federal government cannot establish a national religion. Thomas Jefferson also said, "Can the liberties of a nation be thought secure when we have removed their only firm basis, a conviction in the minds of people that these liberties are a gift of God?" Apparently, he did not believe in the separation of the state from God.

There is nothing, *absolutely nothing*, in the First Amendment—or anywhere else in the Constitution—or in Thomas Jefferson mandating a separation of God and government. The First Amendment prevents the federal government from establishing a national religion. It does not prohibit government references to God or religion from influencing government!

The United States Senate has a paid-by-taxpayers chaplain. In 1983, the United States Supreme Court ruled that congressional chaplains did not violate the First Amendment's Establishment Clause (*Marsh v. Chambers*). Chief Justice Warren Berger wrote, "Clearly, the men who wrote the First Amendment religious clauses did not view paid legislative chaplains and opening prayers as a violation of that amendment."

If paid chaplains do not violate the Constitution, neither does the motto, "In God we trust" on money. The motto "In Jesus Christ we trust" might, but not "In God we trust."

After all, Paul says, "There is no authority except from God, and the authorities that exist are appointed by God" (Rom. 13:1) and the Declaration of Independence mentions God six times.

A Point to Ponder

THE REDEMPTION OF TOOKIE WILLIAMS

Stanley Tookie Williams, the co-founder of the Crips gang (1969), was convicted of killing four people (1979). All appeals have been exhausted. He is scheduled to be executed on December 13, 2005 [and he was]. The only thing that can prevent the courted-ordered execution is a stay of execution by the Governor, Arnold Schwarzenegger.

Some are pleading with the governor to reduce Tookie's sentence to life in prison. They say Tookie has been redeemed. He has repudiated any affiliation with any gang. He has written nine children's books to persuade children not to participate in gangs. He has been nominated for the Nobel Prize for Literature five times and for the Nobel Peace Prize four times. He has been redeemed; he should be given mercy.

Some are opposed to the governor granting clemency in this case. They argue that justice demands that he pay for killing four innocent people. They point out that all it takes to be nominated for one of the Nobel prizes is for one individual to fill out an application. Bill Handel, a Los Angeles talk show host, had somebody nominate him for the Nobel Peace Prize to prove the point. Evidently, Tookie's books have not sold very many copies (one report said only a few hundred) and there is no evidence that he has had any impact on keeping people out of gangs. Steve Lopez, a reporter for the *Los*

A Point to Ponder

Angeles Times, interviewed a member of the Crips gang who is in jail. The gang members said that the young people do not even know who Tookie Williams is. There is no redemption, only a PR campaign. He should be given justice.

When the governor makes his decision, should he base it on justice or mercy?

In my opinion, this decision should be made based on justice. In the first place, I believe the Bible teaches capital punishment. After the Flood, God decreed, "Whoever sheds man's blood, by man his blood shall be shed; For in the image of God He made man" (Gen. 9:6 NKJV). That mandate has not been suspended. The New Testament teaches that God has given government the sword, an instrument of death, and "If you do evil, be afraid; for he (the governor) does not bear the sword in vain; for he is God's minister, an avenger to *execute* wrath on him who practices evil" (Rom. 13:4 NKJV).

In the second place, I believe the Bible teaches redemption but does not teach that redemption eliminates the consequence of a crime. Paul says, "For if I am an offender, or have committed anything deserving of death, I do not object to dying (Acts 25:11 NKJV). Should convicted thieves be released from prison if they get saved? Besides, people receive mercy when they acknowledge they need it. Tookie Williams says in his memoir, *Blue Rage, Black Redemption,* "I will never apologize for crimes I did not commit." He does not qualify for redemption. He should be given justice based on repeated judicial decisions that he is guilty.

A Point to Ponder

IS RELIGION A PROBLEM?

According to some, one of the major problems in the world today is religion. For example, In his book, *The End of Faith: Religion, Terror and the Future of Reason*, Sam Harris writes, "Words like 'God' and 'Allah' must go the way of 'Apollo' and 'Baal,' or they will unmake our world." According to Harris, religious faith is "the devil's masterpiece."

Robert Reich, former Labor Secretary under President Bill Clinton, says, "The great conflict of the 21st century will not be between the West and terrorism," but "between those who give priority to life in this world and those who believe that human life is mere preparation for an existence beyond life; between those who believe in science, reason and logic, and those who believe that truth is revealed through Scripture and religious dogma."

Is religion a problem? Is it the devil's masterpiece? Does it cause conflicts in the world? Absolutely!

In history, some of the most religious people who ever lived were the Pharisees. Paul was a Pharisee. In Philippians 3:4-7, Paul explains just how religious he was. He goes so far as to say that he had more reason than anyone else to have confidence before God because of his religious heredity and heritage (Phil. 3:4). He then lists his religious pedigree (Phil. 3:5-6) and it is impressive, but he single-handedly terrorized the church. As a Pharisee, he consented to the death of Steven (Acts 8:1) and "made havoc of the church,

A Point to Ponder

entering every house, and dragging off men and women, committing *them* to prison" (Acts 8:3).

If religion is a problem, what is the solution?

Paul had religion and personal righteousness to his credit but counted all that lost (Phil. 3:7) and beyond that rubbish (Phil. 3:8). The purpose for such drastic action was "that I may gain Christ and be found in Him, not having my own righteousness which is from the law, but that which is through faith in Christ the righteousness, which is of God by faith" (Phil. 3:9). Paul counted his religion and personal righteousness as garbage to have the righteousness, which is from God (Phil. 3:9).

Let me explain. We are all sinners. Religion does not solve the problem because the penalty of sin is death (Rom. 6:23) and religion does not pay the penalty. When Jesus died on the cross, He died for our sins (1 Cor. 15:3). When we trust Him for the gift of eternal life (1 Tim. 1:16), we are declared righteous (Rom. 5:1). He took our sin; we get His righteousness (2 Cor. 5:21). What a deal, but to obtain the righteousness of Jesus Christ, you must abandon all trust in religion to get you to heaven and trust Jesus Christ and Him alone. Religion is a problem; trusting Christ is the solution.

A Point to Ponder

THE RIGHTS OF THE BORN

Before an audience of 1,300 people, a panel in Washington was discussing politics and faith. The panel consisted of two clergymen with "progressive spiritual leanings," a moderate who is liberal and Catholic, and Anne Lamott, the author of *Plan B: Further Thoughts on Faith*. According to a guest editorial written by Lemott ("The Rights of the Born," *Los Angeles Times*, February 10, 2006, page B13), all was going well until a soft-spoken, neatly dressed, older man asked the panel how they could reconcile their progressive stances on peace and justice with the "murder of a million babies every year in America."

Lemott said, "I sat there simmering." "I wanted to respond by pushing over our table." Then she added, "There was a loud buzzing in my head, the voice of reason that says 'You have the right to remain silent,' but the voice of my conscience was insistent. I wanted to express calmly and eloquently that pro-choice people understand that there are two lives involved in an abortion—one born (the pregnant woman) and one that is not (the fetus)—but the born person must be allowed to decide what is right."

She had other things to say, such as, "Fetuses are not babies yet." "A woman's right to choose was nobody else's Goddamned business." "I am so confused about why we are still having to argue with patriarchal sentimentality about teen weenie so-called babies—some microscopic, some no bigger than the sea monkeys

A Point to Ponder

we used to stand up for—when real, alive, already born women, many of them desperately poor, get such short shaft from the current administration." "As a Christian and a feminist, the most important message I can carry and fight for is the sacredness of each human life, and reproductive rights for all women is a critical part of that." She concluded the article by saying she and an older woman "Eat M&Ms to give us strength. It was a kind of communion for those of us who still believe that civil rights, equality, and even common sense will somehow be sovereign someday."

It would take more space than this article allows (I limit "A Piece of My Mind" to one page) to respond to the nonsense she calls common sense. For example, from a scientific as well as a biblical point of view, a fetus is an actual human being, not just a "so-called" baby. Beyond that essential, critical point, however, is perhaps a more fundamental issue: who has the *right* to decide what is *right*?

This is the most fundamental issue in the abortion debate. According to Lemott, "The born person must be allowed to decide what is right." That reminds me of, "In those days *there was* no king in Israel; everyone did *what was* right in his own eyes" (Judges 21:25 NKJV). According to the Scripture, The Giver of life was the right to say what is right. "There is one Lawgiver, who is able to save and to destroy" (Jas. 4:12 NKJV).

A Point to Ponder

DID YOU HEAR WHAT SHE SAID ABOUT MUSLIMS?

Dr. Wafa Suitan is a Syrian-American psychiatrist who lives in Southern California. On February 21, 2006, she unfavorably compared Muslims to Jews, out loud, in Arabic, on Al-Jazeera, the most widely-seen Arabic television network on the planet. According to an article written by John M. Broder in the *New York Times* and rerun in the *Daily News*, here is what she said.

"The Jews have come from the tragedy (the Holocaust) and forced the world to respect them, with their knowledge, not with their terror, with their work, not with their crying and yelling." She continued, "We have not seen a single Jew blow himself up in a German restaurant. We have not seen a single Jew destroy a church. We have not seen a single Jew protest by killing people." She concluded, "Only the Muslims defend their beliefs by burning down churches, killing people, and destroying embassies. This path will not yield any results. The Muslims must ask themselves what they can do for mankind before they demand that mankind respect them."

You can only imagine the reaction in the Muslim world. Clerics denounced her as an infidel. One said that she had done Islam more damage than the Danish cartoons of the Prophet Muhammad. Dr. Ibrahim al-Khouli, a professor of religious studies, said she had blasphemed Islam, the prophet Mohammed, and the Koran. She

A Point to Ponder

has received numerous death threats.

Who is this lady?! Wafa Suitan grew up in a traditional Muslim family in Syria. Her father was a devout Muslim, and she followed her family's faith into adulthood. She is a psychiatrist, wife, and mother of three children.

How could such a woman come to such conclusions? According to her, her life changed in 1979. She was a medical student at the University of Aleppo in northern Syria. At the time, a radical group called the "Muslim Brotherhood" was using terror to undermine the regime of President Hafez Assad. One day, while she was attending class, gunmen from the Muslim Brotherhood burst into the classroom and killed the professor as she watched. She reported, "They shot hundreds of bullets into him shouting, 'God is Great!' At that point, I lost my trust in their God and began to question all our teachings, and it led me to this point: I had to leave. I had to look for another God." Now she says she is not a Christian, a Muslim, or a Jew; she is a "secular human being."

When I read that story, I had several reactions. She may not be religious, but she is astute, brave, and courageous. If Muslims are opposed to suicide bombings, terrorism, and the killing of innocent people, they should loudly proclaim it. Looking for another God is a great idea. God did not say, "*Die for me* so you can go to heaven." He says, My Son *died for you* so that you might have eternal life (Jn. 3:16).

A Point to Ponder

JUDAS: BETRAYER OR BEST FRIEND?

Have you heard? The latest on Judas is that he was not a traitor; he was Jesus' best friend. Here is the story.

In the 1970s, the *Gospel of Judas* was discovered by looters in the Egyptian desert. An antiquities dealer placed it in a safety deposit box in New York, where it rapidly deteriorated. In 2000, it was purchased by a Swiss antiquities dealer named Frieda Nussberger-Tchacos, who handed it over to the Maecenas Foundation of Ancient Art in Basel, Switzerland. With support from the National Geographic Society and the Waitt Institute of Historical Discovery, the Foundation began the time-consuming, painstaking process of reassembling the estimated 1000 pieces of the manuscript. The manuscript's content was released on April 6, 2006.

Analysis of the paper, ink, and ancient writing style indicates that this manuscript was made around 300 AD (an ancient author refers to it in 180 AD). Scholars agree that it was written by Gnostics, a sect that emphasized spiritual knowledge of God (Gnostics comes from the Greek word *gnosis*, which means "knowledge"). Gnostics believed that the world was created by an inferior god who imprisoned the inner self in a material body. The *Gospel of Judas* clearly reflects the teachings of Gnosticism.

The *Gospel of Judas* consists of conversations that are supposed to have occurred between Jesus and Judas during the last week

A Point to Ponder

of their lives. Jesus is said to share spiritual secrets with Judas, which other disciples do not know. Jesus says to Judas, "Step away from the others and I will tell you the kingdom's mysteries." The manuscript pictures Judas not as a betrayer but as the best friend of Jesus. Purposely, Judas turned Jesus over to the authorities because Jesus asked him to do so! By helping Jesus to rid himself of his flesh, Judas helped him liberate the divine being within Him.

Was Judas a betrayer or the best friend of Jesus? You either believe the Gospels of Matthew, Mark, Luke, and John or the Gospel of Judas.

Matthew, Peter (Mark wrote what Peter preached), and John were constant companions of Jesus (27-30 AD). They were present when Judas betrayed Jesus (30 AD). Matthew wrote his Gospel between 45 and 50 AD. Mark wrote between 61 and 67 AD, and John wrote before 70 AD. Luke, who was not present but did extensive research, wrote his Gospel in 59 AD. What Matthew, Mark, Luke, and John wrote was inspired by the Holy Spirit (2 Tim. 3:16). Paul quotes Luke and calls what he wrote Scripture (See 1 Tim. 5:18).

The Gospel of Judas was written more than a hundred years after the events by those who rejected the basic teachings of the Old Testament and the New Testament. I don't know about you, but given the fact, it is easier for me to believe the Bible—again!

A Point to Ponder

WEEKEND OR WEEK BEGINNING?

We think and speak of the work week and the weekend. Perhaps we should think about the week beginning and the work week. Let me explain.

The Apostle John writes, "For the law was given through Moses, *but* grace and truth came through Jesus Christ" (Jn. 1:17).

The Mosaic legal system contained a provision for observing the Sabbath, Saturday, the seventh day of the week. Moses writes, "Remember the Sabbath day, to keep it holy. Six days, you shall labor and do all your work, but the seventh day *is* the Sabbath of the LORD your God. *In it* you shall do no work: you, nor your son, nor your daughter, nor your male servant, nor your female servant, nor your cattle, nor your stranger who *is* within your gates. For *in* six days, the LORD made the heavens and the earth, the sea, and all that *is* in them, and rested the seventh day. Therefore, the LORD blessed the Sabbath day and hallowed it" (Ex. 20:8-11). The Mosaic legal system is simple enough: work six days and rest on the seventh. It is patterned after the creation work week. God Himself worked and rested on the seventh day.

Jesus flipped it. He brought grace. In the grace system, God gives, and then, we work. In that well-worn passage Paul says, "For by grace you have been saved through faith, and that not of yourselves; *it is* the gift of God, works, lest anyone should boast. For we are His workmanship, created in Christ Jesus for good works, which God prepared beforehand that we should walk in them" (Eph. 2:10). The grace system is simple enough: God saves us by His grace and, then, out of gratitude, we work. It is the exact opposite of the Mosaic Law.

It is no accident that in the New Testament, believers observed Sunday, the first day of the week, rather than Saturday, the seventh day of the week. Luke records, "Now on the first *day* of the week, when the disciples came together to break bread, Paul, ready to depart the next day, spoke to them" (Acts 20:7). Paul instructs the Corinthians, "On the first *day* of the week let each one of you lay something aside, storing up as he may prosper, that there be no collections when I come" (1 Cor. 16:2).

The Sabbath is a day of rest *after* a week of work; Sunday is a day of remembrance *before* the work week.

We need to change the way we think about the week. Instead of thinking, "I have worked hard all week. The weekend is my time off to do what I want." We should think, "Sunday is the day to remember God's gift of His Son, who rose from the dead on the first day of the week." With that attitude adjustment, we are ready to take on a new week with a new attitude of gratitude. That change of thinking will change your whole life, not just your week.

A Point to Ponder

A TRIBUTE TO MY (SPIRITUAL) FATHER

For years, I have been saying things about a man behind his back. I would now like to say them to his face in print. Since most who read this do not know the story, I'll have to begin by explaining a few things.

I grew up in Pensacola, Florida. Since my father immigrated from Greece, I was christened in the Greek Orthodox Church. When I was six years old, my parents were divorced. My mother, who did not attend church, reared me. When I started dating, a girlfriend took me to a Baptist church, where I went forward in an evangelistic meeting but was not saved. Within a few months of graduating from high school, I attended a service at the Central Baptist Church. The teenagers were so friendly I went back.

On April 8, 1958, the pastor of that church, C. Sumner Wemp, led me to Christ. I'm sure I had heard the gospel before, but that night, I understood that Christ died for me for the first time in my life. I had a *dramatic* conversion. At that point in my life, I thought only two people in the world understood the gospel: my pastor and me! I felt it was my responsibility to see to it that everyone in the world heard the gospel. I at least *tried* to let everyone in my world know the good news that Christ paid it all.

I sat in a pew at the Central Baptist Church in Pensacola, Florida, for five short months. The place was ablaze for the Lord. People were coming to Christ. Young people were being called to

A Point to Ponder

ministry. "Brother Wemp," as everyone affectionately called the pastor, was not only a zealous evangelist but also an expositor of the Word. He taught the Bible, book-by-book and verse-by-verse.

In September of 1958, at the advice of "Brother Wemp," I enrolled in a Christian college with the goal of attending the same seminary from which my spiritual father had graduated. I had the privilege of sitting under his ministry for five brief months. Several years later, I returned home for one summer, but the minister and his ministry during those first five months modeled my life.

I owe a great deal to C. Sumner Wemp, my spiritual father. He led me to Christ. By his personal example and his pulpit exhortations, he impressed upon me the thrill of evangelism. He modeled zeal for evangelism that I have never seen equaled. By his personal example and his pulpit expositions, he implanted in me a deep desire to expound the Word of God. His ministry of the Word produced a hunger to know and teach the Word that is with me to this day. As if all that were not enough, he gave me many practical insights into life that I have used and passed on to others. In those areas, I have imitated him in his Christ likeness (1 Cor. 11:1).

Thanks, my spiritual father, for just being you and for all that you taught me by your example and exhortations.

A Point to Ponder

YOUR RELATIONSHIP TO THE WORD

What is your relationship to the Word of God? To help clarify the question, ponder the possibilities. Other possibilities could be added, but this will serve as a starter kit.

1. Oppose it. According to some, the Scripture is nothing more than superstition. Furthermore, it misleads people and, therefore, must be exposed for what it is—a myth.

2. Reject it. Having decided that the Bible is not a Word from God, some reject it. They do not attack it or oppose it. They rejected it and seek an explanation for life and death somewhere else.

3. Pervert it. Who would pervert the Word of God? Cults.

4. Respect it. Many in America respect the Bible. It is recognized as the 'Good Book" and even as great literature.

5. Read it. Many pride themselves on the fact that they read the Bible regularly. With pride, they proclaim, "I have read the Bible through every year for twenty years" (or more).

6. Learn it. If you learn the content of the Bible, you will have knowledge. How is that for saying the obvious? Knowledge of the Bible is helpful, but in and of itself, it is not the objective. It can also be harmful. Paul says, "Knowledge puffs up" (1 Cor. 8:1).

7. Absorb it. God's purpose in giving us His Word is to change us. Paul told Timothy that the Scripture is "able to make you wise for salvation through faith which is in Christ Jesus" (2 Tim. 3:15) and adds, "All Scripture *is* given by inspiration of God, and *is*

profitable for doctrine, for reproof, for correction, for instruction in righteousness" (2 Tim. 3:16). In short, the purpose of the Bible is to give us the good news of salvation and bring us to spiritual maturity. For that to happen, first, we must believe that Jesus Christ died for our sins and rose from the dead, and we must trust Jesus Christ for the gift of eternal life. Then, we must absorb the message of the Word of God to *determine the will of God* for our lives. The process of absorption involves meditation (Ps. 1:2), faith (Heb. 4:2), and obedience (Jn. 14:21, 23). It is when we meditate on, believe, and obey the Word that the Holy Spirit can use it to transform us (2 Cor. 3:18). The test of absorption is transformation (Rom. 12:2). Until the Word is transforming us, we do not have the relationship to it God intends.

To determine your relationship to the Bible, do not look at the time you have logged reading it or even how many verses you have memorized. Ask yourself, "How has it transformed my life?"

If you accept the most important message of the Bible and trust Jesus Christ, you will be given the gift of eternal life. If you are transformed by its message, you will end up spiritually mature in this life and rewarded in the next.

A Point to Ponder

AMERICA'S FOUR GODS

Based on polling conducted by the Gallup Organization and with funding from the John M. Templeton Foundation, Baylor University has just released a study of the perception of God in America. Previous studies by various researchers have found that 85-90% of Americans say they believe in God. This study found that while Americans may say they believe in one God (94.8%), they do not agree on what that God is like. The Baylor study identified four views of God.

The Authoritarian God The authoritarian God is engaged in the daily life of humans but is a judgmental God capable of inflicting punishment on the ungodly and the unfaithful. The study found 31.4% of the respondents believed in such a God.

The Benevolent God The benevolent God is also engaged in the daily life of human beings, but He is not as judgmental. He judges, but He is less likely to be angry or act in wrathful ways. The study found that 23% believe in a benevolent God.

The Critical God The critical God is not engaged in people's lives but is judgmental like the previous two. He watches the world, sometimes unfavorably, but He does not interact with the world. He punishes offenders, eventually. Of the respondents, 16% believe in this kind of God.

The Distant God Like the critical God, the distant God is not engaged in daily life, but unlike the critical God, the distant God is

A Point to Ponder

not judgmental either. He is viewed more as a cosmic force that sets nature's laws in motion. The study found 24.4% of the respondents believed in this version of God (from "America Sees One God, but in Different Ways" by Stephen Padilla in the *Los Angeles Times*, September 16, 2006).

From this study, it appears that only 54.4% of Americans believe God is engaged in the lives of people, but 70.4% believe that He is judgmental. Based on the way the conclusions of this study were presented, only 23% believe that God is benevolent!

The study raises the question, "What is God like?" Is He engaged in the lives of people? Is He judgmental or benevolent? The answer is "All of the above," plus much more. According to the Scripture, God is holy (Lev. 11:44). God is love (1 Jn. 4:8). God judges (Jn. 5:22). God is involved in the lives of people (Mt. 10:30).

God is a Father. God loves you. He sent His Son, Jesus Christ, to die in your place to pay for your sins. If you trust Christ to get you to heaven, you become God's child (Jn. 1:12-13). As a child of God, if you cry, "*Abba*, Father (Gal. 4:6) seeking His face and favor, God the Father will be deeply involved in the details of your life (Mt. 6:9-13). As a father, He also disciplines His children (Heb. 12:6-9) and, yes, one day, all of God's children will stand before the Judgment Seat of Christ (Rom. 14:10).

If you have not trusted Christ, I can see why you might think God is judgmental, critical, and distant. Why not trust Christ and experience the loving care of the Father?

A Point to Ponder

HOW TO DEAL WITH YOUR ENEMIES

Do you have any enemies? Let me ask that question another way. Are there people who hate, curse, or spitefully use you? If so, Jesus has a word for you. He says we are to love our enemies (Mt. 5:44; Lk. 6:27-28). How is it possible to love our enemies?

The place to begin answering that question is with the meaning of "love." There are four different Greek words for love. *Storge* describes family affection. *Eros* is the passion between a man and a woman (always involving sex). *Phila* is the warm and tender affection between close friends. *Agape* is "unconquerable, invincible goodwill" (Barclay). The people who exercise *agape* love do not allow insult, injury, resentment, or bitterness to prevent them from seeking the other person's highest good.

Agape is the word used in the command to love your enemies. In other words, Jesus is not saying we must *like* our enemies or have tender affection toward them, only that we choose to do what is best for them. That may mean we see that the person is punished, but that decision must not be based on our desire for revenge. It will be to make that person a better person. The punishment will be remedial, not retributive.

When Jesus gave the general command to love our enemies, He added several specific ways to do that. He said, "Love your enemies, do good to those who hate you, bless those who curse you, and pray for those who spitefully use you" (Lk. 6:27-28).

A Point to Ponder

To love enemies who hate you, do good to them. "If your enemy is hungry, give him bread to eat; and if he is thirsty, give him water to drink" (Prov. 25:21).

To love enemies who curse you, bless them. The Greek word translated "bless" means "to speak well of, praise." When General Robert E. Lee spoke in complimentary terms about someone, a fellow officer said, "General, do you know that the man you spoke so highly of is one of your worst enemies and that he misses no opportunity to slander you?" "Yes," General Lee said, "but I was asked for my opinion of him, not his opinion of me."

To love enemies who spitefully use you and persecute you, pray for them. The Greek word rendered "spitefully use" means "threaten, revile, abuse." It always refers to speech (Alexander). Hence, spitefully use and persecute are hostile speech and hostile action.

To sum up, the way to deal with your enemies is to seek their highest good, which means praying for them, speaking well about them, and only doing what is good for them. WOW! That is a high standard. That is a tall order! Correct. That is why you will need the grace of God to pull it off (Heb. 4:16). If you do, you will be "perfect (mature), just as your Father in heaven is perfect" (Mt. 5:48).

A Point to Ponder

THE CASE FOR SYSTEMATIC EXPOSITION

The systematic, contextual teaching of the Word from the pulpits of America has fallen on hard times. Modern means of communication have greatly reduced our attention span (to such things as a thirty-minute sitcom) and even our ability to concentrate. The masses want to be entertained, not educated. How many people watch the Discovery Channel or the History Channel? People want to hear something that makes them feel good. In such an environment, who wants to listen to an exposition of an ancient text? That sounds like a history lecture. It gets worse. In the name of being "seeker-friendly," many modern evangelical pastors deliberately avoid such words as sin, judgment, and hell.

It is not popular, but I firmly believe that one of the greatest needs today is for pastors to practice the systematic, contextual teaching of the Word of God. I emphasize contextual because some systematic exposition is based on the pastor's theology, not the passage's context. The systematic, contextual explanation of the Scripture allows it to determine the spiritual diet of the congregation. Topical preaching (preaching on a single topic from several passages) and even most textual preaching (preaching on a single verse) lend themselves to the pastor deciding what to feed the congregation.

This is not to say that topical or textual preaching is wrong. Such sermons can contain spiritual nourishment, but if that is the constant diet, the preacher controls what is taught. The messages the congregation hears are limited to what the pastor thinks is important. As I have practiced the systematic exposition of the books of the Bible, I have found myself speaking on subjects that I would not have chosen to address left to myself. It has forced me to preach the "whole counsel of God" (Acts 20:17). It has stretched me personally and, no doubt, those who listen to me.

Unfortunately, expository preaching has also gotten a bad reputation from its friends, not its foes. Too many (one is too many) so-called expository preachers have been boring and irrelevant. In my opinion, it is a sin to bore people to death with the Living Word from God, whether I do it or someone else does it. I have worked at making it interesting and relevant. I may not have always succeeded, but that has been my aim.

I was told of a seminary professor (I believe it was Dr. Walter C. Kaiser, Jr.) told a group of pastors that once every five years, they should preach a topical sermon and, then, they should get on their knees and repent! That is strong. If taken literally, it is extreme, but he has a point. Pastors need to repent—of their preaching.

I hesitated to send this, fearing people would be critical of their pastor. That is not my intent. You need to pray for your pastor. Nevertheless, in my opinion, one of the greatest needs in America today is for the systematic, contextual teaching of the Word of God. Let us pray.

A Point to Ponder

DON'T MISS THE MESSAGE

It is possible to know the Word of God and miss its message! In Jesus' day, the scribes studied the Law. They delved into the minutiae of the Law, but they never came to grips with the essential message of what God was saying. They were preoccupied with the Law of God and missed the will of God. How is that possible?

The short answer is that people come to the Word with preconceived ideas of what they think it says. For example, Paul says, "Or do you not know that as many of us as were baptized into Christ Jesus were baptized into His death?" (Rom. 6:3). When Baptists see the word "baptism," they automatically think of immersion in water. When Lutherans come upon the term "baptism," they see an infant sprinkled with water. Both believe what they have been taught. Both believe they can "prove" their explanation with evidence that, in their opinion, should convince any "open-minded" soul. Both are so committed to their prejudgment they cannot entertain the possibility that there is another meaning of the word "baptism." Both are wrong. There is a spiritual baptism (1 Cor. 12:13)! It's dry. There is no water involved, pourer or otherwise. Romans 6 is talking about spiritual baptism. It says that we were "baptized into Christ." Spiritual, not water baptism, puts us in Christ (1 Cor. 12:13).

If it is so easy to miss the message of the Word of God, what is the solution? What do believers have to do to understand what God has said?

A Point to Ponder

Believers must come to the Word with a desire to know the *will of God*. Paul prayed that the Colossians would "be filled with the knowledge of His will in all wisdom and spiritual understanding" (Col. 1:9). Granted, the way to know the will of God is the Word of God, but it is possible to know the Word without seeing the essential message concerning *the will of God*.

Believers must come to the Word with a teachable spirit. James instructs us, "Receive with meekness the implanted word" (Jas. 1:21). To receive the Word with meekness is to receive it with a teachable spirit. When we come to the Word, our attitude must not be to prove our point of view, find material to confirm our convictions, or feel good because we did something spiritual. To discover the will of God in the Word of God, the attitude of believers must be, Lord, "Open my eyes, that I may see wondrous things from Your law" (Ps. 119:18).

Believers must come to the Word with faith. The writer to the Hebrews says that the Exodus generation did not know God's ways (Heb. 3:10). He explains that the Word of God did not profit them because it was not "mixed with faith" (Heb. 4:2).

Don't miss the message. When you open your Bible, be bent on seeking and finding the will of God. When you find it, believe it. When you believe it, do it. Then, share it.

A Point to Ponder

I CAN AFFORD IT!

What is your objective in your relationships with other people? The answer varies from person to person and from relationship to relationship.

Is your aim to be right, which is often the case when two people differ on an issue?

Is your intent to control the situation, as in a parent-small child relationship?

Is your objective to comply no matter what because you detest tension and conflict?

Is your purpose to persuade because, in your opinion, that is what the other person needs?

Each of these possibilities needs to be carefully pondered. Given the various relationships we experience, all of us have, no doubt, wrestled with each one of these at one time or another. We need to be honest with ourselves and realistic about our various relationships.

From a biblical point of view, the overriding objective in all relationships is to love the other person. Believers in Jesus Christ need to be loving because they need to be like Christ. That objective overshadows everything.

Granted, there are times when we need to speak the truth. Paul urges us to speak the truth in love (Eph. 4:15), but that should be done in love, not because we have a personal need to be right.

A Point to Ponder

There is a vast difference between speaking the truth *in love* and speaking the truth *because I need to be right*.

Granted, there are occasions when we submit to serve. Paul admonishes us to submit to one another (Eph. 5:21). There is, however, a radical difference between submitting to serve and complying to avoid conflict.

Granted, there is a time and a place to witness. We are to preach the Gospel to the whole world (Mk. 16:15), but we do not do that because we need to persuade anyone of our theological position. We talked to other people about their need for the Lord because they need it!

If we stop and think about it, we who know the Lord can afford to be loving in all about relationships. We have been drenched, soaked, and saturated with so much love we can afford to share it with others. "Beloved, if God so loved us, we also ought to love one another" (1 Jn. 4:11). When done as unto the Lord, when we give love, we get more to take its place. Wow! Under those terms, I can afford to be loving.

Those who need money sometimes manipulate others to get it from them. Those who are rich beyond their capacity to spend can afford to give money away. They have no need to get money; they can afford to give it away. So it is with love. The Lord has loved us beyond what we begin to realize. As we understand how much love we have been given, we can afford to give away much more love than we do. It should be the objective of all our relationships. In the end, we will be better off for the effort. Under the circumstances, we can afford it.

A Point to Ponder

THE GOSPEL ACCORDING TO PATRICIA

My wife, Patricia, did not attend seminary but can think like a theologian. She does not use the vocabulary of a theologian; she explains spiritual truth in ordinary terms. Here is an example. The "Gospel according to Patricia" is salvation is like a wedding ring. It was purchased for a price. In many cases, it was bought at a sacrifice. To obtain it, the recipient simply reached out with an empty hand.

Not bad. Jesus died in our place to pay for our sins. Paul told the elders at Ephesus that the church was "purchased with His (Christ's) own blood" (Acts 20:28) and he wrote that believers are the Lord's "purchased possession" (Eph. 1:14). Furthermore, all we can do is reach out an empty hand, for salvation is without cost to us. Paul plainly says that we are "justified *freely* by His grace through the redemption that is in Christ Jesus" (Rom. 3:24, italics added).

I interrupted Patricia. Like any theologian, she had more to say on the subject. She explains that having obtained it, the recipient should cherish it, honor it, and proudly display it. The proper care of it would include keeping it clean. She is right on again. Paul says, "For you were bought at a price; therefore glorify God in your body and in your spirit, which are God's" (1 Cor. 6:20).

She is not finished. Squeezing even more out of her analogy, she suggests that even if the recipient mistreated the ring, it would

A Point to Ponder

still be hers. Suppose she did not keep it as clean as she should. It still belongs to her! The price was still the same. The gift still belongs to her. The only difference was that she was not honoring it. Paul says, "For the gifts and the calling of God *are* irrevocable" (Rom. 11:29).

Patricia's final point is that the relationship between the recipient and the giver is the motivation for properly caring for the ring. As she made this last point, several passages of Scripture came to my mind. John wrote, "We love Him because He first loved us" (1 Jn. 4:19). Jesus said, "If you love Me, keep My commandments" (Jn. 14:15).

In the final analysis, it is a love relationship, isn't it? Perhaps that is why Paul says marriage illustrates our relationship to the Lord. He writes, "Husbands, love your wives, *just as Christ also loved the church and gave Himself for her*" (Eph. 5:25, italics added) and "Wives, submit to your own husbands, *as to the Lord*" (Eph. 5:22, italics added). Then, he adds, "This is a great mystery, but I speak concerning Christ and the church" (Eph. 5:32).

Every time you see a wedding ring, remember it illustrates several spiritual truths. Above all, it should remind us that salvation is primarily a relationship—a love relationship. It is not about being religious but about having a relationship with Jesus Christ by trusting Him to save us.

A Point to Ponder

THE FUNCTIONAL CHURCH

When Mary and the half-brothers of Jesus came to see Him, He used the occasion to teach a spiritual lesson. Turning to His disciples, He said, "Here are My mother and My brothers! For whoever does the will of My Father in heaven is My brother and sister and mother" (Mt. 12:49-50). That statement contains the seed of a thought that is later developed into a beautiful flower: the church is a spiritual family.

As in human families, we enter the family of God by birth (cf. Jn. 1:12-13). The will of the Father for obtaining eternal life is to believe on His Son (Jn. 6:39-40). This means realizing that Jesus died to pay for your sins and rose from the dead, you trust Him to get you to heaven.

When we trust Christ for eternal life, we are spiritual brothers and sisters with all others who have trusted Christ. Paul told Timothy, "Do not rebuke an older man but exhort *him* as a father, younger men as brothers, older women as mothers, younger as sisters, with all purity" (1 Tim. 5:1-2).

A properly functioning church family is described in Acts. "And they continued steadfastly in the apostles' doctrine and fellowship, in the breaking of bread, and in prayers" (Acts 2:42). They studied the Word together. They fellowshipped together. They shared meals together. They prayed together. The church is a spiritual family where you go to nurture and be nurtured. The church is a spiritual family where you can be loved like a brother or sister. The healthy church is a spiritual family where you can have fellowship like no other place. The church *should* be a family, a caring body of believers who love one another because of their relationship to the Lord. John Calvin said, "The church is the gathering of God's children, where they can be helped and fed like babies and then, guided by her motherly care, grow up to manhood in maturity of faith."

A functional church is a family. It has elders who exercise godly oversight, a pastor/teacher who feeds the flock, sheep who eat, and believers who fellowship with one another and reproduce. The love among the sheep attracts others. "A new commandment I give to you, that you love one another; as I have loved you, that you also love one another. By this all will know that you are My disciples, if you have love for one another" (Jn. 13:34-35).

Unfortunately, a church can be nothing more than a collection of individuals, traditions, preferences, or, worse, prejudices. It is no wonder that power plays and petty feuds characterize such unbiblical collections.

Some dysfunctional churches act like corporations. They have a board of directors. The pastors function as CEOs. They have a marketing plan to attract new customers. The stockholders sit in the pews each week, passing judgment on the performance of the board and CEO. The Lord weeps as a Father who yearns for His children to be a loving family.

A Point to Ponder

WHO WANTS TO DEAL WITH A TAXMAN?

Well, it is tax time again. Who wants to deal with tax collectors? If you think that is bad now, you should reflect on how it once was.

In first-century Palestine, tax officials were detested and classed as the vilest of men. When Jews served as taxmen, they were regarded as outcasts from society. They were disqualified as judges and witnesses in court, and they were excommunicated from the synagogue. By being a tax collector, these Jews were working for the despised Romans.

The other side of the tax coin was the taxes themselves. People never knew how much they had to pay. Tax collectors extracted as much as they possibly could from each individual. They gave the Romans what was required by law. Then, they lined their own pockets with the surplus. Lucian, a Greek writer, ranked tax-gatherers with 'adulterers, panderers, flatterers and sycophants." Who would want to deal with such people?

Jesus. As we all know, Jesus is in the business of saving sinners. So, I guess tax collectors are candidates for the Jesus business. Jesus saved tax collectors alright, but He went way beyond that. He invited one such converted sinner to be an Apostle!

Matthew was a taxman. Jesus invited this social outcast to "Follow Me" (Mt. 9:9) as a disciple. Later, Matthew was appointed to be an Apostle. Barclay says, "Jesus wanted the man no one else

A Point to Ponder

wanted. He offered his friendship to the man whom all others would have scorned to call friend."

Matthew illustrates there is hope for sinners. In fact, being a sinner is part of what it takes to be saved. Jesus saves sinners, not those who think they are righteous. He says, "I did not come to call the righteous, but sinners, to repentance" (Mt. 9:13). Then, lo and behold, Jesus invites those who have trusted Him for the gift of eternal life to follow Him. Jesus wants to save sinners and use them in His service.

Matthew immediately followed Jesus. He gave up his profession to follow Jesus, which was remarkable. Once he gave up his profession, he could not resume it, like a fisherman could, because his position would have been filled.

Matthew left everything but one thing—his pen. His Gospel is one of the most important documents of all history, the first written account of the teaching of Jesus. Barclay observes, "Had Matthew refused the call, he would have had local ill-fame as the follower of a disreputable trade which all men hated; because he answered the call, he gained worldwide fame as the man who gave men the record of the words of Jesus."

There is good news from this tax collector. Matthew's message to you is that he knows from personal experience that if you trust Jesus Christ for the gift of eternal life, you will be given that gift because Jesus died in your place to pay for your sin. This tax collector also has more good news for you. If you follow Christ, He will use you.

A Point to Ponder

VITAL VIRTUES

Some time ago, I wrote an article in which I pointed out that in his book *Mere Christianity*, C. S. Lewis has a chapter on the seven virtues. The three "theological" virtues (faith, hope, and love) are Christian virtues and the four "cardinal" virtues (prudence, temperance, justice, and fortitude) are those all civilized people recognize. After decades of studying the New Testament, I recently realized there are three other virtues I have tried to develop in my life. I call them the "vital virtues." One of the meanings of the English word "vital" is "necessary to the continuation of life." These virtues are necessary for a growing spiritual life.

A Grateful Attitude At a critical point in describing virtues, Paul adds, "Be thankful" (Col. 3:15). He also says, "In everything, give thanks" because that is the will of God for you (1 Thess. 5:18). God puts a premium of being grateful, perhaps because as Cicero points out, "A thankful heart is the parent of all virtues." Paul says people have a chance to know God through creation but do not respond to Him, nor are they thankful (Rom. 1:20-21). Shakespeare wrote, "I hate ingratitude more in a man than lying, vainness, babbling, drunkenness or any taint of vice."

Joyful Outlook At significant junctions in their writings, James, Peter, and Paul speak about handling the trials of life, which include inconveniences, irritations, and interruptions. Each one says the same thing, "count it a joy" (Jas. 1:2; 1 Pet. 1:6; Rom.5:3). The

A Point to Ponder

Greek word rendered "glory" in Rom. 5:3 is the same one translated "rejoice" in Rom. 5:2). They are not saying that the trials, troubles, and tribulations are enjoyable. Peter says they are so painful, they cause grief (1 Pet. 1:6). The Apostles are teaching believers can rejoice, realizing difficulties are opportunities to grow. For example, tribulation produces perseverance (Rom. 5:3) and character (Rom. 5:4).

Servant's Mindset At a strategic place in his Gospel, Mark says, "For even the Son of Man did not come to be served, but to serve, and to give His life a ransom for many" (Mk. 10:45). Paul points out that although Jesus was equal with God, He became a servant (Phil. 2:6-7). Paul exhorts us to have the mind of Christ (Phil. 2:5). The servant's mindset is not to be loved but to love, not to be served but to serve.

These three virtues relate to God (a grateful heart), ourselves (a joyful outlook), and others (a servant's mindset). They are vital because dealing with life means dealing with relationships and problems.

These "vital virtues" need to be deliberately practiced until they become habits that are second nature. When they become second nature, they are *our* virtues. That is what I want to add to my life. How about you?

A Point to Ponder

HAVE YOU GROWN UP YET?

At what age is a person "grown up?" 18? 21? 30? 40? If you're a teenager, you are undoubtedly convinced that when you reach 18, you will have finally "grown up." After all, you are "of age." Even the government recognizes that. You can vote!

Those in their early twenties look back to when they were 18 and are amazed at how much they have grown in a few short years. The same thing could be said of those who reached the milestones of 30, 40, or 50. At what age should we consider ourselves "grown up?" Is it "When you do not unscrew your Oreos anymore?"

Age is not the issue. We have all known eighteen-year-olds who were mature beyond their years and 80-year-olds who were immature. Antonio Villaraigosa, the mayor of Los Angeles, announced that he and his wife were getting a divorce. Some felt that how Villaraigosa handled the press conference, called to announce his divorce, was childish. Steve Lopez, a reporter for the *Los Angeles Times*, wrote an article entitled "Mr. Mayor: Shut Up, Grow Up, Slow Down" (*Los Angeles Times*, June 14, 2007). Villaraigosa is 54 years old! Imagine telling a 54-year-old to shut up and grow up. Come to think of it, maybe there are other "older people" who need that message.

Perhaps it takes longer to grow up than we think. In the Old Testament, a priest had to be thirty years old before he could serve in the Tabernacle (Num. 4:3, 23, 30, 35, 47). Jesus was about thirty

A Point to Ponder

before He began His ministry (Lk. 3:23). The Old Testament does not say how old Moses was when he first attempted to deliver the Israelites from bondage. Stephen says he was forty (Acts 7:23). What is interesting is the way the Old Testament describes the same event. It says, "Now it came to pass in those days, when Moses was grown" (Ex. 2:11). Does that imply that Moses was not "grown up" until he was forty? In his commentary on the book of Acts, Howard Marshall says, "'Forty' was the age at which a person had 'grown up' (Ex. 2:11).

Reaching a certain age is not the criteria for being "grown up." Neither is it graduating from college, having children, being a mayor, or being President of the United States. Young people can make "grown-up" decisions and older people can make foolish decisions. Experience is not the measure of having arrived. Not even suffering will do the trick. As Anne Morrow Lindbergh says, "I do not believe that suffering teaches. If suffering alone taught, all the world would be wise, since everyone suffers. To suffering must be added mourning, understanding, patience, love, openness, and the willingness to remain vulnerable."

Ah, that is it. It is not living enough years. It is not having enough experience. It is not even suffering. It is learning through the years from the experiences and the suffering (Jas. 1:2-8; Rom. 5:1-4; 1 Pet. 1:6-7). Don't just grow older; grow up.

A Point to Ponder

THE VOLUME OF SILENCE

Anyone who knows anything about baseball knows that Hank Aaron hit more home runs than anyone else—755. Sports fans also know that Barry Bonds is chasing that record. At this writing, he has hit 754 home runs in his career, one shy of the all-time record. It is only a matter of time before Bonds slams more balls over the fence and smashes the record.

Barry Bonds may be about to break one of the most sacred records in all of sports, but Bonds has a problem. He is accused of having taken performance-enhancing steroids. In fact, he is currently under investigation for that accusation.

The plot thickens. Bonds, who plays for the Giants, may break the home run record when he plays the Dodgers next week! The San Francisco Giants are the arch-rivals of the Los Angeles Dodgers and have been ever since they were the New York Giants playing the Brooklyn Dodgers. Bill Plaschke, a sports writer for the *Los Angeles Times*, expresses the feelings of many Dodger fans, "The player you despise most, playing for the team you hate most, probably will have the chance to break baseball's greatest record in your backyard." He adds, "If you are there, what will you do?"

What should Dodger fans do if Barry Bonds hits a home run in Dodger Stadium next week that breaks the all-time home-run record? Should they cheer, or should they boo, believing he cheated by using steroids? When Bonds hit home run number 754, one shy

A Point to Ponder

of the all-time record, it was shown on the screen at Angel Stadium. Bonds was booed.

Plaschke says if it happens in Dodger Stadium, booing might seem perfect at the time, but twenty years from now, it will seem petty. He suggests silence. He concludes, "Greet the loudest hit in baseball history with a silence that will fill Dodger Stadium with dignified dissent, a silence that might fill someone's ear hole with a tad of remorse. A silence that will last a lifetime. Talk about a shot heard round the world."

I am not sure what Dodger fans should do if they are faced with a record-breaking home run in their backyard, but I know that silence is sometimes louder than a shout. Every husband knows that when his wife says nothing, she is shouting. If he is smart, he hears volumes. The less she says, the more he hears.

The Scripture recognizes the volume of silence. To wives living with an unbelieving husband, Peter recommends living a godly life and having "a gentle and quiet spirit" (1 Pet. 3:4). He says such is "very precious in the sight of God." Paul urges believers to "aspire to lead a quiet life" and mind their own business (1 Thess 4:11). He also says they should "lead a quiet and peaceable life in all godliness and reverence" (1 Tim. 2:2).

It is appropriate sometimes to be slow to speak (Jas. 1:19) and sometimes to be silent. Silence can speak volumes.

PS: This was written on July 28, 2007. Barry Bonds hit home run number 755 on August 4 in San Diego. His career total was 762. As of the end of the season in 2023, he holds the record.

A Point to Ponder

BIBLICAL ILLITERACY

As the story goes, a pastor visits the children's class. The teacher said, "Pastor, we're studying Joshua this morning." "That's wonderful," said the pastor, "Let's see what you're learning. Who tore down the walls of Jericho?" Little Billy shyly raised his hand and offered, "Pastor, I didn't do it." Taken aback, the pastor asked, "Come on, now, who tore down the walls of Jericho?" The teacher interrupted, "Pastor, Billy's a good boy. If he says he didn't do it, I believe he didn't do it." Flustered, the pastor went to the Sunday school director and related the story to him. The director, looking worried, explained, "Well, sir, we've had some problems with Billy before. Let me talk to him and see what we can do." Really bothered now by the answers of the teacher and the director, the pastor approached the deacons and related the whole story, including the responses of the teacher and the director. A white-haired gentleman thoughtfully stroked his chin and said, "Well, Pastor, I move we just take the money from the general fund to pay for the walls and leave it at that."

Unfortunately, it is not a joke. People in America and even believers in church do not know the Bible. Recently, I was thumbing through a magazine I received, when I found an article that once again documents the lack of knowledge of the Scriptures in this country. It reports that Stephen Prothero, the religion department chair at Boston University, has written a book entitled *Religious*

A Point to Ponder

Literacy: What Every American Needs to Know—and Doesn't. In it, he claims that although the United States is arguably the most religious nation in the developed world, it is also the most religiously ignorant. Here is what Prothero found. Of those polled, less than half could identify the Bible's first book, only half could name one of the four Gospels, and only one in three knew who delivered the Sermon on the Mount. More than 10 percent think that Joan of Arc was Noah's wife. Approximately 75 percent of adults believe the Bible teaches that "God helps those who help themselves." (Benjamin Franklin said that.) Moreover, Prothero also discovered that evangelicals fared only slightly better than non-evangelicals!

How can people consider themselves educated and not know about the all-time best seller? As the article says, "This lack of Biblical proficiency is only one manifestation of a more general decline in the public's cultural and civic knowledge. According to polls conducted by the National Constitution Center, only one-third of Americans can name even one of the rights protected by the First Amendment" ("Ignorance of the Bible Isn't Bliss," *Biblical Archaeology Review*, September/October 2007, p. 15).

It is much more serious than being uneducated. The Word of God tells us how to get to heaven and be spiritually mature (2 Tim. 3:15-17). How can we who know the Lord and be spiritually mature without knowing His Word? We can't.

A Point to Ponder

A MODEST POLITICAL PROPOSAL

Perhaps I should begin with a disclaimer. I am not a politician, a political commentator, or a political science professor. I am a citizen and I vote. That said, I would like to make a modest political proposal.

I propose that every member of every city council, all members of all 50 states' governing bodies, and each member of the US Congress be required to read a bill in its entirety before voting on it. Reading a summary of a bill is not acceptable, nor can they have someone else read it for them. Moreover, to demonstrate that they have read each bill, they must take and pass an exam on it before they are allowed to vote. All who vote must pass the exam one week before they vote to give them time to think about what they are about to do. In addition, they must attend the sessions of their respective bodies or be removed from office the day they arrive at a failing grade in attendance. Finally, they must publish their pork on a website.

I further propose that citizens who vote must take and pass an exam on what every candidate "says" he or she will do once in office before they are allowed to vote. Like politicians, each citizen must pass the exam at least one week before casting a ballot.

I have one more modest political proposal. All who know the Lord should pray for all who are in office at every level of government. The first two proposals are my ideas. The third is God's idea. Paul wrote, "Therefore I exhort first of all that supplications, prayers, intercessions, *and* giving of thanks be made for all men, for kings and all who are in authority, that we may lead a quiet and peaceable life in all godliness and reverence. For this *is* good and acceptable in the sight of God our Savior, who desires all men to be saved and to come to the knowledge of the truth. For *there is* one God and one Mediator between God and men, *the* Man Christ Jesus, who gave Himself a ransom for all" (1 Tim. 2:1-6). The purpose of this kind of praying is that "we" (believers) may lead a quiet and peaceable life in all godliness and reverence, not that "they" (politicians) might lead such a life. In other words, we are to pray that government governs in such a way that we can live in peace. The ultimate purpose of these prayers is that people be saved. God wants all to be saved. Praying for those in authority so that peace will prevail enables the gospel to spread. Freedom from war and persecution facilitates the spread of the gospel (Hendriksen). The book of Acts records, "Then the churches throughout all Judea, Galilee, and Samaria had peace and were edified and walking in the fear of the Lord and in the comfort of the Holy Spirit, they were multiplied" (Acts 9:31).

The objection will no doubt be that it would cost too much to give and grade all those exams. Granted, it would be expensive, but the way it is being done now costs more. Also, prayer does not cost dollars, only time.

A Point to Ponder

HOW TO HANDLE CREDIT CARDS

Credit is an economic fact of life. We are forced to use it. Unless you are exceedingly wealthy, you must use credit to purchase a house or a car.

The problem with credit today is credit cards. On the one hand, it is difficult to function in our society without a credit card. A good credit card repayment history establishes your credit rating, making obtaining a mortgage loan possible. People have been turned down for a mortgage loan because they never had credit card debt. It is harder to get a mortgage loan with no credit history than with a bad credit history! Credit cards make online purchases faster and easier. You need a credit card to rent a car, although most firms allow you to pay the final bill with your debit card. You need a credit card to guarantee a late arrival at a motel.

On the other hand, many do not correctly use credit cards; they abuse them. Wise Solomon warned, "The rich rules over the poor, and the borrower *is* servant to the lender" (Prov. 22:7). Credit is not a sin. Just know that when you borrow, you are working for the lender. As Matthew Henry wrote, "Sell not your liberty to gratify your luxury."

What is the proper use of credit cards? Listen to an expert.

According to the *Guinness Book of Records*, Walter Cavanagh of Santa Clara, California, holds the record for having active credit cards. He has 1496 of them! He has oil company credit cards, bank

A Point to Ponder

credit cards, credit cards from ice cream places, and shoe stores. He even has a card from Harry's shop for big and tall men—although he is neither. With his cards, he has access to $1.7 million in instant credit.

Cavanagh is also the proud owner of the world's largest wallet. It is a custom-made, 38-pound wallet that holds 800 hundred credit cards in plastic sleeves that would stretch 30 stories.

Cavanagh's collection began as a bet. In the early 1970s, he bet with a buddy to see who could collect the most credit cards by the end of the year. The winner won dinner. Cavanagh won. His friend only gathered 138; Cavanagh collected 143. Someone at a party who found out about the collection suggested he notify Guinness. After Guinness entered him into the record book, he realized that to keep up his title, he would have to keep collecting.

Although Cavanagh possesses 1496 credit cards, he is a one-card guy. Furthermore, he pays off that one card in full each month. This retired financial planner says, "What good is putting money in a retirement plan if you're paying 18% on a credit card at the same time?" His philosophy is, "Never use a credit card to buy anything you can't pay off in a couple of months. If you don't have the discipline, you shouldn't have the cards."

We need to learn to use, not abuse, credit cards.

A Point to Ponder

ROMNEY'S RELIGION

As a pastor, I should stay out of politics. However, when politicians make theological statements, it is my duty to clarify, if necessary, theological issues. So here I go again. The last time I did this was when Kerry made an illogical statement concerning a fetus. (See "Kerry's Logic" above.)

Recently, Mitt Romney delivered a defense of religious liberties. He vowed to stand proudly by his beliefs as a member of the Church of Jesus Christ of Latter-Day Saints. He also said, "I believe that Jesus Christ is the Son of God and the Savior of mankind" and "My church's beliefs about Christ may not all be those of other faiths."

Romney is right about his religion; it has different beliefs than the Scripture about Christ and a number of other things. Their official doctrinal statement says:

Article 3   We believe that through the atonement of Christ, all mankind may be saved by obedience to the laws and ordinances of the gospel.

Article 4   We believe that the first principles and ordinances of the gospel are: 1) faith in the Lord Jesus Christ, 2) repentance 3) baptism by immersion for the remission of sins, 4) laying on of hands for the gift of the Holy Ghost.

Article 8   We believe the Bible to be the Word of God as far as it is translated correctly; we also believe the Book of Mormon to be the Word of God.

A Point to Ponder

That is only the beginning. They also believe Adam was God, Jesus was the natural offspring of Adam and Mary, Jesus was a polygamist who married two Marys and Martha and Jesus had children.

What makes Mormonism radically different from biblical Christianity is that the Bible teaches Jesus is God (Jn. 1:1), who became a man (Jn. 1:14—Christmas!), who died for our sins and rose from the dead (1 Cor. 15:3-4—Good Friday and Easter) and that salvation is by faith alone in Christ alone (Eph, 2:8-9). While Mormons *say* they believe in the Trinity and the deity of Christ, they *actually* believe in another Jesus (2 Cor. 11:4) and another Gospel (Gal. 1:6). Mormons are sincere, hardworking, family-oriented people, but *doctrinally* they are just plain wrong.

If nominated and elected, Mitt Romney may make a good president. As a Christian, what bothers me is that a Mormon president would give Mormonism a form of legitimacy in the US and around the world. That is a spiritual issue, not a political one, and spiritual issues should take precedence over all other issues.

A Point to Ponder

CONTINUE!

As I was reading the book of Acts, I was struck by the fact that Paul "persuaded them to continue in the grace of God" (Acts 13:43). He had just preached in the synagogue at Antioch in Pisidia. He told the congregation of Jews and Gentile proselytes that God had raised up a Savior from the lineage of David. He goes on to proclaim the message of "salvation" (Acts 13:26), namely, that Jesus died (Acts 13:27-28, Gal. 3:1), that He was buried (Acts 13:29), that He rose from the dead (Acts 13:30, 33-37) and that He was seen (Acts 13:31). In other words, Paul preached the gospel (1 Cor. 15:1-8). Paul concluded his sermon by telling the congregation that those who believe are forgiven and justified (Acts 13:38). In short, he preached the gospel of the grace of God (Acts 20:24). It was after the service that Paul persuaded those who had believed to continue in the grace of God. That sermon is not recorded. I wish it had been.

What does Paul mean by continuing in the grace of God? Peter says believers are to "grow in the grace and knowledge of our Lord and Savior Jesus Christ" (2 Pet. 3:18). Peter also informs us that if we have "tasted that the Lord *is* gracious" (1 Pet. 2:3), we should lay aside "all malice, all deceit, hypocrisy, envy, and all evil speaking," and "as newborn babes, desire the pure milk of the word" that we may grow (1 Pet 2:1-2). Surely, at least part of growing in the grace of God is setting aside sin and saturating our minds with the Word of God.

A Point to Ponder

There is another element in growing in the grace of God. The writer to the Hebrews urges believers to "come boldly to the throne of grace, that we may obtain mercy and find grace to help in time of need" (Heb. 4:16). It is only as we seek God's grace that we have the power to set aside sin and obey God's will as revealed in and gleaned from His Word. God told Paul, "My grace is sufficient for you" (2 Cor. 12:9). Then He explained to Paul, "For My *strength* is made perfect in weakness" (2 Cor. 12:9, italics added). Paul responded, "Therefore most gladly I will rather boast in my infirmities, that the *power* of Christ may rest upon me" (2 Cor. 12:9, italics added). Paul knew that as he sought the grace of God to do the will of God, He would experience the power of God.

The problem is that believers can fail to avail themselves of the grace and power available to them. That is why the writer to the Hebrews warns believers to be careful "lest anyone fall short of the grace of God" (Heb. 12:15).

Hence, Paul told those saved by God's grace to continue in God's grace. We are saved when we realize that we cannot save ourselves and we must depend on Jesus Christ, the One who died for our sins and rose from the dead, to get us to heaven. Likewise, we *continue* in the grace of God when we realize that without Him, we can do nothing and depend on Him for the grace and power to do His will.

A Point to Ponder

A TRIBUTE TO JACK

Recently, a dear friend of mine went to be with the Lord. Because of some common experience and interest, Jack Moulton was a friend like no other I have ever had.

I met Jack several years ago, but we became fast friends in the last year or so. At the time, he lived in Dallas. Later, when he married Glenda, the love of his life, he moved to Scottsdale, Arizona. We were phone pals. We talked on the phone frequently and at length.

At times, like two old soldiers, Jack and I told war stories. He told me about his numerous campaigns—in Texas, New Mexico, and Arizona. He had a few defeats and many victories. In the battle of life, Jack was a veteran of many crusades. I told him about my battles, scars, and a few successes. I will miss listening to his war stories.

At other times, like two specialists on the New York Stock Exchange floor, Jack and I shared trade secrets. Actually, this was very one-sided. Jack was a veteran with decades of experience. I was the kid sitting at his feet with awe and wonder. When Jack began investing in stocks, better than thirty years ago, the fee per trade was $250. In the last year, he became a day trader, paying $1.00 per trade. I listened and learned a lot. I will miss listening to his financial exploits.

Like two "theologians," Jack and I often grappled with difficult theological issues. We covered a wide range of

A Point to Ponder

theological problems.

The last one we struggled with was, by far and away, the one we delved into the most.

In some circles, the theological issue being debated is how much a person must know to come to Christ. More specifically, must people know about the cross and, if so, how much must they understand about it? Some are saying it is not necessary to know that Jesus died, only that He is the One who grants eternal life.

Because of my involvement in evangelism, people ask me about this issue. As a result, a few months ago, I began an in-depth study of the word "believe" in the Gospel of John. When I told Jack what I was doing, he and I began to discuss it by the hour—on the phone. I shared my conclusions with him, and he shared his insights with me.

For example, one day, Jack called to remind me that Paul spoke of the offense of the cross. Indeed, Paul wrote, "I, brethren, if I still preach circumcision, why do I still suffer persecution? Then the offense of the cross has ceased" (Gal. 5:11). Jack's point was that since it is the cross that offends people if it is possible to lead people to Christ without telling them about the cross, Paul would have done it, but he did not. He was willing to suffer persecution rather than not tell people Jesus died for their sins on the cross. Excellent point, Jack, excellent point!

Jack died clinging to the cross. We should all learn that lesson from my friend, Jack.

A Point to Ponder

WHY GOOD FRIDAY?

A lady asked me, "Why did Jesus have to die for God to forgive us? Why did not God just say, 'You are forgiven' without Jesus having to die?" After all, she argued, "He is God."

Paul answers that question in Romans 3. He explains that "all have sinned and fall short of the glory of God" (Rom. 3:23). To say that all have sinned does not mean that all have committed all sins, but all have committed some sin. Every individual has fallen short of God's perfect standard. Nevertheless, God provides righteousness to all, but it is only available to all who will trust Christ (Rom. 3:22).

This justification is "through the redemption that is in Christ Jesus, whom God set forth to be a propitiation by His blood, through faith" (Rom. 3:24-25, italics added). The means of justification (being declared righteous), redemption (having one's sins paid for), and propitiation (satisfaction) is the death of Christ. The death of Christ satisfied the righteous demand of God that death be paid for sin.

These benefits of His death are personally obtained through faith. In the lyrics of William Cowper, "There is a fountain filled with blood, drawn from Immanuel's veins; and sinners plunged beneath that flood, lose all their guilty stains."

Paul goes on to explain that God did it this way "to demonstrate His righteousness" (Rom. 3:26), that He might be "just and the

A Point to Ponder

justifier of the one who has faith in Jesus" (Rom. 3:26). Because Christ paid for sin, God can be both righteous and at the same time can declare righteous anyone who believes in Christ.

Donald Grey Barnhouse illustrates this by telling the story of an oriental monarch known for his justice. He made a law that certain crimes would be punishable by the criminal losing both eyes. No sooner was the law on the books than someone who had broken that law was brought before his tribunal. The problem was that the guilty criminal was his son. The father commanded that the law be carried out. When one eye of the son was put out, the king stepped from the throne and said, "Release him." He then took his son's place and had one of his own eyes burned out. Thus, the law was upheld, and at the same time, he was able to sacrifice himself for his son. As Barnhouse said, "In a far more wonderful way at the cross, love and justice kissed each other." It is not a perfect illustration. Jesus paid it all. He had both eyes put out, so to speak, but the point is that since the just penalty of sin is death, by sending His Son to die for sin, God is just when He justifies (declares righteous) guilty sinners.

After explaining Romans 3 to the lady who asked the question, I added, "I know of no religion or philosophy that even comes close to explaining justice and love." Good Friday is the good news that love and justice kissed each other.

A Point to Ponder

HAPPY BIRTHDAY

Today is my birthday. I am 50 years old today [April 8, 2008]. Those who know me well will be surprised that I am claiming April 8 as my birthday because they know I was born in September and I am over 50 years old. So, I need to explain.

Fifty years ago today, I was a senior in high school. Because of a girl, I began attending the Central Baptist Church in Pensacola, Florida. That church brought in a visiting pastor named Hugh Pyle to conduct a revival meeting. That did not interest me—at all. However, something the visiting speaker said Sunday morning got my attention. He said that after every weeknight service, he would meet with the teenagers and discuss "Love, Courtship. and Marriage." I attended those weeknight services to hear what he said about love, dating, and marriage.

After the session on Tuesday night, April 8, 1958, I was headed to my car when the pastor of the church, C. Sumner Wemp, stopped me. He asked me if I knew for sure I was going to heaven.

At the time, I thought if anyone had a crack at heaven, I did. Because my father was from Greece and was a Greek Orthodox, I had been baptized in the Greek Orthodox Church. Moreover, when I started dating, a girl took me to a Baptist church, where, at her coaching, I went forward and was baptized. From my point of view, I was a member of two churches. That ought to cover it. Besides, I had been baptized twice. Since the Greek Orthodox practice triune immersion, I had been dipped in baptismal waters four times. Surely I had points in my favor.

Nevertheless, when the pastor asked me if I knew *for sure* I was going to heaven, I had to admit I did not. I gave him my story, but he was unimpressed. So he invited me to his office to tell me how I could know for sure I was going to heaven. Because I was a Greek Orthodox, he used a Catholic Bible to explain to me that I was a sinner, that Jesus suffered and died for my sins, and that I needed to trust Jesus Christ to get to heaven.

I remember realizing that before God, I was a sinner, but what really came through to me that night was that God loved me so much that He sent His Son to die for me (Rom. 5:8). I had known Jesus died, but I had never understood that His death paid for my sins and that it made it possible for me to go to heaven. I was overwhelmed. I wept. I trusted Christ that night and felt as if a heavy weight had been lifted off me. I was overjoyed. Later, when I got home, my mother took one look at me and said, "What happened to you?"

That night, I was born again, this time spiritually. I became a member of God's family. From that night until this day, I have never doubted that God is my Father and heaven is my home. So you see, April 8 is my birthday—my spiritual birthday.

Now, that is what I call a "happy" birthday.

A Point to Ponder

THE MOST IMPORTANT ROOM IN THE HOUSE

Which room in your house would you say is the most important?

A case could be made for the bedroom being the most important. Apartments and houses are known by the number of bedrooms they have. It is the most used room in the house. At least, we spend more time in it than in any other room. In what other room do we spend eight hours a day (OK, a night)?

Many wives and mothers might argue for the kitchen. When they look for a house, they want the right kitchen. The definition of "right" varies from person to person, but whoever does the cooking, whether a man or a woman, believes that the kitchen is important.

Some might suggest that the dining room is critical to family life. Historically, in this country, as well as others, families eat together. Unfortunately, family time around the table has been sacrificed on the altar of busy schedules, but those who experience it when it is done right realize how valuable it is. They cherish those times in the family dining room.

Today, most would probably vote for the den. That is where the family gathers to watch TV or play the Wii. It is the fun room of the house.

Maybe the most important is the one you need at the moment. If you are sleepy, it is the bedroom. If you are hungry, it is the kitchen. If you want to watch a TV program, it is the den or wherever the

A Point to Ponder

TV is located. If you need a shower or if nature is calling, the bathroom is indispensable.

A laundry room is handy. If you have ever had to go out to a Laundromat, you appreciate the laundry room. Those who have and enjoy an exercise room would not want to live in a house that did not have one.

What kind of house would you have if you had the money to build your dream house? How many bedrooms would you have put in it? What other rooms would you include? Would you have an exercise room? A game room? Some houses in Southern California have a movie room, and some even have a bowling alley.

Ideally, every home should have at least a "prayer closet." Jesus taught, "When you pray, you shall not be like the hypocrites. For they love to pray standing in the synagogues and on the corners of the streets, that they may be seen by men. Assuredly, I say to you, they have their reward. But you, when you pray, go into your room, and when you have shut your door, pray to your Father who *is* in the secret *place;* and your Father who sees in secret will reward you openly" (Mt. 6:5-6). For most people, having a separate room just for prayer is impossible, but every home should have a private place where you can pray. Such a place is the most important place in the house.

A Point to Ponder

THE 80-20 RULE

Many years ago, I heard about the 80-20 rule. The 80-20 rule states that 80% of the work is done by 20% of the workers; 80% of the money is given by 20% of givers. Women say they wear 20% of their clothes 80% of the time.

At the time, I was conducting evangelistic meetings. As an evangelist, it was obvious to me that only a small percentage of the people brought most visitors to the services. I used to say that if only a few more people in the church went to work to bring people to the meetings, I would have very successful results.

Recently, I discovered the origin of the 80-20 rule. In the 19th and 20th centuries, Vilfredo Pareto, an Italian economist, wrote about the unequal distribution of wealth. He observed that 80% of income in Italy went to 20% of the population. In 1937, Joseph M. Juran coined the Pareto Principle, named after Vilfredo Pareto. The Pareto Principle, also known as the 80-20 rule, states that 80% of the effect comes from 20% of the cause. Applied to business, it means that 80% of the sales come from 20% of the customers or 80% of production errors come from 20% of the workers. Simply put, the bulk of the effect comes from relatively few contributors. The principle is used in management to separate the "useful many" from the "vital few." In the final analysis, it is a way to focus on what is essential and not get lost in what is not necessary.

It should be pointed out that the 80-20 idea is a principle, not

A Point to Ponder

a law. In real life, 20% of the workers could create 100% of the result—or 80%, 40%, or 20%. At best, the 80-20 rule is a rough guideline. Nevertheless, the point is still well taken: life is not fair; it is uneven. Returns and rewards for effect are not distributed evenly. In a perfect world, every worker would contribute the same amount of work.

If you are in the 20% (Good for you.), don't pay too much attention to the 80% who don't put in the same effort as you do. I have seen faithful workers develop a bad attitude because they felt they had to "do all the work." In the first place, the reality is the *few* do the *most*.

More importantly, if you are a disciple of Jesus Christ and you do all you do as unto Him, you will be rewarded by Him. Paul told slaves to obey their masters, "not with eye-service, as men-pleasers, but in sincerity of heart, fearing God" (Col. 3:22). Then, he added, "and whatever you do, do it heartily, as to the Lord and not to men knowing that from the Lord you will receive the reward of the inheritance; for you serve the Lord Christ" (Col. 3:23-24). Paul told slaves, who had no choice, to obey their masters, but to do everything as if they were working for the Lord. Furthermore, those who do will be rewarded by the Lord. So, be part of the 20%—just make sure you do it as unto the Lord. It will help your attitude now and you will get your reward later.

A Point to Ponder

BE SENSIBLE

May I share a word with you? It is a Greek word that appears sixteen times in the New Testament. Observing its richness of meaning, one scholar observed there are several shades of meaning in it and there is no one precise English equivalent. All attempts at translation prove too narrow. That explains why there are so many different translations of this word in the New Testament, such as *sound mind*, *sober-minded*, *self-controlled*, *temperate*, and *discreet*.

This word means to be sane, that is, being in one's right mind, not being crazy (Mk. 5:15; Lk. 8:35; Acts 26:25; 2 Cor. 5:13), but it is much more than that. It describes a sane, sensible, sober-minded, self-controlled person. In other words, this word has two basic nuances: sound, sane sense and self-control that curbs desires and impulses.

People with this characteristic are not only sane; they are sensible. This word describes someone who is facing things realistically, free from delusion. It is thinking about and evaluating situations maturely and correctly.

People with this characteristic are not only sensible, they are self-controlled. This word depicts sound judgment that exercises restraint and is not impulsive. It does not allow emotion to take over; it keeps cool under pressure. When people with this quality get angry, they control it instead of it controlling them.

Jeremy Taylor says, "It is reason's girdle and passion's bridle."

A Point to Ponder

Barclay says it characterizes people who see what things are important and what things are not important; it is not swept away by sudden and capricious and transitory enthusiasms. It is only when we see the affairs and the activities of earth in the light of eternity that we see them in their proper proportions and their proper importance. It is when God is given His proper place that all things take their proper places.

This is an equal opportunity word. Elders must have it (1 Tim. 3:2; Titus 1:8). Older men should possess it (Titus 2:2), as should older women (Titus 2:5), younger men (Titus 2:6) and younger women (1 Tim. 2:9, 2:15; Titus 2:4). All believers are to think like this (Rom. 12:3) and live like this (Titus 2:12).

In Romans 12:3, this word is rendered "think soberly." When believers first trust Christ, they are given a spiritual gift. That gift should determine their estimate of themselves and their place in the body of Christ. Thus, they will have a sane, sober estimate of themselves and not think too highly of themselves, that is, be puffed up with an idea of their own self-importance.

In short, be sensible. Exercise more self-control. I can imagine someone saying, "I need more of that." There is hope. This same word is used of the way we pray (1 Pet. 4:7) and God grants us the ability to be what He wants us to be (2 Tim. 1:7).

A Point to Ponder

TO BE LIKE CHRIST

The plan of God is for believers *"to be* conformed to the image of His Son" (Rom. 8:29). Just exactly what is true of Christ that is supposed to be true of us? What are the specifics? To define all that is involved in being like Christ and describe what that means in a variety of situations cannot be done in a short article. It would take a book—the New Testament! What *can* be done in a short space is to outline the overall concept.

While Christ has many characteristics, they can be grouped around two concepts. According to John, Jesus, who is God (Jn. 1:1) in the flesh (Jn. 1:14), is full of grace and truth (Jn. 1:17). Around the two fundamental attributes of *grace* and *truth* can be grouped all the qualities of godliness. The Old Testament emphasizes that God is holy (Lev. 11:44) and the New Testament stresses "God is love" (1 Jn. 4:8). Around holiness can be grouped such attributes as truth, justice, and righteousness. Clustered around love is grace and mercy. To be Christ-like, believers must be both holy (truthful, just) and loving (gracious).

When Moses asked to see God, he was given a list of seven characteristics of God (Ex. 34:5-7). The list contains three pairs of characteristics referring to His mercy and a single attribute affirming His justice. Clearly, mercy predominates, but this list is essentially two basic virtues: mercy and justice, which are similar to grace and truth.

A Point to Ponder

The Psalmist said, "For Your mercy *is* great above the heavens, and Your truth *reaches* to the clouds" (Ps. 108:4). Sounds similar to grace and truth. Jesus told the scribes and Pharisees that they "neglected the weightier *matters* of the law: justice and mercy and faith" (Mt. 23:23). He is highlighting the most predominant aspects of the Mosaic Law as justice and mercy. The ultimate in Christ-like maturity is "speaking the truth in love" (Eph. 4:15; cf. 1 Tim. 6:11, 2 Tim. 2:22).

Righteousness is doing what is *right*. Love is doing what is *best* for other people. It is seeking their highest good. Christ-likeness is being both righteous and loving. These two things are not in conflict with each other. What is right is loving and what is truly loving is right.

Instead of developing balance in both facets of godliness, believers often manifest one aspect of godliness without the other. Truth without grace is aloof. It makes one a critical and condemning judge. Righteousness without love is judgmental. Grace without truth is "sloppy agape." It makes one an "enabler." Love without righteousness is sheer sentimentality.

To be Christ-like, believers must be full of grace and truth. To have one without the other is not true Christ-likeness. To have both and have them in their proper place makes one like Christ and one who is a comforter and an encourager to others.

A Point to Ponder

SWEET REASONABLENESS

Many years ago, I stumbled upon a word that greatly impacted me. At the time, I used the King James Version of the Bible. Here is what I read, "Let your moderation be known unto all men. The Lord *is* at hand" (Phil. 4:5 KJV). As I looked at the verse in the Greek text, I discovered that the Greek word translated "moderation" means "fairness, gentleness, moderation." When I dug deeper, I found that Matthew Arnold rendered it "sweet reasonableness."

Sweet reasonableness. Wow! "What a concept," I thought. I want to develop that virtue and have it characterize my life. I think I have managed to become like that to some degree, but not as much as I would like. The Lord will decide just how successful I have been. Nevertheless, I still admire the concept and aim for it to characterize who I am.

While studying the book of Acts, I came across that word again. Paul was arrested in Jerusalem on trumped-up charges and sent to Caesarea to appear before the Roman governor, Felix. Felix summoned Paul's accuser to come state their charges. A committee of religious leaders from Jerusalem showed up with an orator named Tertullus, who was their spokesman, perhaps like their attorney, who would speak for them in court (Acts 24:2). Tertullus began his speech before Felix, thanking him for the peace and prosperity they experienced under his leadership. What Tertullus said was (and still is) a favorite form of flattery. Then, Tertullus asked Felix

A Point to Ponder

to hear him "with courtesy" (Acts 24:4).

I discovered that the Greek word translated "courtesy" was my old friend rendered "moderation" in the King James Version of Philippians 4:5. In his commentary on Acts, Alexander says that the essential idea of the Greek word "is not so much kindness or gentleness, as that of fairness and reasonableness, freedom from extremes of every kind." He adds it is "a particular judicial virtue." So, this is a case of one pagan asking another pagan to be reasonable.

This virtue is more than Paul's exhortation or Tertullus's example. It is the essence of Jesus. When Paul speaks of "the meekness and gentleness of Christ" (2 Cor. 10:1), the Greek word translated "gentleness" is the same one rendered "courtesy" in Acts 24:4 and "moderation" in the King James Version of Philippians 4:5. In fact, in the New King James Version and the New International Version, it is translated "gentleness."

If we are to be like Christ, we must be courteous, gentle, and reasonable. Paul told Titus to remind believers to be gentle (Titus 3:2). James lists gentleness as a characteristic of Godly wisdom (Jas. 3:17). So, as Paul admonishes us, "Let your courtesy, gentleness, sweet reasonableness be known to all men. The Lord *is* at hand" (Phil. 4:5).

A Point to Ponder

THE OTHER BENEFIT OF CHRISTMAS

We all know that because of Christmas, we have a Savior. The shepherds heard, "For there is born to you this day in the city of David, a Savior" (Lk. 2:11). Joseph was told to name the Babe "Jesus," a name that means "Jehovah is Savior," "For He will save His people from their sins" (Mt. 1:21). For Jesus to be our Savior, He had to die for the sin of the world and be raised from the dead. When we trust Him to be our Savior, He saves us from our sins. That is one of the great spiritual benefits of Christmas.

There is another. Jesus is not only a Savior; He is a sympathetic High Priest (Heb. 4:15). As a Savior, He was born to die. As a sympathetic High Priest, He was born to live and experience human life firsthand. Hebrews declares Jesus was tempted in all points as we are (Heb. 4:15). Jesus knows what it is like to be tempted by the Devil (Mt. 4:1-11). Isaiah says, "He is despised and rejected by men, a Man of sorrows and acquainted with grief" (Is. 53:3). Jesus knows what it is like to grieve at a funeral (Jn. 11:34-35).

When Lazarus died and Jesus saw Mary and the others weeping, He groaned in spirit and was troubled (Jn. 11:33). Commenting on this passage, Barclay says, "Jesus shows us a God whose very heart is wrung with anguish, a God who in the most literal way is afflicted by our afflictions."

When Lazarus died, Jesus wept (Jn. 11:35). Warren Wiersbe calls the shortest verse in the Bible ("Jesus wept.") the deepest verse in the Bible. Why did Jesus weep? He knew that He would raise Lazarus from the dead (Jn. 11:11). Wiersbe suggests that His weeping reveals His humanity. As a human, He entered into our experiences. He knows how we feel. His tears assure us of His sympathy.

Jesus can "sympathize with our weaknesses" (Heb. 4:15). The Greek word translated "sympathize" is a compound word made up of the two Greek words: "with" and "suffer." "It expresses not simply the compassion of one who regards suffering from without, but the feeling of one who enters into the suffering and makes it his own" (Westcott). The Greek word translated "weakness" means "without strength." It was used of physical illness (Phil. 2:26) and financial need (Acts 20:35). Yet it is "sufficiently comprehensive to include any form of felt need" (Guthrie). Except for sin, Jesus experienced it all from birth as a babe to the painful death of crucifixion. He knows what it is like to be betrayed by someone close, denied by someone dear, and deserted by virtually all of His followers. Because He was born in Bethlehem two thousand years ago, Jesus understands whatever you are going through today.

Contemplating Jesus as a sympathetic High Priest, the author of Hebrews urges us to come boldly to the throne of grace to obtain mercy (for past failure?) and grace to help in our present need (Heb. 4:16). What a "Christmas" gift!

A Point to Ponder

WHAT DETERMINES WHO OBTAINS ETERNAL LIFE?

Between July 31 and August 10, 2008, the Pew Forum for Religion and Public Life asked 2905 adults in the United States, "What determines who obtains eternal life?" The three options were: 1) actions, 2) belief, 3) a combination of both.

Of all who participated in the poll, 29% said actions, 30% said belief, and 10% said a combination of both.

Of those identifying as white mainline Protestants, 33% said actions, 25% said belief, and 10% said a combination of both.

Of those calling themselves white Catholics, 47% said actions, 13% said belief, and 14% said a combination of both.

Of those classified as white evangelicals, 11% said actions, 64% said belief, and 10% said a combination of both.

Had they asked you, how would you have answered their question? This is more than an issue of passing curiosity. If the issue is eternal life, your personal eternal destiny is at stake. So which is it: behavior, belief, or both?

One person's or group's opinion does not determine the correct answer. That's good because of the vast differences of opinion. Why not ask those who are in the know, figures such as Moses, Jesus, and Paul?

Moses says Abraham "believed in the LORD, and He accounted it to him for righteousness" (Gen. 15:6). Moses votes for belief.

A Point to Ponder

Jesus says, "This is the will of Him who sent Me, that everyone who sees the Son and believes in Him may have everlasting life; and I will raise him up at the last day" (Jn. 6:40). Jesus not only says belief is the answer, He clearly says that the belief is in Him.

Paul says, "Believe on the Lord Jesus Christ, and you will be saved" (Acts 16:31). He agrees with Moses and Jesus.

Salvation is not obtained by actions; that is, something we do. Paul declares, "For if Abraham was justified by works, he has something to boast about, but not before God" (Rom. 4:2).

Salvation is not obtained by belief and actions. Paul explains, "To him who does not work but believes on Him who justifies the ungodly, his faith is accounted for righteousness" (Rom. 4:5).

Salvation is obtained by faith alone. It is a gift. Paul plainly says, "The gift of God is eternal life through Jesus Christ our Lord" (Rom. 6:23). It is not our actions that secure salvation; it is the actions of Jesus, who died for our sins and rose from the dead. All that is left for us to do is trust Jesus Christ for the gift of eternal life.

A large number of Americans, including Protestants, Catholics, and Evangelicals, need some clarification on this issue. Those of us who know should let them know.

A Point to Ponder

THE HEALING TOUCH

Jesus did the unthinkable. He touched an untouchable. To the Jews of Jesus' day, touching a leper was unimaginable, yet when a leper asked to be made clean, "Jesus put out *His* hand and touched him, saying, 'I am willing; be cleansed.' Immediately his leprosy was cleansed" (Mt. 8:3). The additional expression "put out his hand" focuses attention on the act of touching. The result was miraculous; the physically ill, social outcast leper was immediately *cleansed*.

There is more here than physical healing. Jesus could have healed him by just speaking. He did not just talk; He *touched* him. The touch had social implications. The leper was not just healed, he was cleansed. He was healed of a physical disease and cleansed from his social disgrace and his spiritual defilement.

The leper was healed and helped when Jesus touched him because Jesus, as God in the flesh, had the power to do that. We do not have that kind of power, but the story reminds us of the healing power of touch.

In his book *Love and Survival*, Dr. Dean Ornish, the famous heart doctor, writes, "The simple act of touching someone is a powerful way to begin healing loneliness and isolation. While the most important benefits of touching may be beyond measurement, some can be observed and studied. The experience of being in an intensive care unit is a powerfully isolating one for many people because they spend much of their time alone. When a doctor or nurse or technician appears, the tubes and wires and machinery often become the focus of most of their time and attention" (Ornish, *Love and Survival*, p. 70).

Ornish cites a series of studies of intensive care units by Dr. James Lynch and his colleagues, who studied men and women who had significant irregular heartbeats called ventricular arrhythmias and were under constant monitoring in the coronary care unit. "They found a significant reduction in irregular heartbeats occurred when the nurse or doctor touched the patients to take their pulse. In some of these patients, pulse taking had the power to suppress irregular heartbeats that had previously been occurring completely." Dr. Lynch has written a book about this entitled *The Broken Heart: The Medical Consequences of Loneliness*. Lynch says, "Reflected in our hearts there is a biological basis for our need to form loving human relationships. If we fail to fulfill that need, our health is in peril" (Lynch, cited by Ornish, *Love and Survival*, p. 70).

As the phone company used to say, "Reach out and touch someone." Do more than shake hands. Hug. Touch someone on the shoulder. Pat people on the back—literally!

Obviously, all of this needs to be done selectively and with sensitivity, but with those we know, our family, close friends, and, in some cases, people we just meet, we need to touch them. It heals—them and us.

A Point to Ponder

THE FUNCTION OF DYSFUNCTION

"Sacramento is dysfunctional" has become a cliché in California. Speaking to the San Francisco Commonwealth Club while launching his campaign for six budget measures on the May 19, 2009, special election ballot, Governor Arnold Schwarzenegger said: "Our state capital is a town that feeds on dysfunction. The special interests, left and right, need the process to be dysfunctional. This is how they control Sacramento. This is how they prevent change."

The word "dysfunction" is used in different ways, including describing an organ unable to function regularly because of disease, an organization that is failing to perform as expected, and people who cannot function emotionally or socially.

Schwarzenegger is using the word of an organization, if you can call the California government that. In the process, he makes an interesting observation about dysfunction. He says dysfunction controls and prevents change. George Skelton, writing on Schwarzenegger's speech, entitled the article, "The Function of Dysfunction." The function of dysfunction is to control and prevent change.

That applies to other areas of dysfunction. A *functional* family is one in which the members of the family function in an emotionally mature manner toward each other. Consequently, they know how to relate to each other, empathize with each other, and care for each other. As a result, they know how to relate to those outside the family.

A Point to Ponder

It has been suggested that children who grow up in a dysfunctional family adopt one or more of six roles: "The Good Child" (the child assumes the parental role), "The Problem Child" (the child is blamed for most problems, in spite of often being the only emotionally stable one in the family), "The Caretaker" (the child takes responsibility for the emotional well-being of the family), "The Lost Child" (the inconspicuous, quiet child, whose needs are often ignored or hidden), "The Mascot" (the child uses <u>comedy</u> to divert attention away from the increasingly dysfunctional family system), or "The Mastermind" (the opportunist child capitalizes on the other family members faults in order to get whatever he/she wants). (www.nationmaster.com/encyclopedia/Dysfunctional-family, acessed 3/21/09). Did you recognize yourself?

People growing up in dysfunctional families end up dysfunctional individuals. As adults, their dysfunction controls them, preventing them from change, and is used to control situations and people, especially those close to them.

The function of dysfunction may be to control and prevent change, but that does not mean dysfunction *has* to control people all their lives. Being aware of what we are doing is a first step out of the control of dysfunction. Focusing on being Christ-like is the next. By the grace of God, we can be functioning, loving, empathic, caring people. Paul said, "I am what I am by the grace of God" (1 Cor. 15:10).

A Point to Ponder

WHEN YOUR WORLD FALLS APART

For many, their world is falling apart. In the first few months of our young year, a whole town has been wiped off the map by a tornado, many have lost their homes due to a fire, millions have lost their jobs, and all who have money in a retirement plan have lost, thousands, and in some cases millions of dollars. Because of what has happened in the stock market, instead of retiring now, some will have to work for the rest of their lives. Then, there are those who have lost a near and dear significant person in their life or they have been told they have a terminal illness.

What do you do when your world falls apart? In his day, Habakkuk was confronted with a falling-apart world. The Babylonians were about to destroy his country! Here is how he handled it: "Though the fig tree may not blossom nor fruit be on the vine; though the labor of the olive may fail, and the fields yield no food; though the flocks be cut off from the fold, and there be no herd in the stalls—yet I will rejoice in the Lord, I will joy in the God of my salvation. The Lord God is my strength; He will make my feet like deer's feet and He will make me walk on my high hills" (Hab. 3:17-19).

Even though the Babylonians may destroy the fig tree, the vines, the olive trees, the fields, and the flocks of the herds, Habakkuk is determined to rejoice in the Lord and his salvation. He decides he will trust the Lord no matter the circumstances or the consequences.

A Point to Ponder

The Lord will be his source of strength and sustaining power, enabling him to rejoice in the face of coming destruction. The Lord will give him steadiness and surefootedness like a deer. He will have such sureness of step, he will be able to walk on high hills, an Old Testament figure for victory.

Erwin Lutzer, the Pastor of the Moody Church in Chicago, gives these verses a contemporary twist: "Though the stock market fluctuates, though I have just been fired from my job, and I don't know how God is going to supply my needs; though my body is falling apart, yet I will rejoice in the Lord. I will take joy in the God of my salvation. God is going to be my strength. He's going to see me through this time. God is going to deliver me in the midst of the trouble that is coming."

This is not a head-in-the-sand response to life. Being fully aware of what was about to happen, Habakkuk stared the raw reality of this world in the face and looked beyond the external world to see the eternal God. Paul had the same approach to life. When he experienced a painful thorn in his flesh, he learned that God's grace would give him the strength to handle it (2 Cor. 12:7-10). Job did the same thing. When he lost everything, including his wealth and his health, his siblings and the support of his wife, when he had virtually nothing left, he said, "Though He slay me, yet will I trust Him" (Job 13:15).

When your world falls apart, trust the Lord for the strength to face it and cope with it.

A Point to Ponder

24-7-365

Living the Christian life is a 24-hour-a-day, seven-days-a-week, 365-days-a-year affair.

The psalmist says completely happy people are those who meditate in the Law of the Lord "day and night" (Ps. 1:2). The expression "day and night" is a reference to all the waken hours of the day. Thinking about the Lord and His Word is a full-time job, from the time we get up in the morning until we go to bed at night.

Paul exhorts believers to "pray without ceasing" (1 Thess. 5:18). Years ago, I heard a Greek professor suggest that the expression "without ceasing" was used of a hacking cough. In other words, it is not praying like a running faucet but like a dripping faucet. It may not be continuous, but it is constant. There is not a lot of time lapse between drips!

Living a spiritual life is like being a clerk serving one customer after another in a long line—the job is never done. It is like driving a car: you must have both hands on the wheel, your foot on the pedal, and your eyes on the road—at all times. It is like breathing—if you stop, you're in trouble.

There are no breaks. There's no "time out" for an extended lunch. There are no vacations. It sounds so demanding, even oppressive. Demanding? Yes. Oppressive? No! No! No! A thousand times, "NO!"

Living the Christian life is, first and foremost, a *relationship* with a *Person*. This relationship is with a Person who loved us so much He died for our sins! How could you not love a Person like that? He loved us, therefore, we love Him (1 Jn. 4:19). We love Him, so we crave communion with Him. Because we love Him, His commandments are not burdensome (1 Jn. 5:3).

Living the Christian life is like falling in love and wanting to be with your beloved 24/7/365. When you are in love and apart, all you think about is being together. When you are apart, you email, talk on the phone, and send text messages and pictures. It never occurs to you that doing so is demanding or oppressive.

If you, as a believer, feel that living the Christian life is a drudgery, not a delight, maybe it is because you have lost your first love. In Revelation, Jesus told the Ephesians, "I know your works, your labor, your patience, and that you cannot bear those who are evil. And you have tested those who say they are apostles and are not, and have found them liars; and you have persevered and have patience, and have labored for My name's sake and have not become weary. Nevertheless, I have *this* against you, that you have left your first love. Remember therefore from where you have fallen; repent and do the first works, or else I will come to you quickly and remove your lampstand from its place—unless you repent" (Rev. 2:2-5). Notice: 1) They were working for the Lord, 2) they could not bear those who were evil, and 3) they had left their first love. Jesus did not say they lost it; He said they left it!

If you have left your first love, you need to remember, repent, and redo those things you did when you first fell in love. Then you can enjoy the Lord again—24-7-365.

A Point to Ponder

TO COMPLAIN OR NOT COMPLAIN

The Scripture warns us not to complain. In reviewing Old Testament events, which Paul says were written for our learning, he cites a case of the children of Israel complaining. He says, "nor complain, as some of them also complained, and were destroyed by the destroyer" (1 Cor. 10:10). The Israelites murmured about the water (Ex. 15:22-27), about food (Ex. 16:2-3), about water again (Ex. 17:7), and about the Promised Land itself (Num. 14:2). Consequently, the whole nation, except Joshua and Caleb, died in the wilderness (cf. Num. 14:26-29; Moses didn't enter the land because he struck the rock twice when he was told to do it once). The destroyer mentioned here is a destroying angel sent by God.

On the other hand, being content and not complaining is pleasing to the Lord. It is also more pleasant for those around us. There could be other advantages.

Having recently graduated from Fordham, 21-year-old Vin Scully was eager to break into the announcing business. Red Barber tapped him to announce the Maryland-Boston University football game on November 12, 1949, at Fenway Park. At that time, Barber was the announcer for the Brooklyn Dodgers and host of a college football roundup show on the CBS radio network. Assuming that he would be in a warm broadcast booth, Scully left his coat, hat, and gloves in his hotel room.

A Point to Ponder

When he arrived at Fenway Park, he discovered that he would call the game from the roof, exposed to the elements. On that mid-November day, the temperature in Boston never climbed above 45°. As darkness fell, with the wind blowing off the Charles River, Scully was freezing, but throughout the broadcast, he never once mentioned his discomfort or working conditions to his listeners.

Meanwhile, since the other games being broadcast by CBS that day were not nearly as competitive as the Maryland-BU game, Barber frequently returned to Scully to carry the broadcast. Maryland won the game, but Scully felt that he had blown a golden opportunity because he was frozen.

Two days later, a Boston University official phoned Barber to apologize for the shoddy treatment of their network announcer, explaining the circumstances under which Scully had to broadcast. Barber had been unaware of what happened. In his autobiography, Barber writes, "Vin did a sound job, even though it was bitterly cold and he had to work with a hand mike on the exposed roof. The wind even blew his papers away, but he didn't complain." Barber was so impressed that he asked Scully to announce the Harvard-Yale game and, two months later, to join the team calling the Dodger games. The rest, as they say, is history. For the next 60 years (and still going), Scully announced the Dodgers' games. [Scully was the Dodger announcer for 67 years, from 1950 to 2016.]

Scully got his break because he didn't complain. We who know the Lord should follow Scully's example concerning complaining, not just because it might get us a break or make us more pleasant to be around, but, in the final analysis, because it pleases the Lord.

A Point to Ponder

"SUGGESTIONS!"

Having been invited to speak in Macon, Georgia, Patricia and I decided to go a few days early to do some sightseeing. We flew to Atlanta, rented a car, and headed for the Smoky Mountains. After driving through the beautiful Smoky Mountains, we had to either retrace our steps back through the Smokys or take the long way back through North and South Carolina. We opted for the latter. We drove through Ashville, North Carolina, and the Cove, the Billy Graham Training Center. We also drove through Greenville, South Carolina, and Bob Jones University.

We were impressed with the traffic. We connected with the interstate system while we were still in Tennessee. Over the decades, as I have traveled hundreds of thousands of miles on interstate highways, I set the speed control about four miles above the speed limit and enjoy the trip. When I do that, every car going my way passes me like I am sitting still. But as soon as I entered North Carolina, no one passed me! I was shocked. To add more intrigue to the trip, everything on the road flew past me as soon as I crossed the border into South Carolina.

We stopped for the night in Anderson, South Carolina. The next day, I asked someone why nobody passed me in North Carolina and everybody passed me in South Carolina. He did not know what was happening in North Carolina (I never got an explanation), but he did have an explanation for South Carolina. He informed me that

A Point to Ponder

the good citizens of South Carolina thought that the speed limit signs were suggestions!

God gave Ten Commandments (Exod. 20:3-17), not Ten Suggestions. Jesus gave a New Commandment (Jn. 13:14), not a New Suggestion. The Bible is full of commands we treat as suggestions. Did God command or suggest that we "pray without ceasing" (1 Thess. 5:17)? That we "In everything give thanks" (1 Thess. 5:18), and "Rejoice always" (1 Thess. 5:16)? To the list could be added "preach the gospel to every creature" (Mk. 16:15), "Love one another; as I have loved you" (Jn. 13:34), and "be patient, brethren, until the coming of the Lord" (Jas. 5:7). There are many, many more.

May I suggest that you compile your own list? Select a book of the Bible. Read it with a highlighter and highlight all the commands. Choose a short book, such as James, Philippians, or Colossians. Then, focus on obeying each command one at a time. Ask God for His grace to enable you to do what He asked you to do (Heb. 4:16).

I suspect the people in North Carolina obey the speed limit because they discovered the hard way that it is costly to disobey.

A Point to Ponder

MAKING A MARK

On August 8, 1963, a 15-member gang robbed a Royal Mail train traveling from Glasgow, Scotland to London. They beat the train driver with an iron bar before making off with 2.6 million pounds (in August 2009 US dollars, well over $65 million). The driver never fully recovered from his injuries. Most of the money was never recovered. At the time, it was the largest robbery in British history.

Thirteen gang members were caught, tried, and sentenced on April 16, 1964. One of the robbers was Ronnie Biggs. After serving 15 months of a 30-year sentence, Biggs escaped from prison, fleeing to Paris, where he acquired a new identity and underwent plastic surgery. In 1970, he moved to Australia and later to Rio de Janeiro, Brazil. Because of extradition laws in Brazil, he had legal immunity. He lived in Rio for many years. He developed a cult-like status for his open defiance of British authorities. He lived a playboy lifestyle, recorded with the Sex Pistols ("No One Is Innocent"), charged tourists to spend time with him, and made TV commercials for hair replacement.

Biggs, 71, returned to Britain in May 2001, knowing he would be arrested, to receive health care. However, according to his Brazilian son, Michael, health care was available in Brazil and he had many friends who would have contributed to such expenses. Biggs proclaimed he wanted to walk into a pub again to order a pint! He did not make it to the pub. He was arrested and returned to prison to serve the 28 years remaining in his sentence.

By August 2009, weakened by three strokes and suffering from pneumonia, he was unable to walk or feed himself. Since he was unlikely to recover and did not pose a threat to society, on August 6, 2009, officials granted him an early release, citing "compassionate grounds." On August 8, 2009, Briggs was 80 years old.

Briggs remained defiant. On July 1, 2009, a judge rejected his plea for early release, saying he remained "wholly unrepentant." Briggs said, "I don't regret being involved in the train robbery.... I'm quite pleased with the idea I was involved because it's given me a little place in history." He once told an interviewer, "I've made a mark for myself."

What an attitude! He made a mark alright. By heaven's standards, it was a black mark. All of us have marks we would like to erase. Thank God for His forgiveness, but our attitude ought to be shame for the black marks and concern that we leave some white marks.

Briggs' problem was that instead of looking at the past, he should have been concerned about a future appointment—the one we all have to give an account to a holy God. "So then each of us shall give an account of himself to God" (Rom. 14:12). Briggs was proud of his past and ignorant of the future.

A Point to Ponder

GOD'S TIMING

Has God's timing ever bothered you? Have you ever prayed and didn't get an answer in what you thought was a timely manner? Have you ever felt that God was late? An incident in the ministry of Jesus puts God's timing into perspective.

As John tells the story, "Now a certain *man* was sick, Lazarus of Bethany, the town of Mary and her sister Martha. It was *that* Mary who anointed the Lord with fragrant oil and wiped His feet with her hair, whose brother Lazarus was sick. Therefore the sisters sent to Him, saying, 'Lord, behold, he whom You love is sick'" (Jn. 11:1-3). There is no request or plea, yet the message implies a belief that Jesus could and would heal him.

Instead of immediately rushing to the scene, "When He (Jesus) heard that he (Lazarus) was sick, He stayed two more days in the place where He was. Then after this, He said to *the* disciples, 'Let us go to Judea again'" (Jn. 11:6-7). Jesus deliberately waited for *two days* before seeing Mary and Martha!

When Jesus finally arrived on the scene, He was greeted by Martha, who said to Him, "Lord, if You had been here, my brother would not have died. But even now, I know that whatever You ask of God, God will give You" (Jn. 11:21-22). Later, when He met Mary, she said, "Lord, if You had been here, my brother would not have died" (Jn. 11:32). Both sisters said the exact same thing. They were not rebuking the Lord; they were expressing regret, but they

A Point to Ponder

must have felt that His timing was tardy.

Why did not Jesus come sooner? John records Jesus's reaction when He first heard the news. Jesus said, "This sickness is not unto death, but for the glory of God, that the Son of God may be glorified in it" (Jn. 11:4). John adds, "Now Jesus loved Martha and her sister and Lazarus" (Jn. 11:5). First, Jesus said the sickness was not unto death, that is, it was not to have death as its final result. Instead, it was for the glory of God, meaning the Son of God might be manifested by it. By raising him from the dead, Jesus would demonstrate His deity. Second, Jesus loved Lazarus and his sisters; therefore, He waited. The Greek word used for "love" here is different from the one used in verse 3. The one in verse 3 denotes passionate, emotional warmth. It is the affection of lovers, parents, etc. The Greek word for love used in verse 5 is choosing to do what is best for the person loved. The sisters used the more emotional word; John used the loftier and yet less impulsive word. Jesus waited for the glory of God and the good of Mary and Martha. Waiting was good for them because, in the end, their faith was strengthened by what happened.

In other words, God's timing is perfect for accomplishing His purpose (Plummer, Morris). In this case, His purpose was to glorify His Son and to cause them to grow (cf. Jn. 11:4-15). Had He immediately rushed to Lazarus' bedside and healed him, he would not have died and Jesus would not have been able to manifest Himself in the greater miracle of resurrecting Lazarus from the dead.

A Point to Ponder

JESUS WEPT

The shortest verse in the Bible is, "Jesus wept" (Jn. 11:35). Why was Jesus weeping? When He wept, He was standing outside the tomb of His beloved friend Lazarus. The verses following John 11:35 suggest that His friend's death personally moved Jesus. When the Jews saw Him weeping, they said, "See how He loved him!" (Jn. 11:36).

This, the shortest verse in the Bible, has been called the "deepest verse in the Bible." Is there something deeper here than personal grief at a funeral?

Many have suggested that His weeping reveals His humanity. That is no doubt true. He was a "man of sorrows and acquitted with *grief*" (Is. 23:3; italics added). He is a merciful High Priest who can be touched with the feelings of our infirmities (Heb. 4:14-16).

It has also been suggested that His weeping reveals His deity. Barclay says, "To the Greeks, the primary characteristic of God was what he called apatheia, which means total inability to feel any emotion whatsoever. How did the Greeks come to attribute such a characteristic to God? They argued like this. If we can feel sorrow or joy, gladness or grief, it means that someone can have an effect upon us. Now, if a person has an effect upon us, it means that, for the moment, that person has power over us. No one can have any power over God and this must mean that God is essentially incapable of feeling any emotion whatsoever. The Greeks believed in an isolated, passionless, and compassionless God. What a different picture Jesus gave" (Barclay, italics his).

There is more. The verses just prior to the famous verse about Jesus weeping say, "Therefore, when Jesus saw her (Mary) weeping, and the Jews who came with her weeping, He groaned in the spirit and was troubled. And He said, 'Where have you laid him?' They said to Him, 'Lord, come and see'" (Jn. 11:33-34). When Jesus saw the scene, He was deeply moved emotionally. An authority on Greek words says that the Greek word translated "groaned" means "such deep emotion seized Jesus that an involuntary groan was wrung from His heart." He adds, "So deeply did Jesus enter into men's sorrows that his heart was wrung with anguish" (Barclay). The Greek word translated "trouble" means "to be disturbed, stirred up." "Jesus was profoundly moved" (Morris).

Based on the prior verses, it is safe to say that, moved by the mourning of others, Jesus wept. It is interesting to note that several Greek words are used to describe weeping in this passage. The mourners, including Mary, wept out loud. The Greek word used of Jesus weeping indicates that He did not weep out loud like the others. Tears trickled down His cheeks. At any rate, the point is He could sympathize with the intensity of His friend's grief. He wept with those who weep.

In the book of Romans, Paul exhorts all of us to "rejoice with those to rejoice and weep with those who weep" (Rom. 12:15). Many get it backward. They rejoice with those who weep and weep with those who rejoice. Jesus did not do that. Nor does Christ-like love do that today. Let us be like Christ, weeping with those who weep.

A Point to Ponder

ANDREW

In the Gospel of John, each time Andrew is mentioned, he is introducing somebody to Jesus. After spending the day with Jesus, Andrew first found his brother Simon and exclaimed, "We have found the Messiah!" (Jn. 1:39, 41). Simon, of course, is the man who became the Apostle Peter. Andrew introduced Peter to Christ. Sometime later, Andrew was present when a great multitude of people had to be fed, but there was no food. Andrew introduced the lad with five barley loves and two small fish to Jesus (Jn. 6:9). At the end of the public ministry of Jesus, some Greeks who had come to Jerusalem to worship sought to see Jesus. When they approached Phillip, Phillip went to get Andrew and Phillip and Andrew introduced the Greeks to Jesus (Jn. 12:22).

Andrew introduced Peter to Jesus. When Peter preached on the day of Pentecost, 3000 people were saved (Acts 2:41). When he preached in the home of Cornelius, the first Gentiles entered the church (Acts 10:1-11:18). Peter also wrote two New Testament books. A Sunday school teacher, Ezra Kimball, introduced D. L. Moody to Christ. Moody brought thousands to Christ across two continents.

Andrew introduced a small boy with a small lunch basket to Jesus. As a result, 5000 people were fed and 12 baskets full of food were left over after everyone had eaten (Jn. 6:10, 13). Moishe Rosen, the founder of Jews for Jesus, said that his wife, Ceil, "is not much of a soul winner. The only people she ever won to Christ are her daughters and me!" Through Rosen, many thousands came to Christ.

Andrew introduced Greeks to Christ. In the Gospel of John, the author includes that seemingly insignificant story because part of his point is that Jesus is the Savior of the world, not just the Jews (cf. Jn. 1:29; 3:16; 4:42; 6:33; 8:12; see also 10:16 and 11:51-52).

Andrew was not famous for his preaching. Andrew was not the author of any New Testament book. As far as is recorded, all he did was introduce three people to Jesus. If all he did in his entire lifetime was introduce three people to Christ, it was quite an accomplishment.

Thank God Andrew did not have spiritual lockjaw.

D. L. Moody tells of being impressed by a painting of a woman coming out of the water clinging to a cross with both hands. It stirred him greatly until he came upon another picture that spoiled the first. It was the picture of a person coming out of the waters with one hand clutching to a cross and the other lifting a drowning victim out of the water. With one hand on the cross, reach out to introduce others to the Savior.

A Point to Ponder

THE COST OF SERVICE

When someone serves us, it costs us. We tip the witness and the parking attendant when we valet park. Serving also costs the server. After raising Lazarus from the dead, Jesus attended a diner in Bethany (Jn. 12:1). John records, "There they made Him a supper and Martha served, but Lazarus was one of those who sat at the table with Him" (Jn. 12:2). Martha served. That cost her. It cost her time, effort, and energy. Sometimes, she was out of the room, missing the conversation between Jesus and the others around the table. When the dinner was over, the guest felt full and refreshed. Martha felt tired and spent. Serving is costly.

John goes on to say, "Then Mary took a pound of very costly oil of spikenard, anointed the feet of Jesus, and wiped His feet with her hair. And the house was filled with the fragrance of the oil" (Jn. 12:3). Like her sister Martha, Mary served the Lord and she paid for the privilege. She used twelve ounces of very costly, undiluted oil. (The word "spikenard" is uncertain; it probably means unadulterated). John goes out of his way to emphasize the cost (Morris). This large amount of unmixed fragrance was expensive. It cost 300 denarii (cf. Jn. 12:5). According to Matthew 20:2, one denarius was one day's wage. Therefore, the price was the equivalent of a working man's wage for a year.

Mary's service costs more than money. As if the precious perfume were only common water, Mary poured it over the feet

A Point to Ponder

of Jesus in such abundance that it was as if she bathed Him with it. So, she was obligated to wipe His feet. For this, she used her hair. Barclay says, "On the day a girl was married, her hair was bound up and never again would she be seen in public with her long tresses flowing loose. It was the sign of an immoral woman to appear in public with her hair unbound." In other words, what Mary did cost her; it cost her pride. No sacrifice was too costly for her purse; no service was too lowly for her person.

What did Mary get for this sacrificial service? Applause from the guest? Praise from the Apostles? No. For her extraordinary service, she received criticism! "But one of His disciples, Judas Iscariot, Simon's *son*, who would betray Him, said, 'Why was this fragrant oil not sold for three hundred denarii and given to the poor?'" (Jn. 12:4-5).

If service is so costly and all you get is criticism, why serve? Let Mary answer that. In her day, the custom was that on a feast day, the *heads* of the guests were anointed with perfume. Mary anointed His *feet* as well as His head. Anointing His head was an act of honor; anointing His feet a display of devotion. Mary did it simply because she loved Him. All she was and had was His. Because of her love, the cost was a small price to pay. Love is not love if it calculates the cost (Barclay).

Let us sacrificially serve—out of love and with great joy for the privilege.

A Point to Ponder

AWARENESS OF SIN

Over the years, Paul became more and more aware of his sinfulness. In 57 A.D., he said, "I am the least of the apostles" (1 Cor. 15:9). In 61 A.D., he wrote, "I am the very least of all the saints" (Eph. 3:8). In 62 A.D., he felt he was the chief of sinners (1 Tim. 1:15). When Paul said that he was the least of the apostles and later said he was the least of the saints and still later that he was the chief of sinners, he did not mean that he sinned more; he meant he became more aware of his sinfulness. What causes believers to become more and more aware of their sinfulness?

We do not understand just how sinful we are until we see ourselves as compared to the Lord. He is the standard (Rom. 3:23). The more we grow in the grace and knowledge of the Lord, the more we understand what sin is and how just how sinful we are. First John 1:9 says if we confess our sins, the Lord is faithful and just to forgive us our sins. What is often overlooked is that the context of that passage says God is light (1 Jn. 1:5) and that "If we walk in the light as He is in the light, we have fellowship with one another (1 Jn. 1:7). In other words, as we walk in the light, our sin is exposed.

The more we understand God's holiness, the more we become aware of our sinfulness. Isaiah wrote, "In the year that King Uzziah died, I saw the Lord sitting on a throne, high and lifted up, and the train of His *robe* filled the temple. Above it stood seraphim; each one

A Point to Ponder

had six wings: with two he covered his face, with two he covered his feet, and with two he flew. And one cried to another and said: 'Holy, holy, holy *is* the LORD of hosts; The whole earth *is* full of His glory!' And the posts of the door were shaken by the voice of him who cried out, and the house was filled with smoke. So I said: 'Woe *is* me, for I am undone! Because I *am* a man of unclean lips, And I dwell in the midst of a people of unclean lips; For my eyes have seen the King, The LORD of hosts'" (Isa. 6:1-5).

Luke records Peter's experience. "When He [Jesus] had stopped speaking, He said to Simon, 'Launch out into the deep and let down your nets for a catch.' But Simon answered and said to Him, 'Master, we have toiled all night and caught nothing; nevertheless, at Your word, I will let down the net.' And when they had done this, they caught a great number of fish, and their net was breaking. So they signaled to *their* partners in the other boat to come and help them. And they came and filled both the boats, so that they began to sink. When Simon Peter saw *it*, he fell down at Jesus' knees, saying, 'Depart from me, for I am a sinful man, O Lord!' For he and all who were with him were astonished at the catch of fish which they had taken" (Lk. 5:4-9).

Job said, "I have heard of You by the hearing of the ear, But now my eye sees You. Therefore, I abhor *myself,* And repent in dust and ashes" (Job 42:5-6).

The awareness of our sinfulness often follows the path that begins with seeing the sinfulness of our speech (Isaiah) and then the sinfulness of our behavior (Peter), followed by the sinfulness of our attitude (Job).

INDEX

Genesis 2:24	131, 188
Genesis 9:6	238
Exodus 2:11	272
Exodus 20:2	220
Exodus 20:8-11	247
Exodus 20:12	214
Leviticus 18:22	195
Deuteronomy 6:5-7	189
Deuteronomy 6:7-9	177
Judges 21:25	242
1 Chronciles 29:11-12	142
2 Kings 5:16	234
Habakkuk 3:17-19	309
Job 13:15	310
Job 42:5-6	328
Psalm 1:1	113
Psalm 1:1-2	69
Psalm 1:2	113, 311
Psalm 2:1	97
Psalm 9:7	92
Psalm 21:1	123
Psalm 27:7	164
Psalm 33:13	61
Psalm 106:30-31	153

A Point to Ponder

Psalm 119:105	55
Proverbs 4:5	57
Proverbs 22:7	279
Nehemiah 1:8	65
Isaiah 6:1-5	328
Jonah 4:10-11	106
Nahum 1:3	89
Malachi 2:14, 16	107
Matthew 5:44	255
Matthew 6:5-6	292
Matthew 6:7	111
Matthew 6:9-13	254
Matthew 6:19-20	128
Matthew 6:33	228
Matthew 8:3	305
Matthew 7:12	228
Matthew 9:9	267
Matthew 12:49-50	265
Matthew 16:15-16, 18	221
Matthew 19:9	136
Matthew 23:15	122
Mark 6:43	157
Mark 10:45	158, 270
Mark 11:24	49
Luke 1:41, 44	203
Luke 5:4-9	328

Luke 5:5	45
Luke 6:27-28	255
Luke 8:14	208
Luke 13:1-5	120, 231
Luke 16:10	100
John 1:17	247
John 1:41	323
John 3:16	244
John 7:24	43
John 8:30-31	147
John 11:1-7	319
John 11:35	321
John 12:1-5	325
John 13:34	266
Acts 1:8	41, 176
Acts 2:4	87
Acts 2:23	192
Acts 2:38	84
Acts 8:30	67
Acts 9:31	278
Acts 13:43	283
Acts 19:2	85
Acts 20:7	248
Acts 20:17	258
Acts 20:28	263
Acts 25:11	238

A Point to Ponder

Romans 1:11-12	150
Romans 2:2	144
Romans 3:24-25	287
Romans 4:5	304
Romans 5:2-3	146
Romans 5:8	224, 290
Romans 6:14	172
Romans 7:15, 19	166
Romans 14:7	94, 207
Romans 14:12	318
Romans 12:1	118
Romans 12:1-3	79
Romans 12:18	180
Romans 13:1	236
Romans 13:7	169
Romans 13:11	104
Romans 14:5	155
1 Corinthians 7:39	200
1 Corinthians 9:24-26	205
1 Corinthians 10:10	313
1 Corinthians 10:13	15
1 Corinthians 11:1	250
1 Corinthians 15:7	75
1 Corinthians 15:10	308
1 Corinthians 16:2	248
2 Corinthians 3:18	77

2 Corinthians 4:8-9	17
2 Corinthians 3:18	80
2 Corinthians 4:4	230
2 Corinthians 4:16-18	140
2 Corinthians 11:2	182
2 Corinthians 11:4	282
2 Corinthians 12:10	216
Galatians 1:6	282
Galatians 5:11	286
Galatians 5:22-23	210
Galatians 6:9	9
Galatians 6:10	109, 186
Ephesians 2:8-9	174
Ephesians 5:15	5
Ephesians 5:15-16	168
Ephesians 5:20	126
Ephesians 6:15	115
Philippians 1:21	160
Philippians 2:14	152
Philippians 3:3-9	240
Philippians 4:4	21
Philippians 4:5	300
Philippians 4:8	134, 218
Colossians 1:9	260
Colossians 2:2-3	95
Colossians 3:9	194

A Point to Ponder

Colossians 3:13	19
Colossians 3:15	269
Colossians 3:23-24	147
1 Thessalonians 5:16	59
1 Thessalonians 5:17	11
1 Thessalonians 5:18	63, 311
1 Thessalonians 5:16-18	183
1 Thessalonians 5:25	71
1 Thessalonians 5:26	81
2 Thessalonians 2:1-2	13
1 Timothy 2:1-6	278
1 Timothy 5:18	246
1 Timothy 6:12	23
2 Timothy 3:15-17	25, 276
2 Timothy 3:16	246
Titus 1:8	102
Titus 2:6	27
Titus 2:12	296
Philemon 17-19	3
Hebrews 4:15	302
Hebrews 13:5	51
James 1:2	269
James 1:2-4	7
James 4:12	242
1 Peter 2:1-3	35
1 Peter 2:17-18	212

A Point to Ponder

1 Peter 3:4	274
1 Peter 5:3	226
2 Peter 1:5-7	209
2 Peter 3:18	38
1 John 1:8	137
1 John 1:8	137
1 John 1:8-9	29
1 John 3:18	73
1 John 4:11	262
1 John 4:19	312
1 John 5:3	312
2 John 10-11	31
3 John 5-8	33
Jude 20-21	39
Revelation 3:20	54

A Point to Ponder

About The Author

G. Michael Cocoris is a gifted communicator. He can make even complicated subjects simple, clear, and practical. His breadth of experience has allowed him to relate to a wide range of audiences.

Michael received a Bachelor of Arts degree from Tennessee Temple University, a Master of Theology degree from Dallas Seminary, and a Doctorate of Divinity from Biola University. He traveled the United States for over a dozen years as a speaker. He has also been a seminary professor, visiting lecturer, and world traveler, including hosting tours to Israel and China.

Michael has pastored three churches, including a rural church when he was in seminary, an urban church, the historic Church of the Open Door, first in downtown Los Angeles and later in Glendora, California, and a suburban church, the Lindley Church in Tarzana California, a suburb of Los Angeles. While at the Church of Open Door, he had a daily radio broadcast.

Michael has written numerous magazine articles, mainly for *Biblical Research Monthly*. He has authored a number of books, including *Seventy Years on Hope Street, A History of the Church of the Open Door*; *The Spiritual Life, Clarifying the Confusion; Repentance, The Most Misunderstood Word in the Bible; Evangelism: A Biblical Approach; The Salvation Controversy; Lordship Salvation: Is It Biblical?; The Books of the Bible, the Subject, Structure, Situation, and Significant Verses of Each Book; Psalms, A Song for Every Situation, Each Summarized on One Page; and Counseling Theories: A Simple Explanation and Biblical Evaluation*. In addition, he was a contributor to The *NKJV Study Bible* and Nelson's New Illustrated Bible Commentary.

Michael is the pastor of the Lindley Church in Tarzana, California. He and his wife, Patricia, lived in Santa Monica, California.

www.ingramcontent.com/pod-product-compliance
Lightning Source LLC
Chambersburg PA
CBHW070046080526
44586CB00013B/934